Legal Aspects of the Conservation of Wetlands

Aspects juridiques de la protection des zones humides

IUCN - The World Conservation Union

Founded in 1948, IUCN - The World Conservation Union - is a membership organization comprising governments, non-governmental organizations (NGOs), research institutions, and conservation agencies in more than 100 countries. The Union's objective is to promote and encourage the protection and sustainable utilization of living resources.

Several thousand scientists and experts from all continents form part of a network supporting the work of its six Commissions: threatened species, protected areas, ecology, environmental strategy and planning, environmental law, and environmental education and communication. Its thematic programmes include forest conservation, wetlands, marine ecosystems, plants, the Sahel, Antarctica, as well as population and natural resources. These activities enable IUCN and its members to develop sound policies and programmes for the conservation of biological diversity and sustainable use of natural resources.

UICN - Union mondiale pour la nature

Fondée en 1948, l'UICN - Union mondiale pour la nature - est une organisation qui compte parmi ses membres des Etats, des organisations non gouvernementales (ONG), des institutions de recherche, ainsi que des organismes de conservation, répartis dans plus de 100 pays. L'Union a pour objectif de promouvoir la protection et l'utilisation durable des ressources vivantes.

Plusieurs milliers de scientifiques et d'experts des cinq continents forment un réseau sur lequel s'appuient les six commissions de l'UICN; espèces menacées, aires protégées, écologie, stratégies et planification de l'environnement, droit de l'environnement, et éducation et communication. Ses programmes spéciaux comprennent la conservation des forêts, les zones humides, les écosystèmes marins, les plantes, le Sahel, l'Antarctique, ainsi que la population et les ressources naturelles. Grâce à ces activités, l'UICN et ses membres sont en mesure d'établir des politiques et des programmes pour la conservation de la diversité biologique et l'utilisation durable des resources naturelles.

Legal Aspects of the Conservation of Wetlands

Aspects juridiques de la protection des zones humides

Papers presented at an international conference held in Lyon, 23-26 September 1987

Communications présentées à la conférence internationale de Lyon, 23-26 Septembre 1987

Scientific Direction/Direction scientifique: Jean Untermaier

Société Française pour le Droit de l'Environnement

IUCN Commission on Environmental Policy, Law and Administration

IUCN Environmental Policy and Law Paper No. 25

IUCN - The World Conservation Union
UICN - Union mondiale pour la nature

1991

Published by IUCN, Gland, Switzerland and Cambridge, UK. / Publié par UICN, Gland, Suisse et Cambridge, R-U.

IUCN Environmental Policy and Law Paper No. 25

IUCN Environmental Law Centre / UICN Centre du droit de l'environnement, Adenauerallee 214, D-5300 Bonn 1, Germany/Allemagne.

Citation: Untermaier, J. (Scientific Director/Directeur scientifique). 1991. *Legal Aspects of the Conservation of Wetlands / Aspects juridiques de la protection des zones humides*. IUCN, Gland, Switzerland and Cambridge, UK / UICN, Gland, Suisse et Cambridge, R-U. x + 202 pp.

ISBN 2-8317-0073-6

Printed by / Imprimé par: Page Bros. (Norwich) Ltd.

Cover photograph / Photo en couverture: Forest lake in primary forest, Poland. Photo: WWF/W. Lapinski

Available from / Disponible auprès de: IUCN Publications Services Unit, 219c Huntingdon Road, Cambridge CB3 0DL, UK.

Préface

La protection des zones humides se heurte à des difficultés d'ordre juridique, aussi bien en droit interne qu'en droit international.

Ainsi, les législations de nombreux Etats contiennent encore des dispositions qui encouragent le drainage des marais, des prairies inondables ou qui, d'une manière générale, favorisent la disparition des zones humides. Ces dernières sont souvent pénalisées par une fiscalité qui, par ailleurs, incite à les transformer en terres cultivées, en terrains à bâtir ou en décharges de déchets ménagers.

Ces facteurs négatifs rendent nécessaire un examen des situations nationales, et un suivi de leur évolution.

Un des objectifs de la Conférence de Lyon était d'obtenir un aperçu de ces problèmes dans nombre d'Etats.

Toutefois, recenser les obstacles n'est pas un but en soi; dans une perspective prospective, il convient également de réfléchir aux instruments juridiques indispensables à une gestion écologiquement satisfaisante. Cette démarche suppose une information sur le statut foncier et administratif des zones humides et sur les régimes de protection applicables dans le plus grand nombre de systèmes juridiques possible, ainsi qu'une analyse de ces éléments.

Un autre objectif de la Conférence de Lyon était donc également d'obtenir le plus d'informations possible sur ces différents points, et ainsi d'apporter des éléments de réflexion à ceux qui cherchent à traduire dans les normes et les institutions les principes d'une bonne gestion des zones humides.

La Conférence, patronnée par la Société française pour le droit de l'environnement (Groupe "Zones Humides") et l'UICN, l'Union mondiale pour la Nature (Commission des politiques, du droit et de l'administration de l'environnement), fut organisée sous la direction scientifique de Jean Untermaier, Professeur de droit de l'environnement à l'Université de Lyon III.

Nombre de spécialistes participèrent à sa préparation en répondant au questionnaire (voir pp. 179-188) qui servit de base à la collecte des informations nécessaires; de nombreux experts y participèrent, et contribuèrent à faire de la Conférence un succès.

Des difficultés nous ont empêché de publier les communications présentées à la Conférence dans les délais prévus. Il nous a semblé, cependant, que malgré le temps écoulé depuis la Conférence, ces documents, dans leur essence, et par leur qualité, restaient d'actualité.

Cette opinion a été confirmée par les demandes que de nombreuses personnes, désireuses de les obtenir, continuent de nous adresser. Nous nous réjouissons donc de voir enfin ce volume sortir de presse.

Les organisateurs

Preface

The protection of wetlands presents a number of difficulties from the legal point of view, both at national and international levels.

Thus, the legislation of many countries still contains provisions that encourage the draining of marshes and water meadows, or that in general promote the disappearance of wetlands. Such areas frequently suffer from a fiscal regime which, among other things, promotes the transformation of wetlands into agricultural land, building land, or sites for the disposal of waste.

These negative factors make it necessary to examine the various national situations, and to monitor their evolution.

One of the objectives of the Lyon Conference, therefore, was to obtain an overview of these problems in a number of countries.

Merely to record the obstacles to wetland conservation, however, is not enough; with an eye to the future, it is just as important to consider what legal instruments are essential to ensure the management of wetlands on an ecologically sound basis. To do this requires on the one hand information on the treatment of wetlands in property law and administrative law, and on the other hand a comparison and analysis of the systems of protection in as many legal systems as possible.

Another objective of the Lyon Conference, therefore, was to obtain as much information as possible on these different topics, and thus provide food for thought to those who seek to translate the principles of sound wetland management into legal norms and institutions.

The Conference, sponsored by the French Society for Environmental Law (Group on Wetlands) and IUCN - The World Conservation Union (Commission on Environmental Law, Policy and Administration), was organized under the scientific direction of Jean Untermaier, Professor of Environmental Law at the University of Lyon III.

A number of specialists participated in the preparation of the Conference by answering the questionnaire (see pp. 189-198), which served as a basis for collecting the necessary information; many experts participated in the Conference itself, and contributed to make it a success.

Difficulties have prevented us from publishing the papers presented to the Conference within the period originally planned. Nevertheless, we believe that, despite the time that has elapsed since the Conference, these papers are still of great interest because of their subject matter and their quality.

This opinion has been confirmed by the requests we have received from many individuals for copies of the papers. We are therefore very pleased to see this book finally available.

The Organizers

Contents
Table des matières

Country Reports

Conclusions

Annexes

Introductory Address

WOLFGANG E. BURHENNE

Chairman, IUCN Commission on Policy, Law and Administration, Bonn, Germany

It is a pleasure for me to be able to greet the participants to this Conference in the name of IUCN. It is an added pleasure to see that the efforts in setting up this Conference have been rewarded, and that the subject has attracted so many participants.

This meeting takes place within the framework of the joint IUCN/World Wildlife Fund Wetland Programme; IUCN is grateful to WWF-France for their support to this meeting. IUCN is also pleased to have the partnership of the *Société française pour le droit de l'environnement* and of its *Groupe des zones humides*, which collaborated in the design of the meeting.

IUCN's concern on wetlands goes back a long time. It was brought to the forefront of attention in 1962, when Project MAR—on the conservation and management of marshes, bogs and other wetlands in temperate zones—was launched. In the proceedings of the 1962 MAR Conference, you will come across a remark which I feel is appropriate today: in his introduction to the Conference, Max Nicholson, the far-sighted British conservationist, suggested that "Discussion should be focused mainly on the problem of how to produce the most useful and comprehensive advice, which might be disseminated for the use of those who may have to deal with problems of creating wetlands refuges or reserves". In contrast he observed, and I quote, "It would probably not be profitable at such a meeting to discuss in detail the differences in organization, law, and management techniques which may be related to accidental local factors or to national tradition in different countries. It might", he added, "be useful to discuss the possibility of creating a panel or ring of authorities and individuals who would be prepared to give more detailed advice on particular problems or might in special cases even be willing to send experts to make surveys or recommendations on the spot".

Twenty-five years have passed, and many things have evolved; some progress has even been made!

This is clearly true with respect to the technical and scientific fields related to wetland conservation, but it is also true of the legal and administrative aspects. Who would have thought, 25 years ago, that legislation on wetland conservation would no longer be restricted to laws on protected areas? Who would have thought, 25 years ago, that these legal matters would have become so interesting and important that lawyers from a wide variety of countries would hold a meeting to compare notes? Twenty-five years ago, there were, indeed, very few notes to compare in this field!

This evolution is due to the combined efforts of both non-governmental organizations and governments, at international and national levels. Indeed, this cocktail of efforts is reflected in the diversity of the contributors to this conference: I have already mentioned WWF and the *Groupe des zones humides* of the *Société française pour le droit de l'environnement*; I would also like to mention the *Institut de droit de l'environnement* of the University which is our host. The Institute has provided the logistics and has worked hard to enable us to be here today. Jean Untermaier, head of both the Institute and of the *Groupe des zones humides*, has played a key role in the design and organization of this event. I want to thank him personally for his efforts. I am sure that we will feel at home at the Université Jean Moulin Lyon III. How could it be otherwise, when this is one of the few universities in France and in Europe having an institute devoted to environmental law? Many thanks are due also to our hosts, the Administrators of the University.

Finally, it is gratifying to note that the Ministry of the Environment of France has agreed to become the patron of this Conference; their generous cooperation with our endeavour is a reflection of the fact that France has become a leading nation in the field of environmental and conservation law.

We expect a lot from the participants of this Conference, but we expect just as much from its patrons, sponsors and organizers. We need the continued support of everyone. We need a continuous dialogue and in effect a permanent conference on legal aspects of conservation. I hope that these ideas and many others will be discussed in the course of this meeting, and wish you a successful conference.

Discours d'ouverture

CLAUDE LAMBRECHTS

Secrétaire générale de la Société française pour le droit de l'environnement, Strasbourg, France

Le Président Prieur est actuellement en mission aux Etats-Unis, ce qui me vaut le plaisir et le privilège de souhaiter la bienvenue à tous les participants à cette Conférence au nom de la Société française pour le droit de l'environnement.

Je voudrais remercier tout d'abord M. le Président de l'Université Jean Moulin, qui nous reçoit ici, ainsi que tous ceux qui ont participé à tous les niveaux à l'organisation de cette Conférence.

La plupart des colloques et tables rondes de la Société française pour le droit de l'environnement ont été organisés en liaison avec des organismes universitaires (ainsi le Colloque de 1979 sur le contrôle des pollutions industrielles organisé ici même). Mais il faut se féliciter particulièrement de la nouvelle ouverture que représente l'organisation de la Conférence qui débute aujourd'hui et de la collaboration qui s'est instaurée, à l'occasion de cette Conférence, entre l'Union internationale pour la conservation de la nature et la Société française pour le droit de l'environnement à travers son groupe "Zones humides" avec le parrainage du Ministère de l'environnement, dont le représentant se trouve également assis à cette table, et le soutien actif, financier et scientifique, du Fonds mondial pour la nature (WWF) France.

Une telle collaboration, du reste, est bien conforme à la vocation de la Société française pour le droit de l'environnement. Cette association à but scientifique a été créée en 1975 par un petit groupe de juristes de tous horizons qui avaient pris conscience du rôle que pouvait et devait jouer le droit dans la protection de l'environnement et la conservation de la nature. L'association a rapidement regroupé tous les juristes qui, en France, prennent une part active à la réflexion sur le droit de l'environnement, son élaboration, sa mise en oeuvre.

Cette réflexion ne s'est pas faite en vase clos, à l'intérieur d'un cercle de spécialistes du droit, mais toujours au contact des réalités concrètes de la protection et en liaison avec les "gens de terrain", les milieux scientifiques, les administrations, les associations ... C'est ainsi que la SFDE a tissé des liens de plus en plus étroits avec les organisations internationales et nationales de conservation de la nature et avec les associations qui, à l'étranger, poursuivent des buts analogues aux siens, et qu'elle est membre, notamment, de l'Union internationale pour la conservation de la nature, du Bureau européen de l'environnement et de la Fédération française des sociétés de protection de la nature.

Quant à l'intérêt manifesté par la SFDE pour le problème de la protection des zones humides, il s'est concrétisé, comme vous le savez, par la création en 1984 d'un groupe "Zones humides" sous l'impulsion et la responsabilité scientifique du Professeur Untermaier.

Une double vocation lui était assignée:

● celle d'être un groupe de recherche attaché à l'étude systématique de ces zones, de leur conservation et de leur gestion—en France et à l'étranger—, en droit communautaire et en droit international.

● celle d'être un groupe d'experts examinant les cas concrets qui lui étaient soumis et leur proposant des solutions avec l'aide de différents experts.

La Conférence d'aujourd'hui s'inscrit dans le droit fil de la mission qu'il s'était donnée.

Il faut se féliciter aussi de ce que cette Conférence reconnaisse et même consacre le rôle du droit dans le protection de la nature. En effet, on ne mesure peut-être pas toujours suffisamment la place du droit en tant qu'instrument de la protection de l'environnement. On entend souvent douter de l'efficacité des réglementations, souligner les difficultés de leur application, affirmer que le droit n'est rien sans une volonté politique souvent défaillante ...

En réalité, le rôle du droit est plus subtil, plus ambigu et plus complexe qu'il n'y paraît et la question de la protection des zones humides est peut-être à cet égard exemplaire.

En effet, le droit peut créer des obstacles à la conservation des milieux naturels, quand il n'incite pas directement à les détruire. Les exemples abondent en France comme à l'étranger de mesures législatives encourageant le drainage des prairies, l'assèchement des marais, offrant une protection insuffisante aux zones littorales, objet de multiples pressions et convoitises ...

Mais aussi, le droit peut devenir l'instrument d'une bonne gestion écologique, quand ce ne serait que par la force des engagements internationaux.

Ce sera l'objet de nos travaux de démonter ces mécanismes et de proposer des éléments de solutions grâce à l'apport des expériences qui vous seront présentées—et il ne me reste plus qu'à former les voeux les plus chaleureux pour le succès de cette rencontre.

The World's Wetland Resources—Status and Trends

PATRICK J. DUGAN

Wetlands Programme Coordinator, IUCN, Gland, Switzerland

Wetland diversity and value

Wetlands are diverse. Mountain lakes, rivers, flood-plains, mangroves and estuaries are but a few of the major types of wetland ecosystems. Indeed, the Convention on Wetlands of International Importance Especially as Waterfowl Habitat defines wetlands as "areas of marsh, fen, peatland or water, whether natural or artificial, permanent or temporary, with water that is static or flowing, fresh, brackish or salt, including areas of marine water the depth of which at low tide does not exceed six metres", thus encompassing a vast range of freshwater and coastal habitats.

More important than this diversity, however, is the value of wetlands to human society. Though often poorly appreciated, these ecosystems play a crucially important role in our daily lives. Species which grow up in tidal areas and then swim to open sea account for two-thirds of the world's fish harvest. In particular, shrimp exports from developing to developed countries earns at least US$ 900 million a year. World exports of cod and herring are worth more than $580 million.

Wetlands also limit the ravages of floods, and provide water during droughts. For example, on the Charles River in Massachusetts, the U.S. Army Corps of Engineers recommended that the most cost-effective means of flood control was to protect the existing wetlands, which naturally absorb flood-waters, rather than to build dams or dykes. And in India, where the city of Calcutta has no chemical waste-treatment plants, a series of salt lake wetlands has for 50 years been used to treat sewage and support fish farms which produce 6,000 tons of fish annually.

In addition, many coastal wetlands are now recognized as providing important protection from storms. Thus in the U.S.A., federal regulations state that insured communities shall prohibit the destruction of mangroves, or else lose federal flood insurance. This has come too late for large areas of mangrove fringe cleared in Florida for resorts and other development.

Threats and conservation measures

As recognition of the diverse values of wetlands has grown, so has alarm at the loss of these habitats. Once seen as being of little value, or even dangerous, major efforts have been made to convert wetlands to "more productive" use. Throughout the world flood plains have been drained and converted for intensive agriculture, mangroves and other coastal systems have been converted for construction of shrimp ponds and salt pans, rivers have been regulated, and their waters have been polluted with industrial and domestic effluent and with agricultural run-off. However, as perceptions of wetlands have changed, so have efforts to address these issues and to conserve these resources for future generations.

Over the past 25 years, a wide range of national and international organizations has focused increasing attention on the conservation of the world's wetland resources. Among the first major initiatives in this field were the initiation of Project AQUA in 1961, designed by the *Societas Internationalis Limnologiae* (SIL) and the United Nations Educational, Cultural and Scientific Organization (UNESCO) to identify lakes and rivers of great conservation importance; and the 1962 MAR Conference called by the IUCN, the International Waterfowl Research Bureau (IWRB), and the International Council for Bird Preservation (ICBP) to focus attention and coordinate action on the conservation of Palearctic wetlands. Subsequently, through the continued pioneering work of IWRB, ICBP and IUCN, the Convention on Wetlands of International Importance Especially as Waterfowl Habitat was developed. Following its adoption in Ramsar, Iran, in 1971, it entered into force in December 1975. As the first global environmental convention, the Ramsar Convention has done much to focus the attention of governments and the conservation community on the international significance of wetland resources, and of the migratory birds which depend upon these resources.

Building upon this international interest, the past ten years have witnessed a significant growth in action on wetland conservation at the national level. In Europe, governments have established and are managing a growing number of reserves, while NGOs are increasingly lobbying governments to manage these reserves more effectively and to change policies which contribute to loss of wetlands. In North America, similar progress has been made, at both the governmental and non-governmental level, with over 12 million hectares of wetland protected in Canada alone under the Ramsar Convention. Similarly, increasing effort is now being made to ensure that industrialized countries pay greater attention to the impact of development assistance policies upon wetland resources in the developing world.

Today's concerns

Despite the clear progress which has been made in wetland conservation in recent years, there is concern today that the successes achieved to date fall far short of what is needed to effectively maintain wetland resources for present and future generations. There is concern that much of what has been done has been retroactive rather than designed to pre-empt major wetland losses. Equally, there is concern that many apparent successes are cosmetic and have done little to reduce the loss of the services which wetlands provide to human society. The remainder of this paper will consider some of the reasons for these concerns, and review actions now being taken, and which need to be promoted, in order to address this effectively.

The first question to ask is whether the apparent successes have deluded the conservation community into a false sense of security. While there is general agreement today that the rate of wetland loss has declined, and that the conservation movement has played an important role in achieving this, there is no room for complacency. On a global scale some experts estimate that 50% of the wetlands which once existed have now been lost.

While this may be an overestimate, it is well documented that some countries have indeed suffered this level of loss. In the United States alone, 87 million hectares (54%) of the original wetlands have been lost, without mentioning those which have been degraded. In Europe, the loss may be even more severe, and some particular types of wetlands have been almost totally destroyed. For example, in Scotland and Northern England, a survey of 120 raised bogs has shown that their total area has declined by 87% between 1850 and 1978.

Given this situation, there seems little doubt that in the industrialized world a major factor contributing to today's lower rate of wetland loss is that most sites which are readily accessible and which can be reclaimed cheaply have already been lost. In other words, much of the decline in pressure upon wetlands should not be attributed to concern for conservation, but is rather the result of concern at the investment required to convert additional sites.

The second point of particular importance is that the focus on conservation efforts in Europe and North America has tended to be upon sites of international importance. While this has often been successful and played a major role in building public awareness of the value of wetlands, the focus on a small number of large sites has neglected the equally important and more difficult problem posed by the continuous, insidious loss of smaller, dispersed sites. Although these sites may be of relatively little importance individually, together they constitute a wetland resource of major local, national and often international significance. Indeed, in many areas, it is these small sites which together provide major benefits, such as flood control, to human society. These wetlands are usually privately owned, but provide public services. And as they have been lost, these vital public services have had to be paid for. As a result the U.S. Government has removed federal aid for drainage activities and now refuses crop subsidies to those land-owners who drain wetlands on their own land.

In summary, large areas of wetlands in the developed world have been lost. In response to this loss, a network of protected areas containing many sites of international importance has been established. Each year millions of dollars are spent on its upkeep. However, these protected areas cover only a small proportion of the total wetland area of conservation concern. Outside these parks and reserves, wetlands continue to be lost. With this loss of habitat, ecological services that were once provided free have had to be replaced artificially and paid for by human society, normally in the form of taxation. These losses and the associated costs are now so great that major legislative steps are being taken to conserve the remaining wetlands as functioning units in the landscape.

While there is much to applaud in the progress made in the industrialized world, this northern model is of questionable value for the developing world. If in Europe and North America vast sums are now spent on wetland preservation, restoration and creation, and upon replacing the ecological services once provided by natural wetlands, it is necesary to ask whether developing countries can afford to do the same.

There is no doubt that the developing countries, in particular those in the tropics, today contain the majority of the world's remaining wetlands. And throughout Africa, Asia and Latin America, rural and urban communities are closely dependent upon these wetland resources.

However, given the size of these wetlands, and given the economic conditions in the countries where they occur, the pressures are intense. Indeed, in some countries it is probable that the rate of wetland loss is increasing, while the pressure in others will increase when economic conditions improve. The consequences of wetland loss for the rural economies of the developing nations are, however, more severe than in the developed world. While in Europe and North America the strong industrial economies and the relatively wealthy population can absorb the costs of replacing wetland services, this is rarely the case in developing countries. There the long-term consequences of wetland loss are felt directly by the local population, which cannot pay for action to mitigate against this. In Europe artificial flood control structures are installed to compensate for wetland loss, and paid for through taxation, but such structures are rarely built in developing countries. While this saves public expenditure, it is ultimately paid for in human life.

Thus, if developing countries are to suffer the level of wetland loss tolerated in developed countries, this will lead not only to loss of biological diversity and ecological services, but also to human suffering among the rural populations that depend on these resources. The focus of wetland conservation in the developing world must therefore be to preserve these systems as functioning units in the landscape. And while protected areas have an important role to play, the levels of investment associated with protected areas in the developed world are inappropriate. Innovative measures for establishing and managing protected wetlands on a low-cost basis are needed in developing countries in order that these wetlands can continue to bring tangible socio-economic benefits to human society.

Approaches to the problem

In response to the concerns expressed above, major efforts are now being made worldwide to focus the attention of the conservation community upon action designed to address these issues. In particular IUCN, through its Wetlands Conservation Programme, is addressing four major areas:

1. Information

In order to build a stronger conservation case a major effort is being made to improve the quantity and quality of available information on wetland ecosystems and the functions and values that they provide.

In addressing this particular issue, the U.S.A. and Canada have played a pioneering role. A comprehensive inventory of the country's wetland resources is now underway in the U.S.A., while in both countries a study of the functions and values of small dispersed wetlands, e.g. in regulating river flow and in improving water quality, is well advanced and expanding. Similarly, legislation based upon this work and designed to preserve wetlands as functioning units in the landscape is particularly well advanced. However, much more needs to be done to develop this approach further and to modify it for application in other countries. An inventory alone is an enormous task and the level of detail sought needs to be adapted to national needs and realities. Assessment of wetlands also needs to be adapted to local conditions and the information generated used in the application of existing legislation and in the development of new legal instruments.

2. Field Action

As indicated above, innovative approaches to management need to be developed if protected areas are to contribute fully to wetland conservation in developing countries. Accordingly, IUCN is carrying out a series of field projects designed to identify how wetland conservation can be pursued most effectively and integrated with the development process. Our role is to develop and to promote these projects so that governments and the development assistance community can follow their example, and so use wetlands wisely for the benefit of present and future generations.

3. Training

In support of the field activities, a major effort is being devoted to increasing the quality and quantity of training opportunities in wetland management. In particular, attention is being devoted to providing planners and resource managers with guidance on integrating wetland conservation with development, not only through establishment and management of protected areas, but also through environmentally sound management—"wise use"—of wetlands throughout the national landscape.

4. Supporting the conservation network

The scale of the global wetland problem is enormous. Yet the resources of conservation organizations are very limited. Only if we work together to address the issues identified here, and in particular learn from the experience of others, can we begin to make real progress. A major role of the IUCN Wetlands Programme is therefore to promote collaboration on wetland issues within and between the conservation and development communities. The present meeting is one example of such collaboration.

The role of law

In the next few days, we will discuss in detail the contribution that legal mechanisms can make to wetland conservation. In closing, I would like to draw attention to two points which I believe to be of particular importance.

First, while the traditional focus of wetland conservation efforts has been on protected areas, much greater attention today is being put on the preservation of wetlands as functioning units in the landscape. As in the U.S.A., such an approach requires innovative legislation to ensure that wetland conservation becomes the responsibility of all those who use our landscape, not only of protected area managers.

Second, while there is no doubt that protected areas will continue to play a major role in maintaining wetlands, innovative approaches are required to their management. In particular, in many cases much greater responsibility for management of the resources needs to be given to the users, namely the rural communities, many of which have used these wetlands for centuries. However, to achieve this, existing legislation will need to be modified in order to favour greater local control over resource use.

In both of these areas, there is clearly a major role for environmental lawyers to provide resource managers with the legislative basis for conservation action. In doing so, the lessons of one country have much to teach others and it is to be hoped that the present meeting will be the first of many at which wetland specialists and lawyers come together to address the legal aspects of wetland conservation and development.

Les problèmes juridiques de protection des zones humides

Rapport introductif

JEAN UNTERMAIER
Professeur à l'Université Jean Moulin Lyon III, Lyon, France

Au départ, le présent rapport avait pour ambition de présenter la problématique juridique de la protection des zones humides à travers les résultats du questionnaire préparatoire[1]. A la réflexion, l'exercice s'est avéré infaisable pour des raisons d'ailleurs fort instructives au regard de l'état du droit de l'environnement, qu'il conviendra d'exposer après avoir rappelé les objectifs de la Conférence.

Les objectifs de la Conférence

Dans le monde entier, la protection des zones humides se heurte à des obstacles d'ordre juridique: elle pose des problèmes juridiques qui appellent des solutions juridiques. Il importe, en conséquence, de comparer nos législations en ce domaine, de confronter nos difficultés et de réfléchir aux moyens de les surmonter.

La même démarche s'impose en droit international car de ce point de vue, il existe aussi des problèmes par exemple: gestion des zones humides transfrontalières, impact d'aménagements hydrauliques sur les zones humides d'un Etat tiers—et des dispositions spécifiques, parmi lesquelles figure bien sûr la Convention de Ramsar. Initialement, la Conférence de Lyon devait contribuer à la préparation de la Conférence des Parties organisée à Regina (Canada) en juin 1987. Les aléas du calendrier et diverses contraintes ne l'ont pas permis. Dès lors, il s'agit de tirer les enseignements de Regina dans la perspective, entre autres, de la prochaine réunion.

Notre préoccupation première est donc d'ordre technique: forger des outils au service de la conservation des zones humides, rendre plus performants ceux dont nous disposons. La tâche n'est pas simple et apporter une contribution en ce sens serait déjà un succès.

Néanmoins, il semble que nous pouvons être plus ambitieux encore et que le droit, et partant la Conférence, ne doivent pas se satisfaire de fournir quelques recettes d'aménagement de la nature. Sans la moindre modestie, nous pensons servir également et de plusieurs manières, le progrès de la science juridique.

Il est clair, tout d'abord, que nos travaux soulèvent fréquemment des questions d'ordre général et théorique. Ainsi, les réflexions concernant le niveau de décision en matière de gestion des zones humides[2] sont à verser au débat, si important dans certains pays aujourd'hui, sur la décentralisation. Elles concernent aussi le fédéralisme.

Ensuite, nos analyses peuvent aider à définir les politiques d'environnement. Ordinairement, les problèmes de protection se posent en termes écologiques, socio-économiques et politiques. "Voilà ce marais, avec sa flore et sa colonie de hérons, qu'il est question d'assécher à des fins agricoles". L'Administration, les défenseurs du marais et les aménageurs s'affrontent en un combat où l'on se renvoie des quintaux de maïs, des rendements à l'hectare et des listes d'espèces rares. Lorsque tout est dit, souvent trop tard d'ailleurs, on appelle le juriste de l'environnement. Et le juriste—qui de surcroît n'est peut-être pas un vrai juriste mais un ingénieur quelconque simplement muni d'un code—arrive alors, avec une réserve naturelle, une étude d'impact pour les travaux hydrauliques et des statuts pour le comité de gestion. La fonction habituelle du droit s'exerce ainsi, au terme ultime du processus décisionnel. Une telle situation n'a certes rien d'infamant. Au plus s'avère-t-elle parfois inconfortable car on a facilement tendance, en cas d'échec, à incriminer la partie visible du compromis, c'est-à-dire l'institution de protection et la réglementation.

Il n'empêche que la science juridique et le droit de l'environnement sont largement sous-employés. Car ils pourraient en effet, au même titre que les autres sciences humaines ou l'écologie, aider à mieux comprendre l'environnement, les relations de celui-ci avec la société; et par conséquent, contribuer plus activement à définir et à orienter les actions en faveur de la conservation.

Un exemple français illustre bien ces potentialités ignorées. Dans un arrêt relativement récent[3], le Conseil d'Etat s'est penché sur le cas de l'écureuil et du hérisson, espèces protégées par un arrêté ministériel du 17 avril 1981 dont la légalité justement était contestée par une fédération de chasseurs et une association de taxidermistes. L'arrêté en cause tient son fondement de la loi du 10 juillet 1976 sur la protection de la nature (article 3) qui envisage des mesures au bénéfice des espèces dont la conservation est justifiée par "un intérêt scientifique particulier" ou par "les nécessités de la préservation du patrimoine biologique national". Or, l'écureuil et le hérisson, dont on ne voit pas quel "intérêt scientifique particulier" ils pourraient présenter, ne sont en aucune manière des animaux rares ou menacés de disparition.

La Haute Juridiction administrative a maintenu l'arrêté du 17 avril 1981, mais sans répondre à la question: "Pourquoi au fait, protéger l'écureuil et le hérisson"? En l'état actuel, ce ne peut être pour des raisons scientifiques, mais bien parce qu'il s'agit d'animaux sympathiques et qu'ils ont nourri nos contes et histoires d'enfants. Parce qu'en somme ils font partie de notre culture.

Ainsi l'analyse juridique révèle que la protection de la nature ne peut plus reposer uniquement sur des considération écologiques et qu'il serait utile, sinon urgent, de lui apporter d'autres justifications, culturelles notamment, qui viendraient s'ajouter aux exigences biologiques. En ce sens, les juristes peuvent contribuer à l'amélioration des politiques de conservation, en particulier par l'approfondissement de leur réflexion sur des concepts tels que le paysage, le patrimoine ou le territoire.

Ce plaidoyer, qui paraîtra à certains un peu corporatiste, témoigne de la façon dont nous avons entendu traiter les matériaux ayant servi à la préparation de la Conférence.

Le questionnaire

Adressé à plusieurs dizaines de spécialistes dans une majorité des Etats possédant des zones humides, il a été rempli par dix-huit personnes que les organisateurs tiennent à remercier chaleureusement à nouveau.

Ce résultat n'est pas négligeable. Il l'est d'autant moins que l'exercice s'est avéré difficile, au point que le principal responsable n'hésite pas à dire, en confidence, qu'il n'est pas absolument sûr d'avoir donné toutes les réponses justes en ce qui concerne la France.

Pourtant, l'échantillon reste trop restreint et insuffisamment représentatif en dehors de l'Europe et du continent nord-américain. De plus, malgré son volume (treize pages et plusieurs tableaux parfois impressionnants ...), le questionnaire n'entre guère dans les détails. On remarquera, par exemple, qu'à propos des zones humides protégées (question 3-3), rien n'a été demandé sur les modalités de leur gestion ou le régime des activités à l'intérieur des parcs.

Enfin, malgré les définitions données in fine, des problèmes d'interprétation n'ont pas manqué de surgir. Un concept comme celui de chose commune (res communis) utilisé dans la question 2-1-4 n'est apparemment pas admis de façon générale. D'autres encore n'ont pas été compris de manière uniforme par les consultants.

Il n'empêche que les indications fournies furent précieuses. Elles nous ont permis de nous orienter dans cette mosaïque de textes et de situations que constitue le droit comparé des zones humides. Elles nous ont aussi donné des idées que nos travaux et les recherches qui les prolongeront permettront de vérifier et d'approfondir. Et s'il n'apparaît donc pas possible de réaliser une véritable synthèse, il en ressort néanmoins quelques constatations qui autorisent des suggestions.

I. Le droit des zones humides: tout est dans tout mais la réciproque n'est pas vraie.

Ce n'est pas un message codé, mais il faut expliquer ...

A. Tout est dans tout.

1. Le droit comparé révèle d'abord certaines constantes, qui sont la plupart du temps des évidences. Ainsi tous les Etats concernés par le questionnaire interviennent pour la protection des zones humides (cf. tableau 1). De même, dans tous les pays (sauf la Pologne), la fiscalité est perçue comme défavorable ou sans influence positive pour les zones humides.

A l'inverse, les réponses révèlent parfois des situations contrastées dont il est impossible de déduire un quelconque enseignement. Partout, il est

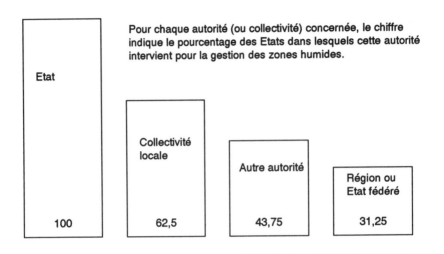

Pour chaque autorité (ou collectivité) concernée, le chiffre indique le pourcentage des Etats dans lesquels cette autorité intervient pour la gestion des zones humides.

Tableau 1

Les autorités de protection des zones humides

des zones qui sont la propriété de personnes privées, d'autres qui appartiennent à l'Etat ou à une collectivité publique. "Et alors?", est-on tenté de dire ...

2. Les instruments de protection sont nombreux et presque tous utilisés de façon très générale, par presque tous les Etats. Certes, il est quelques institutions ou techniques présentées au tableau 2 qui n'existent pas dans tel ou tel pays mais ces lacunes sont rares et vraisemblablement non significatives. En tout cas, la totalité des Etats offre plusieurs illustrations de chacun des trois grands types de mécanismes: aires protégées, procédures de contrôle des activités dangereuses, techniques non contraignantes.

3. Sauf exception[4], aucune technique de protection ne concerne spécifiquement les zones humides.

    Qu'il s'agisse des multiples variétés de parcs naturels ou de réserves, de l'étude d'impact ou des autres formes d'encadrement des entreprises menaçantes, ou encore des politiques foncières, toutes s'appliquent aussi à d'autres milieux naturels. Corrélativement, une forte majorité des Etats consultés estiment qu'il n'est pas nécessaire, pour sauvegarder leurs zones humides, d'élaborer une législation spécifique.

Tableau 2

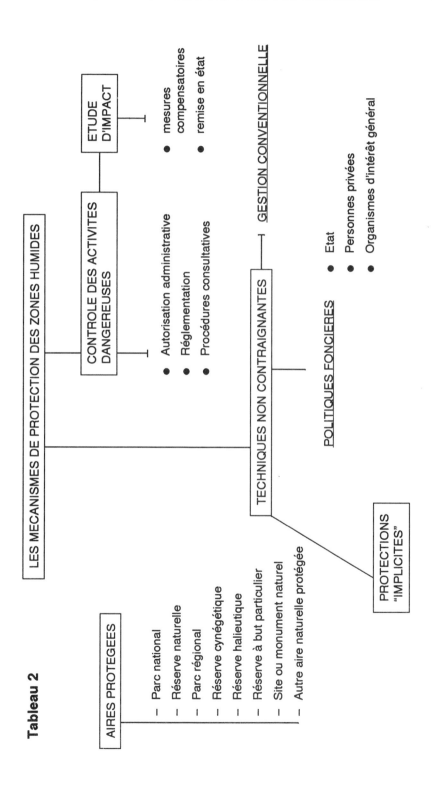

LES MECANISMES DE PROTECTION DES ZONES HUMIDES

AIRES PROTEGEES
- Parc national
- Réserve naturelle
- Parc régional
- Réserve cynégétique
- Réserve halieutique
- Réserve à but particulier
- Site ou monument naturel
- Autre aire naturelle protégée

CONTROLE DES ACTIVITES DANGEREUSES
- Autorisation administrative
- Réglementation
- Procédures consultatives

ETUDE D'IMPACT
- mesures compensatoires
- remise en état

TECHNIQUES NON CONTRAIGNANTES

POLITIQUES FONCIERES

GESTION CONVENTIONNELLE
- Etat
- Personnes privées
- Organismes d'intérêt général

PROTECTIONS "IMPLICITES"

B. La réciproque n'est pas vraie

C'est une manière de dire que lorsque l'on passe de l'approche globale du droit comparé, presque statistique—ainsi avons-nous calculé les pourcentages d'utilisation de ces instruments—à une vision analytique par pays, puis dans chaque pays par type de zone, pour arriver aux cas concrets, c'est-à-dire aux problèmes de gestion d'une zone déterminée, la panoplie paraît infiniment moins riche. Sur le terrain, le choix d'un instrument approprié se révèle fort limité et toujours difficile.

1. Ce constat appelle une remarque apparentée à un postulat: les techniques de protection ont une spécificité.

Au point de vue physique et écologique en effet, les zones humides se caractérisent par une extrême diversité. Quelle ressemblance pourrait rapprocher une mangrove d'une plaine alluviale de l'Europe moyenne et dans un même pays, qu'y a-t-il de commun entre une vasière intertidale et une tourbière ou un marais de l'intérieur? Quant au contexte

---

Tableau 3

Les obstacles à la protection des zones humides

Les opérations d'assèchement

peuvent être imposées pour des motifs:		*peuvent bénéficier d'aides financières de:*	
Agricoles	100 *	Etat	100 *
Sanitaires	61.5	Etat fédéré ou région	45.4
Protection contre les eaux	77	Autre autorité publique	54.5
De production d'énergie	77	Organisme d'interêt général	18.2
Autres	61.5	Organisation internationale	54.5
N'importe quel motif d'intérêt général	23		

---

* en pourcentages des Etats concernés par le questionnaire

socio-économique et politique, il présente des variations plus importantes encore. Dès lors, au regard de la protection envisagée individuellement, il est de bons instruments et d'autres qui ne conviennent pas. Et sans doute avons-nous tous présents à l'esprit des cas où aucune solution ne s'avère réellement satisfaisante au plan juridique.

2. De ce postulat découle une proposition: il convient de réfléchir aux stratégies juridiques, et s'attacher en quelque sorte à l'étude rationnelle des choix en matière de protection. Le choix qui aboutit par exemple à ériger une région d'étangs en parc national ou à soumettre seulement certains de ces étangs au statut de réserve naturelle, voire à ne pas édicter de protection du tout, appartient évidemment aux autorités politiques ou administratives. Or les décisions de ce genre constituent un terrain dont les juristes comme les spécialistes en science administrative sont pour le moment absents. Ils ont tort, car la recherche en ce domaine non seulement rendrait la conservation plus rationnelle et plus efficace mais, au plan scientifique, permettrait d'approfondir la connaissance du droit positif, notamment en incitant à porter davantage d'attention aux pratiques administratives et aux modalités d'application du droit. Au surplus, elle ne manquerait pas de contribuer à l'enrichissement des sciences de la décision.

II. Elargir la réflexion sur les obstacles à la protection des zones humides

C'est une évidence: il est encore très fréquent que la législation encourage la disparition des zones humides.

A. Les obstacles

Ainsi l'assèchement peut être imposé à des fins agricoles dans tous les Etats consultés, cependant qu'il est souvent assorti d'avantages financiers et/ou fiscaux (cf. tableau 3).

Nul ne conteste que ces obstacles, il faut tenter de les faire disparaître. Les efforts en ce sens constituent le passage obligé de toute entreprise visant à perfectionner le droit des zones humides.

B. En revanche, on ne remarque guère qu'il conviendrait également de s'attacher aux **mécanismes juridiques favorables à la protection,** et de se demander comment leur pérennité pourrait être assurée.

Ces mécanismes sont généralement de simples techniques, des dispositions qui indirectement engendrent pour les marais ou les milieux de ce type des effets positifs. Plus rarement, en tout cas dans les pays fortement industrialisés, il s'agit d'un système socio-économique reposant dans son ensemble sur la présence d'une zone humide importante.

1. Les règles protégeant le champ d'inondation des cours d'eau offrent une bonne illustration du premier cas de figure. Elles ont pour objectif de limiter: d'une part, les incidences des crues en accélérant l'écoulement

de l'eau; d'autre part, les dommages résultant du phénomène. Elles se traduisent par l'interdiction ou la réglementation sévère, en zone inondable, de multiples activités telles que la construction, les implantations industrielles, voire les plantations. L'élevage extensif constitue habituellement la vocation économique esentielle de ces milieux dans lesquels la présence périodique de l'eau exclut la plupart des cultures les clôtures étant par ailleurs prohibées.

Ce faisant, un tel statut caractérisé encore assez fréquemment par l'existence de vastes superficies appartenant à la communauté des habitants et par des pratiques d'utilisation collective (pâturage), contribue au maintien en l'état des plaines alluviales. Celles-ci se trouvent en somme protégées, non par une quelconque institution du type parc ou réserve, mais simplement par l'application du droit commun.

2. Avec la Dombes, plateau de 112.000 hectares à proximité immédiate de Lyon, l'écologie et l'agriculture se rejoignent pour constituer un véritable système[5].

Cette région prospère se caractérise en effet par la présence d'un millier d'étangs[6] qui lui confèrent un exceptionnel intérêt biologique, en particulier ornithologique.

Au plan juridique, on remarque l'absence presque totale du droit de l'environnement: là encore, il n'existe pour le moment ni parc national ou régional, ni réserve naturelle, mais seulement une réserve cynégétique. Pourtant la Dombes est parvenue à préserver jusqu'à présent l'essentiel de son patrimoine naturel, alors même que sa situation par rapport à Lyon l'expose à une forte pression d'urbanisation et que l'agriculture traditionnelle recule presque partout en France devant des activités plus rémunératrices mais aussi moins respectueuses de l'environnement.

En réalité, ce "miracle" doit beaucoup aux modalités d'exploitation des étangs qui, selon un cycle de quelques années, sont alternativement en eau et en assec. Lorsqu'ils sont asséchés, le fond est mis en culture. En période d'évolage (c'est-à-dire remplis), on y pratique la pisciculture et ils sont chassés. Ainsi, l'agro-écosystème dombiste fonctionne dans la mesure où ces deux activités, d'une rentabilité élevée, valorisent l'agriculture traditionnelle et lui permettent de résister aux transformations.

3. L'objectivité oblige cependant à souligner que ce système de **protection implicite** de la nature n'est sans doute pas la panacée. En regardant de plus près, on constate que la Dombes n'est pas à l'abri de certaines agressions: çà et là l'environnement est rongé par quelques poussées d'urbanisation et l'agriculture s'intensifie d'une manière générale.

Il n'empêche que de telles situations méritent un examen approfondi. Il est de toute manière passionnant d'étudier leurs fondements juridiques qui réservent maintes surprises, et important de réfléchir au moyen sinon de les conserver, du moins de leur trouver, lorsque les mutations s'avèrent inéluctables, des substituts qui assureraient le maintien de leurs caractéristiques écologiques essentielles.

III. Adapter les instruments juridiques à l'analyse globale et au long terme

La science juridique devrait enfin s'attacher à conformer le droit aux particularismes socio-économiques des zones humides qui rendent leur protection si difficile.

A. Les obstacles économiques à la conservation des zones humides

1. L'intérêt économique des zones humides est difficile à mettre en évidence.

   Indépendamment des utilisations agricoles traditionnelles dont elles font l'objet, les zones humides assurent de multiples fonctions. La productivité des pêcheries et des installations de conchyliculture par exemple, est largement tributaire des matières organiques que les marais côtiers et les estuaires déversent dans les eaux littorales. Le phénomène des crues concourt à la fertilisation des plaines alluviales et les marais ont souvent un rôle important dans la régulation du régime hydrique.

   Ces "bienfaits" sont connus depuis longtemps mais leur mesure demeure difficile, sinon impossible. La science économique est en effet mal outillée pour apprécier, a fortiori comptabiliser, des valeurs collectives, surtout lorsqu'elles se situent dans le long terme. Son impuissance est manifeste, en particulier, s'agissant de chiffrer l'impact négatif de l'assèchement d'une zone humide littorale sur la productivité des cultures marines qui en dépendent.

2. A l'inverse, les opérations qui menacent les zones humides sont en général d'une rentabilité plus visible et à plus court terme. Déterminer le rapport d'un champ de maïs ou les bénéfices que la réalisation d'un ensemble immobilier procurera au constructeur ne présente guère de difficulté.

B. Dès lors, il est urgent de trouver les mécanismes, les institutions aptes à corriger ce handicap des zones humides, de façon à les **intégrer à leur vraie valeur dans les processus décisionnels.**

1. Il existe déjà des ébauches de réponse au plan institutionnel. Il est ainsi envisageable de reconsidérer les structures administratives et de déterminer le champ de leur compétence territoriale en fonction de critères géographiques, physiques et écologiques. Certains pays se sont engagés dans cette voie en créant, pour la gestion des ressources en eau et la lutte contre la pollution, des institutions dans le cadre du bassin

fluvial[7]. Une réforme de ce type pourrait être transposée à la gestion des zones humides, notamment littorales, afin de traiter globalement les problèmes d'aménagement de la frange côtière et de l'arrière-pays.

2. L'essentiel cependant, reste à imaginer. A cet égard, un développement de recherches pluridisciplinaires, conjuguant au minimum les approches écologique, économique et juridique, s'impose. D'aucuns ne manqueront pas de contester le caractère utopique d'une démarche dont le but est de trouver une institution de gestion idéale pour les milieux naturels.

En fait elle n'est nullement déraisonnable, à la condition bien sûr de ne pas oublier qu'il n'existera jamais de machine à aménager écologiquement le territoire.

Notes

1. Cf. infra, annexe 1.

2. Cf. infra, dans cette publication: Françoise et Wolfgang Burhenne, Autorités compétentes et niveaux de décision en matière de gestion et de conservation des zones humides.

3. Conseil d'Etat, 14 novembre 1984, Syndicat des naturalistes de France et Fédération départementale des chasseurs d'Eure-et-Loire, *Actualité juridique de droit administratif*, février 1985, J., p. 96, conclusions Denoix de Saint-Marc; *Bulletin de l'Institut de droit de l'environnement (Lyon)*, 1985, no 2, p. 16, note J. Untermaier.

4. L'une de ces exceptions résulte, semble-t-il, de la législation danoise qui prévoit expressément le classement des zones humides, mais dans le cadre de la loi (générale) sur la conservation de la nature de 1969. Sur ces problèmes, cf. C. de Klemm, *La protection juridique des zones humides en droit comparé*, Soc. française pour le droit de l'environnement, Groupe Zones Humides, exposé prononcé lors de la réunion de Strasbourg (18.10.1984); *La conservation des zones humides, techniques juridiques et problèmes d'aménagement*, Conférence des Parties à la Convention de Ramsar, Groningue (Pays-Bas), 4 mai 1984, Doc. C2.10.

5. La journée d'étude par laquelle s'est achevée la Conférence de Lyon s'est déroulée en Dombes et dans le Val de Saône.

6. Ces étangs sont d'ailleurs d'origine artificielle. Créés au Moyen Age par des communautés monastiques, à partir des XIIè et XIIIè siècles, ils ont permis l'assainissement des terres dombistes très marécageuses jusqu'alors et la constitution de grands domaines agricoles.

7. Voir la loi française du 16 décembre 1964 relative au régime et à la répartition des eaux et à la lutte contre leur pollution.

Une image du contexte international de la Convention de Ramsar

ALEXANDRE KISS

Directeur de recherche au Centre national de la recherche scientifique, Strasbourg, France

Le présent rapport a pour objectif de donner une image du contexte international de la Convention de Ramsar, étant entendu que cette convention qui est au coeur même de la protection des zones humides, sera traitée par un autre rapporteur.

Pour commencer, il convient de rappeler l'évolution intervenue dans le domaine de la protection de la nature, spécialement dans la législation internationale. Le 19e siècle a déjà connu des conventions internationales relatives à l'exploitation de certaines espèces—poissons, phoques à fourrure—mais il s'agissait essentiellement d'une finalité économique dans la répartition des ressources. Avec le 20e siècle apparaissent les premiers traités visant à la conservation des espèces de la faune sauvage. Cependant ces textes sont encore imprégnés d'un fort anthropocentrisme et d'une méconnaissance des véritables données du problème : on fait une distinction entre espèces "utiles" et "nuisibles", seules les premières étant protégées, les secondes pouvant et devant être détruites. La prochaine étape de l'évolution interviendra à la fin des années 1960 avec la compréhension que les espèces ne peuvent pas être isolées les unes des autres et que, en outre, les mesures d'interdiction ne suffisent pas, qu'il est nécessaire d'assurer les conditions de survie des espèces menacées d'extinction, autrement dit qu'il faut aussi conserver leur habitat. Enfin, la dernière phase s'est ouverte il y a quelque années à peine: on parle de plus en plus de la conservation du patrimoine génétique dans son ensemble. Il y a donc de plus en plus une vue globale sur le problème de la conservation de la nature : des espèces, on est passé aux espaces avec tout ce que ces derniers contiennent.

Cette évolution est bien reflétée par des principes qu'énoncent des textes internationaux. La Déclaration de la Conférence de Stockholm de juin 1972 parle de la préservation des "échantillons représentatifs des écosystèmes naturels" dans l'intérêt des générations présentes et à venir (principe 2) et proclame la responsabilité particulière de l'homme pour sauvegarder et gérer avec sagesse le patrimoine constitué par la flore et la faune sauvages et leur habitat (principe 4). La recommandation no 99 du Plan d'action qui accompagne la Déclaration de Stockholm envisage, par ailleurs, déjà expressément les zones humides.

Après la Conférence de Stockholm, de nombreux traités ont trait, explicitement ou implicitement, aux zones humides: l'essentiel du présent rapport comportera leur examen. Parmi les textes non-obligatoires mais importants intervenus dans ce domaine, il convient de signaler dès maintenant, car il s'agit de solutions de principes, la Stratégie mondiale de la conservation élaborée par l'UICN et lancée en 1980. En parlant d'un des principes fondamentaux de la conservation, le maintien des processus écologiques essentiels, la Stratégie déclare que l'expression "systèmes entretenant la vie" désigne les plus importants de ces écosystèmes comme les forêts des bassins versant ou les zones humides côtières (estuaires, mangroves), particulièrement menacées.

Enfin, la Charte mondiale de la nature, adoptée et solennellement proclamée par l'Assemblée générale des Nations unies, le 28 octobre 1982, déclare que la viabilité génétique de la terre ne sera pas compromise; que la population de chaque espèce, sauvage ou domestique, sera maintenue au moins à un niveau suffisant pour en assurer la survie et que les habitats nécessaires à cette fin seront sauvegardés (principe 20). Un autre principe ajoute qu'une protection spéciale sera accordée aux parties de la surface de la planète qui sont uniques: échantillons représentatifs de tous les différents types d'écosystèmes et habitats des espèces rares ou menacées.

Ces principes étant affirmés, dans la Convention de Ramsar elle-même on trouve une double méthode de conservation. D'un côté, l'article 1 décrit les zones à conserver à cause de leur importance internationale "au point de vue écologique, botanique, zoologique, limnologique ou hydrologique". On peut y ajouter que le préambule du traité parle aussi des fonctions écologiques fondamentales des zones humides en tant que régulateurs du régime des eaux. D'un autre côté, on souligne l'importance de ces zones "en tant qu'habitats des oiseaux d'eau". Dans le premier cas, la conservation sera donc fondée sur des qualités qui sont en quelque sorte propres et intrinsèques, dans la deuxième sur des fonctions précises des zones humides dans la conservation des oiseaux d'eau.

Cette double méthode permet de faire une distinction parmi les nombreuses dispositions conventionnelles qui peuvent être appliquées pour sauvegarder des zones humides. Il convient de rappeler d'abord celles qui envisagent la conservation de zones à cause de leurs vertus globales, ensuite de passer en revue celles qui protègent certaines espèces, étant entendu que cette protection comprend celle de leur habitat—en particulier de zones humides.

Protection de zones à cause de leur valeur globale intrinsèque

Le premier instrument qui vient à l'esprit est, bien entendu, la Convention de l'UNESCO concernant la protection du patrimoine mondial, culturel et naturel. La définition donnée par l'article 2 du "patrimoine naturel" parle de "zones naturelles" qui ont une valeur universelle exceptionnelle du point de vue de la science, de la conservation ou de la beauté naturelle. Des zones humides—pas toutes, bien entendu—pourraient donc être protégées à ce titre, étant entendu que les conditions de protection dont bénéficieraient alors ces espaces sont supérieures à celles prévues par la Convention de Ramsar. Aussi, les zones humides ainsi protégées devraient être bien moins nombreuses: face aux 321 zones actuellement inscrites sur la liste de Ramsar, les espaces naturels figurant sur celle de l'UNESCO sont au total quelques dizaines seulement, dont tous ne sont pas des zones humides.

Plusieurs conventions régionales peuvent également venir en ligne de compte à cet égard, sans toutefois oublier que celle de Ramsar a une vocation universelle. Ainsi, la Convention africaine sur la conservation de la nature et des ressources naturelles, adoptées à Alger le 15 septembre 1968, prévoit aussi la création de réserves naturelles intégrales et de parcs nationaux ainsi que de réserves spéciales pour la conservation de la faune, des sols, des eaux, des forêts, etc. (art. 3). De même, la Convention d'Apia du 12 juin 1976 sur la protection de la nature dans le Pacifique Sud parle de la sauvegarde d'échantillons représentatifs d'écosystèmes naturels et de régions présentant un intérêt scientifique et prévoit la création de parcs nationaux et de réserves nationales.

Bien plus intéressant est le Protocole de Genève du 3 avril 1982 relatif aux aires spécialement protégées de la Méditerranée, un instrument intervenu dans le cadre des conventions protégeant la Méditerranée. Il prévoit la protection des aires marines importantes pour la sauvegarde des ressources naturelles et des sites naturels de la Méditerranée, étant entendu que de telles zones peuvent se situer entièrement ou partiellement en-deçà de la ligne de base, et des zones humides désignées par chacun des états contractants (art. 2). L'objectif est de sauvegarder des sites présentant une valeur biologique et écologique, la diversité génétique des espèces, ainsi que des niveaux satisfaisants pour leur population, leurs zones de reproduction et leurs habitats ainsi que des types représentatifs d'écosystèmes et les processus écologiques (art. 3).

La convention ASEAN (Association des nations de l'Asie du Sud-Est) sur la conservation de la nature et des ressources naturelles, adoptée à Kuala Lumpur le 9 juin 1985, prévoit également le maintien des processus écologiques essentiels et des systèmes entretenant la vie pour préserver la diversité génétique dans un langage dérivé directement de la Stratégie mondiale de la conservation. Dans cette perspective, l'article 13 engage les états à créer des parcs nationaux ou des réserves, ces dernières peuvent être dédiées à un objectif précis, comme la conservation d'un écosystème ou d'intérêts scientifiques, esthétiques, culturels ou éducatifs.

Dans tous ces cas, des zones humides peuvent être protégées en tant que telles, même si leur rôle en tant qu'habitat des oiseaux d'eau n'est pas le véritable fondement de la protection. Il en va autrement en ce qui concerne l'autre approche.

La protection de zones humides en tant qu'habitat d'espèces déterminées

Cette forme de protection peut être retrouvée dans toutes les conventions internationales qui protègent des espèces déterminées et leur habitat. Ainsi, la Convention de Bonn du 23 juin 1979 sur la conservation des espèces migratrices appartenant à la faune sauvage prévoit la protection des habitats des espèces menacées (art. 4). Or, de nombreuses espèces d'oiseaux d'eau figurent dans les annexes énumérant les espèces d'oiseaux et autres animaux migrateurs à protéger. Il en est ainsi de la Convention de Berne du 19 septembre 1979 relative à la conservation de la vie sauvage et du milieu naturel de l'Europe. L'article 4 prévoit la protection des "habitats des espèces sauvages de la flore et de la faune, en particulier de celles énumérées dans les annexes". Ces dernières comprennent de nombreuses espèces d'oiseaux d'eau.

La protection de zones humides en tant qu'habitat d'espèces à protéger joue un rôle particulièrement important dans la Directive du 2 avril 1979 du Conseil des Communautés européennes (J.O. no L 103 du 25.4.1979) concernant la conservation des oiseaux sauvages. L'article 3 de ce texte vise au maintien et au rétablissement d'une diversité et d'une superficie suffisantes d'habitats pour toutes les espèces d'oiseaux vivant naturellement à l'état sauvage en Europe et en particulier la création de zones de protection, l'entretien et l'aménagement des habitats, le rétablissement des biotopes détruits et la création de biotopes. Des zones de protection spéciale doivent être créées pour les espèces figurant à l'annexe I—dont de nombreuses espèces sont des oiseaux d'eau. Des mesures similaires doivent être adoptées à l'égard des espèces migratrices non visées à l'annexe I, compte tenu des besoins de protection dans la zone géographique d'application de la directive "en ce qui concerne leurs aires de reproduction, de mue et d'hivernage et les zones de relais dans leur aire de migration. A cette fin, les Etats membres attachent une importance particulière à la protection des zones humides et tout particulièrement de celles d'importance internationale" (art. 4 al. 2)."

Les mesures à prendre à cet égard doivent tendre à éviter la pollution ou la détérioration des habitats ainsi que les perturbations touchant les oiseaux.

Une résolution du Conseil du même jour (J.O. no L. 103 du 25.4.1979) invite, en outre, les Etats membres à communiquer, dans un délai de 24 mois, les zones de protection spéciale qu'ils classent et en particulier les zones qu'ils ont retenues ou qu'ils ont l'intention de retenir en tant que zones humides d'importance internationale.

En fait, la protection des zones humides en tant qu'habitat d'espèces protégées apparaît aussi dans des traités qui prévoient la protection directe de ces zones en raison de leur valeur intrinsèque. La Convention de l'UNESCO sur le patrimoine mondial parle aussi de zones constituant l'habitat d'espèces animales et végétales menacées, qui ont une valeur universelle exceptionnelle au point de vue de la science ou de la conservation (art. 2 al. 2). Il en est de même de la Convention africaine du 15 septembre 1968, également citée, dont l'article 8 vise à la protection particulière des espèces menacées d'extinction ainsi que de l'habitat nécessaire à leur survie. La liste de ces espèces contient également de nombreuses espèces d'oiseaux d'eau. Enfin, la Convention ASEAN du 9 juin 1985 envisage aussi la protection des espèces et de leurs habitats (art. 3) et cherche à assurer des dimensions suffisantes à ces habitats (art. 5, al. 1, c). On doit rappeler que le principe fondamental en matière de conservation des espèces est, dans le système de cette convention, la sauvegarde de la diversité génétique.

Il est bien entendu que la Convention de Ramsar occupe une place centrale dans cet ensemble d'instruments diplomatiques en ce qui concerne la protection des zones humides. La question qui se pose, toutefois, est de savoir comment ces dispositions plus ou moins convergentes se situent les unes par rapport aux autres.

La réponse nous semble être que rien n'interdit le cumul des dispositions à appliquer à une même situation. En dehors de l'inscription d'une zone sur la liste de la Convention de Ramsar, des mesures de protection peuvent être prises dans le contexte des conventions mondiales ou encore en vertu d'une mesure protégeant une ou plusieurs espèces en application d'une convention régionale ou de la directive de la CEE. Cette situation fait penser à des hôtels, restaurants, ou magasins recommandés par plusieurs guides où le client peut choisir soit d'utiliser la recommandation d'un guide, soit faire état de l'ensemble.

Cette image permet aussi de mieux comprendre le rôle de toutes ces dispositions convergentes. En droit international public, il est toujours tentant de conclure de l'existence de clauses plus ou moins analogues à celle d'une règle coutumière de droit international. Toutefois, c'est un exercice périlleux, car précisément on peut aussi affirmer que, s'il y a tant de règles conventionnelles, c'est parce que le droit coutumier n'en contient aucune dans le domaine visé. Par contre, ce que l'on peut dire sans risquer de se tromper, c'est que les dispositions cherchant à atteindre le même objectif, d'une façon directe ou indirecte, valorisent cet objectif. Pour les zones humides, cette valorisation est extrêmement importante car, dans une large mesure, elle correspond à une réhabilitation aux yeux de l'opinion publique: les zones tenues pour malsaines, dangereuses, menaçantes, sont ainsi considérées de plus en plus comme des éléments essentiels des écosystèmes et, pour une part, le berceau et la garantie du patrimoine génétique.

Protection of Wetlands in International Law

ALEXANDRE S. TIMOSHENKO

Institute of State and Law, Academy of Sciences of the U.S.S.R., Moscow*

General comments

According to Article 1 of the 1971 Ramsar Convention, wetlands are understood as areas of marsh, fen, peatland or water (including areas of marine water), the depth of which at low tide does not exceed six metres. Wetlands are found in practically all regions of the world and provide important ecological services. They regulate hydrology regimes and thus favour climatic stability. They serve as habitats for many bird species, including migrating birds. They also represent an important resource for genetic diversity.

Wetlands are ecologically very fragile, yet they have been an object of human activities for a long time. As a result, in the last hundred years alone, the total world area of wetlands has been reduced by half. The process of intensive destruction of wetlands continues without any serious evaluation of possible environmental consequences. To give an example, in nearly 200 large-scale polder (wetland reclamation) projects now completed or underway worldwide, only in nine cases has any serious study been made of environmental and ecological consequences[1].

The special characteristics of wetlands require that their effective protection should be mainly in the form of conservation. This also follows from the text of the Ramsar Convention where the term "conservation" is used. Therefore, the notion of "wise use" may have only a limited application in this field of environmental protection.

Wetlands may have international importance in two cases: when they serve as habitat for migrating birds or when they are situated simultaneously on the territories of two or more States.

The most important factor of international significance about wetlands is their role as habitat for migrating birds, mainly waterfowl. Conservation of these birds is the principal objective of the Ramsar Convention, which is the only multilateral treaty regulating protection of this category of natural objects. In the system of international environmental law, the Ramsar Convention was one of the first

---

* *Now* UNEP Environmental Law and Institutions Unit (ELIU)

international agreements with global coverage[2]. In a narrower sense, it is one of the important legal instruments of international wildlife law[3].

Under the Ramsar Convention the Contracting Parties, while considering their international responsibility for the conservation, management and wise use of migratory stocks of waterfowl, designate suitable wetlands within their territories for inclusion in the List of Wetlands of International Importance. The inclusion of a wetland into the List does not prejudice the exclusive sovereign rights of the Contracting Parties in whose territories the wetland is situated. The Contracting Parties formulate and implement their planning so as to promote the conservation of wetlands included in the List and, as far as possible, the wise use of wetlands in their territories. Meanwhile the Convention gives preference, in the list of other protection measures, to the establishment of nature reserves. In the case where a wetland extends over the territories of more than one State, the Contracting Parties concerned shall consult each other. They must also co-ordinate their present and future policies and regulations concerning the conservation of wetlands and their flora and fauna. The Contracting Parties, as the necessity arises, also convene conferences on the conservation of wetlands and waterfowl.

The Ramsar Convention entered into force in December 1975 and so has been operating for more than a decade. During this period the number of Contracting Parties has grown to exceed 40. The List of Wetlands of International Importance includes more than 300 territories covering over 20 million hectares. Two Conferences of the Contracting Parties have taken place and the third is forthcoming. In 1982 the Paris Protocol was signed (in force since the end of 1986), which regulates the procedures of introducing amendments to the Convention.

Critical analysis

The only basis for strengthening the effectiveness of wetland protection by means of international law is the critical analysis of the content of the pertinent international rules now in force and of their application. In this sense the main object for the current analysis is the Ramsar Convention itself. The effectiveness of an international norm can be determined in the first place by the sphere of its application. In this respect the Ramsar Convention does not yet comprise a sufficient number of countries (about 40 countries compared with 90 countries* participating in the CITES, for example). No less important was the fact that until recently, such major countries as the U.S.A. and France did not participate in the Convention. Among the non-participants there are still a considerable number of developing countries possessing many wetlands which might be of international importance.

The Ramsar Convention is justly seen as the first international environmental treaty of truly global coverage, and as the first agreement aimed exclusively at wildlife habitat protection[4]. At the same time the content of the Convention

---

* Now 62 compared to 110.

reflects certain deficiencies in the juridical approach to environmental problems typical of the beginning of the 1970s. For example, the Convention does not exhaustively stipulate the legal status of wetlands of international importance, does not project the required degree of unified State actions for wetland conservation, and has a number of lacunae in its procedural clauses.

The Ramsar Convention attempts to reconcile the exclusive sovereign rights of a State over its natural resources with the State's responsibility for environmental protection and rational use. This conception is a cornerstone for the entire body of international environmental law. A year later it was more or less adequately formulated in Principle 21 of the Stockholm Declaration. Under the Ramsar Convention territorial sovereignty over wetlands of international importance is linked to state responsibility for protection and wise use of migrating waterfowl.

The formulation of Article 2 of the Convention gives every reason to believe that even a wetland of international importance is treated in the category of national resources. At the same time Article 5 indicates that individual wetlands can extend over the territories of more than one State. This means that such wetlands aquire the status of a shared natural resource or, according to the terminology proposed within the framework of the World Commission on Environment and Development, the status of a transboundary resource[5]. It may also be assumed that individual wetlands covered by the Ramsar Convention, due to their unique characteristics, might have such ecological value that their conservation would affect common interests of the international community as a whole. In such a case a conception of "common heritage of mankind" or "common property" can be applied. We cannot exclude this future possibility since the "common heritage" concept gets more and more international recognition (although its paramount application has not been confirmed by *opinio juris*).

As stated earlier, protection of wetlands is seen primarily as conservation. Nevertheless, according to Article 2 of the Ramsar Convention, wetland conservation is envisaged as working in parallel with "wise use". In this context, the very possibility of coupling effective conservation of a wetland (as an integral ecosystem) with any intensive use (even when it is considered to be wise) sounds doubtful. Besides, it is not clear what the exact scientific and legal meaning of the term "wise use" itself is, taking into account that the even more widespead term "rational use" of natural resources is still far from a uniform interpretation in international law. The content of the term "wise use" seems to be especially vague. It is understandable that this notion had been introduced into the Ramsar Convention with the aim of establishing certain limits to human utilization of wetlands. However, in view of the reasons given above, practical application of these limits seems questionable.

The lacunae in the Ramsar Convention are not limited to insufficient determination of the status of wetlands of international importance. This deficiency is objectively conditioned by the fact that the Convention had been elaborated before the concepts of "shared resources", "world heritage" or "biosphere reserves" were developed. At the present stage of development of international environmental law, the international quality of wetlands to be included on the Ramsar List might be formulated more clearly. Consequently the conservation of wetlands of international importance should not only be ensured by the States on whose territories such wetlands are situated: it is also necessary to stipulate the exact obligations of all States when an activity significantly affecting the ecological quality of a wetland of international importance takes place on their territory, or is under their control. In other words, international legal guarantees of the effective conservation of wetlands having international importance against negative transboundary interferences must be established. In this context it is appropriate to refer to the statement made by the delegation of Sweden at the Groningen Conference of the Contracting Parties: the statement indicated close interdependence between conservation of wetlands of international importance and the "acid rain" problem caused by activities under the control of other countries[6].

Certain difficulties in the application of the Ramsar Convention were created by the fact that the text of the Convention had not stipulated the procedure for introducing amendments to the Convention. Part of the experience gained in the field of international environmental treaties is the ability to evolve according to changing external factors: accumulation of knowledge, technological developments, evolution of the political situation, etc. As a result, necessary amendments to the treaty should be introduced with the aim to ensure optimal correlation between the treaty's provisions and the external "techno-socio-political environment". These changes in the treaty provisions may take the form of amendments, annexes and other similar acts. It is not by chance that in the field of environmental protection the so-called "framework conventions" are so widespread. The reason is that such conventions presuppose further development in the international legal regulation of certain aspects of environmental protection, as external conditions change.

The necessity of introducing special amendment procedures to the Ramsar Convention had been indicated at the Cagliari and Groningen conferences of the Contracting Partiers. By now this problem has been settled in principle by the signature and entry into force of the Paris Protocol. As a result it may be expected that a number of recommendations proposed at the Cagliari and Groningen conferences have been transformed into legal rules. But immediately a question arises: how to apply these new norms, since not all Contracting Parties to the Ramsar Convention are signatories to the Paris Protocol.

In a formal juridical sense this question is to be settled according to the relevant provisions of the Vienna Convention on the Law of Treaties (Arts. 30, 40), which provide that "in relations between a State party to both treaties and a State party to only one of the treaties, the treaty to which both States are parties governs the mutual rights and obligations". This means that in relations between a State Party to only the Ramsar Convention and a State Party to the Convention and the Paris Protocol as well, their mutual rights and obligations are governed exclusively by the Ramsar provisions.

In other words, a problem of limited application of possible amendments to the Ramsar Convention arises. This problem extends beyond the frames of jurisprudence. The effectiveness of a legal rule directly depends on the number of States which accept its obligatory character—and also depends on the degree of uniformity of the activities of those participating in international relations. In the sphere of international environmental protection, such uniformity is particularly important, since the non-participation of a certain number of States to agreed measures to protect the environment may substantially reduce the effect of these measures or nullify them.

Thus the process of practical application of the Paris Protocol demands not only the settlement of purely juridical problems but also calls for justified evaluation of the positions of the majority of States with respect to the possible amendments to the Ramsar Convention. It is necessary to take into account the views not only of current members but also of potential participants to the Convention. Otherwise introduction of "unpopular" amendments may negatively influence both the accession of new participants to the Convention and the inclusion of new sites into the List of Wetlands of International Importance. Every amendment to the Ramsar Convention should adequately reflect the balance of what must be done and of what can be done in existing conditions. Only the collective wisdom of the Contracting Parties may secure further improvement of the Ramsar Convention's effectiveness.

The U.S.S.R.'s participation in the Ramsar Convention

The Convention on Wetlands of International Importance Especially as Waterfowl Habitat was signed by the U.S.S.R. on 15 February 1974 and ratified on 26 December 1975. At the time of signature the following statement was made:

> "The Government of the Union of the Soviet Socialist Republics deems it necessary to state that the provisions of Article 9 of the Convention limiting participation of certain States is in contradiction with the universally recognized principle of sovereign equality of States".

The U.S.S.R. ratification instruments were deposited on 11 October 1976. In accordance with Article 10 the Convention entered into force for the Soviet Union from 11 February 1977.

To perform its obligations under the Ramsar Convention, the U.S.S.R. carried out a number of activities at national level. Firstly, the U.S.S.R. Council of Ministers adopted the Decree of 26 December 1975 "On measures to carry out the obligation of the Soviet part under the Convention on Wetlands of International Importance Especially as Waterfowl Habitat". The Decree gave the Ministry of Agriculture (now Gosagroprom) functions to carry out the responsibilities related to implementation of the Ramsar Convention and pertinent control[7].

The Council of Ministers of the Union Republics, the Minister of Agriculture and the U.S.S.R. Academy of Sciences were made responsible for securing wetland protection under the Ramsar Convention and for carrying out the necessary scientific research. The national List of Wetlands of International Importance was adopted; it includes the following territories: Kandfalaksha Bay of the White Sea, Matsaalu Bay of the Baltic Sea, Volga River Delta, Kirov Bay, Krasnovodsk Bay and North Chelenk Bay of the Caspian Sea, Karkin Bay of the Black Sea, Danube River downstream marshes, Khanka la Issyk-Kul Lake, Kurgaldjin, Teghis, Turgaj and Irghis Rivers downstream[8].

These wetlands are major reserves and habitats for migratory waterfowl. The protection of these species must be also secured in their habitats situated in other countries.

As stated by the Soviet delegation at the Groningen Conference, besides the 12 wetlands included into the Ramsar List in the Soviet Union, 16 additional wetlands, covering nearly three million hectares, fitted the Ramsar criteria of wetlands of international importance. All these wetlands are treated as nature reserves and protected in state zapovednics and zakazniks. The report of the U.S.S.R. delegation also outlined an impressive range of studies to identify and describe 300 sites of international or national importance beyond the additional 16 sites[9].

Conclusions

The Ramsar Convention is an important international instrument in the sphere of environmental protection and a unique document in the field of wetland conservation. Wetlands are places of great significance for a number of ecological processes. The birth of the Ramsar Convention coincided with the initial period of vigorous development of environmental treaties. The Convention served as a useful model for the elaboration of other important international treaties as, for example, the UNESCO Convention on World Heritage, the Bonn Convention on Migratory Species, and such important international programmes as MAB, creating the biosphere reserves network. In recent State practice one can find a number of instruments analogous to both the fundamental conception and separate provisions of the Ramsar Convention. While utilizing this valuable experience States have been taking into consideration both the advantages and the shortcomings of the Convention.

The Ramsar Convention, like any international treaty based on the compromise of different state interests, is not free of drawbacks. Nevertheless, after more than a decade of practical application of the Convention, the rise in number of Contracting Parties and the expansion of the territory of wetlands protected in accordance with the Ramsar List give a convincing example of the great practical value of this international treaty. The juridical and political processes of the Ramsar Convention continue and are in general of a positive character. The basis of these processes should be an understanding that the efficacy of the protection of wetlands of international importance can be secured only by the maximum possible participation of the overwhelming majority of States.

The following problems on the protection of wetlands of international importance are still unsettled; these problems have both a juridical and a political character:

● the increase in number of the Ramsar Convention participants;

● the achievement of maximum uniformity with regard to activities according to the Convention provisions;

- a more precise definition of criteria of the wetlands of international importance, of their status and regime both under national and international law;

- a more precise definition of the regime of the wetlands falling under the category of shared natural resources;

- ensuring the protection of wetlands of international importance from significant negative transboundary impacts;

- strengthening the conservation of wetlands as an important resource of biological diversity.

Notes

1. Stoel, T.B. 1985, Pulling out the plug, *IUCN Bulletin*, No. 10/12, p. 114.

2. See: Kolbasov, O.S. 1982, *Miezdunarodno-pravovaja ochrana okruzhajushej sredy (International Legal Protection of Environment)*, Moscow, p. 135-136; Johnson-Theutenberg B. 1976, *International Environmental Law*, Stockholm, p. 62-63; Kiss, A. 1976, *Survey of Current Developments in International Environmental Law*, Morges, p. 86-87.

3. Lyster, S. 1985, *International Wildlife Law*, Grotius, Cambridge, p. 183-207.

4. See, for example, Lyster, *op. cit.*, p. 206.

5. WCED Doc. WCED/86/23/Add. I.

6. Convention on Wetlands of International Importance, Especially as Waterfowl Habitat, Conference of the Contracting Parties, Groningen, 7-12 May 1984, Doc. Plen. C2.4, p. 3.

7. See Sbornik Postanovlenij (the USSR collected decrees), 1976, N. 4, st. 16.

8. *Ob Ochrane Okruzhajushej sredy 1986, Sbornik documentov partii i pratel tela tya (On the Environment, collected Documents of the CPSU and Soviet Government)*, Moscow, p. 408.

9. Conference of the Contracting Parties, Groningen. Doc. Plen. C2.3, p. 9, 10.

The Ramsar Convention Today

DANIEL NAVID
IUCN, Gland, Switzerland*

Introduction

I have been asked by the Conference organizers to speak on the theme of the Ramsar Convention. I have done so several times in the recent past at scientific meetings where it has been necessary to go into considerable detail about the role and functioning of international law. Needless to say, I am delighted to have the chance to speak at this time to a conference for lawyers and policy-makers. As the participants are no doubt familiar with the provisions and history of the Convention, I do not intend to go into any great detail for those points and certainly will not attempt to lecture you on theories of international law.

A Convention brochure is available in three languages which explains all that you need to know about the Ramsar Convention. Copies have been circulated here. By the way, in one respect that brochure is happily out-of-date. Now there are 45 Contracting Parties and Ghana, we understand, will be the 46th Member State in the very near future**.

So, the purpose of this presentation will be to:

- Give a limited general overview about the provisions of the Ramsar Convention;

- Provide a brief report on the results of this year's third Meeting of the Conference of the Parties at Regina in Canada; and

- Make some observations about current national applications of the Convention for wetland conservation—and to suggest further requirements in this regard.

Limited overview on the provisions of the Convention

The Ramsar Convention, or as it is formally known, the Convention on Wetlands of International Importance especially as Waterfowl Habitat, has a good deal to offer. It was the first modern global nature conservation treaty; it remains the only one which is dedicated to the conservation of selected ecosystems types, in this

---

* Now Secretary General, Ramsar Convention Bureau, Gland, Switzerland
** Now 62 Contracting Parties

case wetlands, and to the species dependent upon them, and it is predicated upon the promotion of international cooperation for nature conservation rather than confrontation, which has characterized certain subsequent international conservation agreements.

The Ramsar Convention is now undergoing an exciting period of growth. States in both the industrialized and developing worlds are finding that the Convention provides considerable benefits for international cooperation. Presently, as noted above, there are some 45 Contracting Parties throughout the world and many more States are expected to join in the near future.

The Ramsar Convention was adopted following a series of international conferences and technical meetings mainly held under the auspices of the International Waterfowl Research Bureau (IWRB). It entered into force in late 1975 upon the deposit of an instrument of ratification by Greece, the seventh State to do so.

The Secretariat, or Bureau as it is referred to in Article 8 of the Convention, is provided by my organization, the International Union for Conservation of Nature and Natural Resources (IUCN). We have been assisted in this task by the IWRB as Scientific Advisor. At the Regina Conference steps were taken to formalize this cooperation. The Governing Body of the Convention, the Conference of the Contracting Parties, meets periodically to review developments under the treaty. The First Regular Conference was held in Italy in 1980, the Second in the Netherlands in 1984 and, as I have mentioned, the Third was held in Regina, Canada, this past spring[*].

The broad objectives of the Convention are to stem the loss of wetlands and to ensure their conservation in view of their importance for ecological processes as well as for their rich fauna and flora. To meet these objectives, the Convention provides for general obligations relating to the conservation of wetlands throughout the territory of the Contracting Parties and for special obligations pertaining to those wetlands which have been designated in a "List of Wetlands of International Importance".

The Convention takes an extremely broad approach in defining the "wetlands" to be covered under its ambit. Wetlands, as defined in Article 1, are "areas of marsh, fen, peatland or water, whether natural or artificial, permanent or temporary, with water that is static or flowing, fresh, brackish or salt, including areas of marine waters the depth of which at low tide does not exceed six metres". In addition, Article 2 provides that wetlands covered "may incorporate riparian and coastal zones adjacent to the wetlands and islands or bodies of marine water deeper than six metres at low tide lying within the wetlands".

As a result of these provisions, the coverage of the Convention extends to a wide variety of habitat types including rivers, coastal areas—and even coral reefs!

There is a general obligation, as noted above, for the Contracting Parties to include wetland conservation considerations within their national planning. According to Article 3, para. 1, "The Contracting Parties shall formulate and implement their planning so as to promote ... as far as possible the wise use of

---

[*]   The Fourth has been held in Montreux, Switzerland, in July 1990.

wetlands in their territory". The Contracting Parties interpreted this wise use requirement to mean the maintenance of the ecological character of wetlands (Recommendation 1.5 of the First Conference of the Contracting Parties, Cagliari, 1980). Major attention was given to this requirement at the Regina Conference, and this will be discussed below.

A second obligation under the Convention is the designation of wetlands for inclusion in a "List of Wetlands of International Importance" maintained by IUCN. Specific conservation duties pertain to the listed sites. At least one site must be designated by each Contracting Party (Article 2, para. 4) with selection based on "international significance in terms of ecology, botany, zoology, limnology or hydrology" (Article 2, para. 2). Criteria for selection, with greatest relevance to importance for waterfowl, were adopted by the Contracting Parties at their 1980 Conference and modified at Regina better to cover other wetland values.

Finally, Contracting Parties are obliged to promote the conservation of wetlands in their territory through the establishment of nature reserves. This applies to wetlands whether or not included on the "List".

Of all the aspects of the Convention, the List of Wetlands of International Importance has attracted the most international attention. In practice, the Contracting Parties have gone far beyond the mandatory designation of only one site; presently 381 sites covering well over 25,500,000 hectares* have been designated for the List. Furthermore, no site has been deleted from the List and replaced by another, despite the possibility that this might be done by a "Contracting Party in its urgent national interest" (Article 4, para. 2).

Although most Contracting Parties have designated wetlands sites on the basis of their importance for waterfowl, other faunal and floral interests are being taken into consideration and presently a rather comprehensive selection of major wetland types is included in the Ramsar List, especially for the Western Palearctic region.

Brief report on the Regina Conference results

The Third Meeting of the Conference of the Contracting Parties marked a turning point in the history of the Ramsar Convention.

After many years of effort by the Contracting Parties and by IUCN and IWRB, the administrative provisions of the Convention were strengthened—provisions which were criticized in the World Conservation Strategy in 1980 as follows:

> "Experience has shown that an international Convention must have a (permanent, secure) secretariat and a financial mechanism to be effective, but the Wetlands Convention lacks both".

Although this assessment was a bit harsh, in so far as the Contracting Parties were able nonetheless to achieve considerable conservation gains via the Ramsar Convention, it has been evident that much more could be done if the administrative problems were solved. I am sure that you are all well aware of the long history of

---

* Now 533 sites covering over 32,000,000 ha

efforts to remedy the administrative shortcomings in the Convention. The first Conference of the Parties in 1980 issued the call for necessary Convention amendments, and for the immediate provision of voluntary funding to the interim secretariat until such time as an amendment providing for a sound financial base might become operative. Contributions were therefore forthcoming from several of the Contracting Parties. However, due to legal and constitutional impediments to voluntary financing by many other Contracting Parties, it became clear that adequate financial support and hence administrative continuity could be ensured following the formal amendment of the Convention.

In December 1982, an Extraordinary Conference of the Contracting Parties was held in Paris. Here a Protocol was adopted, providing for the needed amendment procedure and for additional official language versions of the Convention. This Protocol entered into force in October 1986, and thus provided the basis for the convening of an Extraordinary Conference at Regina to adopt needed administrative amendments to the Convention.

In the meantime, the Contracting Parties worked towards the elaboration of the required administrative regime. Discussions on the subject were held at the Second Conference of the Contracting Parties at Groningen, Netherlands, in 1984. Thereafter a Task Force led by the Netherlands developed recommendations for the Contracting Parties on future secretariat requirements, the text of necessary Convention amendments, fixed Rules of Procedure for meetings of the Conference of the Parties and the need for a Standing Committee to act on behalf of the Parties inbetween meetings of the Conference.

To those not involved in inter-governmental work, it might seem that it took an inordinate amount of time to achieve the changes everyone wanted under the Ramsar Convention. Unfortunately, there was no alternative, following the identification of the problems in 1980, to arrive at the required solutions. International law seems to move rather slowly or not at all!

Ultimately, on 28 May 1987, the Extraordinary Conference was held at Regina to adopt a series of administrative amendments.

The expeditious adoption of these amendments was accomplished only because of the good will of the Contracting Parties and because of the legal gymnastics of several of the delegates, including a few of the participants at this meeting, who represented countries such as Denmark, France, the Netherlands and Sweden at the Regina Conference. This was the case because that Conference faced significant problems of a legal nature concerning voting rights, size of the meeting quorum, provisional application of the amendments, etc.

In any event, the following is a brief description of what was accomplished in Regina:

A. Administrative measures

Convention Amendments. Amendments to the Convention were adopted providing for improved organization and increased authority for the Conference of the Contracting Parties, including provisions for the adoption of a financial regime based upon mandatory contributions from the Contracting Parties.

Secretariat. Based upon these Amendments, the Parties decided to establish permanent secretariat arrangements with an independent office created at IUCN Headquarters to deal with administrative, diplomatic and legal matters, assisted by a unit of the Secretariat based at the IWRB with primary responsibility for technical and scientific matters[*].

Budget. A Convention budget for the next triennium totalling US$ 1.2 million[**] was also adopted. This budget is to be funded by contributions from the 45 Contracting Parties determined by reference to a ratio of payments based upon the United Nations scale of contributions. Furthermore, pledges of additional support have been given by non-governmental organizations including WWF-US and the Royal Society for the Protection of Birds (UK). In anticipation of these funds flowing in 1988, the Secretariat has already received considerable voluntary funding and project support from several of the Contracting Parties.

Standing Committee. A Standing Committee was formed to serve as an Executive Body to guide the work of the Convention between the Conferences of the Contracting Parties. It is comprised of Pakistan (Chairman), Canada (Vice-Chairman), Chile, the Netherlands, New Zealand, Poland, Tunisia, Switzerland and the U.S.A.

Next Conference of the Parties. The next meeting of the Conference of the Parties will be held in 1990 in Switzerland.

B. Conservation Matters

The Conference did not only address administrative requirements; significant time was also devoted to conservation issues as follows:

Workshops. Detailed technical workshops were held on the subjects of:

● Criteria for identifying wetlands of international importance;

● Migratory bird flyway and reserve network;

● Wise use of wetlands; and

● The Ramsar Convention as a vehicle for linking wetland conservation and development.

Recommendations. A thorough review was given to the status of wetlands in all regions of the world. Conference recommendations were passed on a variety of conservation topics, including the need for measures to deal with conservation problems facing particular wetlands (e.g. Azraq in Jordan), procedures and proposals on increased development assistance to enhance the conservation of

---

[*] Now combined at IUCN headquarters.
[**] Now approximately US$ 2.25 million.

wetlands, increased involvement in the Convention by developing country nations, and the need for refined criteria for the selection of wetlands for the Ramsar List, as well as improved management procedures for wetland conservation and development.

North America Day. A special day at the Conference was devoted to a review of wetland conservation problems and opportunities in North America. In this connection, the host government of Canada announced the addition of 11 new sites for the Ramsar List, with the United States announcing the addition of 2 more U.S. sites. Also on the occasion of "North America Day", the Conference was addressed by HRH The Duke of Edinburgh with a call for increased international efforts to help conserve wetlands and wetland species.

A "preliminary proceedings" volume is scheduled to be released in autumn 1987, followed by the full proceedings with all scientific papers in spring 1988.

This dry recital of facts and figures does not begin to give the flavour of the Regina Meeting. The Contracting Parties have established a very full agenda for conservation work in the next triennium. The management of specific sites and the development of national wetland policies have been highlighted for action. Hence the Ramsar Bureau views this present meeting on legal requirements for wetland conservation with extreme importance. We are eager to move forward to implement the programme of work adopted at Regina on the basis of expert input such as that available from this Conference.

Uses of the Convention at national level

As this meeting considers legal tools to help conserve wetlands, I think that it would be enlightening to consider various national experiences under the Ramsar Convention.

A few extracts from the National Reports provided to the Regina Conference demonstrate the range of values which countries perceive from being members of the Convention:

1. The opportunity to fulfil existing agenda

The report from the U.S.A. noted that:

> "The Convention is an appropriate organization for sharing techno-
> logy related to wetland conservation, management and research and
> it complements U.S. concerns for wetlands protection in the U.S., in
> the Western Hemisphere and throughout the world".

The U.S.A. went on to state that "the Convention provides an extremely useful tool for flyway states to coordinate and manage shared migratory resources, to share data on habitats and populations necessary to the wise use of wetlands in ways compatible with environmental and non-government programs".

2. The prestige value for implementing national programmes

The Danish report for the Regina Conference indicated:

> "In Denmark there have been only minor problems with implementation of the Convention probably because the Ramsar Convention has been one of the oldest and most spectacular of the nature conservation conventions that Denmark has ratified".

3. As a tool to promote conservation against other interests

The Belgian report stated:

> "The Ramsar Convention has proved useful as a moral support in the struggle for the protection of our wetlands. Ramsar should be sufficiently powerful to realize a restriction of the agricultural optimalisation politics in areas with mixed nature conservation and agricultural functions".

4. As a basis for international support

A fourth and final perspective can be seen in the Moroccan report:

> "Ratification of the Convention enables the Government to concentrate efforts for the protection of certain wetlands and to benefit from financial and technical assistance".

Given these perceived benefits, the question that needs to be posed is how do the Parties actually implement the Convention? We have found that in the vast majority of cases implementation is handled through existing national legislation, with greatest emphasis upon the protection of the Ramsar sites in the country concerned. Indeed the overview of National Reports prepared for the Regina Conference noted that

> "It seems that few, if any, Contracting Parties have adopted detailed, clearly formulated national wetland policies. Nevertheless, many Contracting Parties give details of measures and legislation going well beyond the scope of classic nature conservation which affect wetlands".

From the Regina Conference National Reports we can examine examples of national experience whereby wetland conservation has been enhanced.

1. Site-specific protection

Because of Ramsar designation, the U.S.S.R. has given protection to Lake Khanka, portions of which were not previously protected; Denmark has noted that Ramsar Convention designation has facilitated arguments for conservation of particular sites; and Australia has remarked that sites on the Ramsar List generally have greater priority for research and management funding.

Perhaps more dramatic have been court cases in Austria (Hainburg) and Greece (Nestos Delta), where Ramsar designation has been determinative in providing protection to a specific site.

2. Trans-border cooperation

The specific role of the Convention to promote border cooperation has also been cited by various Contracting Parties. For example, the Federal Republic of Germany has reported cooperation with the Netherlands over a Ramsar site near the border between the two countries (unterer Niederrhein), where joint efforts are underway for waterfowl conservation.

More difficult have been cases related by Iran concerning the diversion of water supplies to a Ramsar site (Lake Hamoun) caused by disturbances across the border in Afghanistan, and the destruction of wetland resources as a result of Iraqi chemical warfare. Nonetheless it is interesting indeed to see that Iran has raised the application of the Convention as a means that might be used to deal with these situations.

3. Wise use of wetlands

Despite the ways in which national legislation has been used to implement site conservation under the Ramsar Convention and despite some limited progress in transboundary cooperation for wetland conservation under the Ramsar Convention, more innovative legal mechanisms are required to give full effect at national level to the Convention. In particular, more must be done to help implement the "wise use" provisions of the Convention.

The Regina Conference adopted a resolution which helped to define what is needed in this regard, especially for the adoption of national wetland policies. There is considerable scope for legal innovation in such work.

This matter is especially important for developing country Parties to the Convention. In order to achieve the greatest conservation and development benefits from wetland resources for developing countries, the "wise use" provision of the Ramsar Convention is of paramount importance.

Conclusion

The Ramsar Convention faces a very bright future following the successful Regina Conference of the Parties. The likelihood of considerably more Contracting Parties as well as more effective conservation measures under the Convention is great. To help realize this potential, however, there is a very important role to be played by legal experts to help frame the most appropriate provisions for the implementation of the Convention at national level. Thus, this present Conference is extremely pertinent. I look forward to having the chance for individual talks with several of you as well as to receiving the conclusions of the meeting. I should very much like to convey those conclusions to the Ramsar Convention Standing Committee when it next meets in late January 1988 at San José in Costa Rica.

Competent Authorities and Levels of Decision-making in Wetland Protection

FRANÇOISE BURHENNE-GUILMIN
Head, IUCN Environmental Law Centre, Bonn, Germany

and WOLFGANG BURHENNE
Chairman, IUCN Commission on Environmental Policy, Law and Administration, Bonn, Germany

Introduction

The questionnaire which was prepared during the preparatory phase of this Conference contained three questions related to "Authorities with Responsibility for Protection" as follows:

1. Is the protection of wetlands the responsibility of the State or of another public authority (State/region or component state/local authority/other authority)?

2. When the State has responsibility for the protection of wetlands, is this responsibility exercised at the Central level or devolved upon other authorities?

3. Are the responsibilities of the State discharged by a Minister with specific responsibility for the protection of nature or by another Minister?

Although some replies give valuable information on the institutional aspects of wetland protection, many of them use the "yes or no" technique, leaving the reader "*sur sa faim*".

Yet the replies and other information available on relevant national legislation allow the making of several observations at the outset:

1. It is of course necessary to distinguish between the authority to legislate and the authority to implement, a fact which was not reflected in the questionnaire;

2. The authority (both to legislate and to implement) depends, within one jurisdiction, on the type of protection instruments available, and varies with them;

3. Each country is a case in itself, thus making a general overview more or less impossible;

4. Little information is available on this subject, and practically none on a comparative basis[1].

We shall try to justify these observations below, with examples chosen from a variety of jurisdictions[2].

A variety of situations and a variety of responses

In order to describe with some accuracy the situation in various jurisdictions, it is important to distinguish between the different techniques of wetland protection. Three main techniques will be examined here separately: protected areas, general protection of habitat types, and planning controls, although their use may be interlinked.

Protected areas

It is not the purpose of this paper to study the various kinds of protected areas which may exist at national level. Another presentation to this Conference will examine their usefulness for wetlands, and related problems such as financing and land ownership.

Suffice it to say here that including wetlands in protected areas such as national parks and reserves remains a powerful way of achieving the protection of important wetlands, a factor which tends to be overlooked at a time when other protection techniques are emerging.

Virtually all legal systems allow giving specific areas special protective status with a (perhaps illusory) greater degree of permanency than other planning controls. The legislative authority relating to them differs, and so does the implementation powers; we have selected a few examples.

In **Denmark**[3], where legislative authority for nature conservation is centralized, it is interesting to note that the National Forest and Nature Protection Agency of the Ministry of the Environment has no competence with regard to individual conservation orders (instituting a set of rules for a given site using, more or less, an easement technique) although 3.5% of the area in Denmark is covered by such measures.

Denmark is divided into 25 conservation districts, roughly corresponding to the court districts of the country. These districts each have an independent special Conservation Board chaired by the local judge. The Conservation Board is competent to take individual conservation orders. Proposals may be made to the Boards by the local communities, the national conservation authorities, and one NGO (the Danish Nature Conservation Society).

The decision of these Boards may be appealed to a Main Conservation Board in Copenhagen, composed of some ten members including judges of the Supreme Court as well as representatives of political parties. A judge chairs the Main Conservation Board. This system has provided great stability to the system of individual conservation orders (which, incidently, are regarded as "a taking" and thus subject to compensation).

By contrast, the Minister of the Environment may impose conservation measures over areas of the Danish territorial waters (Art. 60, National Conservation Act).

In **France**[4], the regime of National Parks is established by the Act of 22 July 1960. The initiative for the creation of a Park is taken by the Minister of the Environment. Local authorities are consulted as to the principle of the creation and a public inquiry follows; the park is then established by *Décret en Conseil d'Etat*.

The management and administration of each Park, as well as the regulations applicable to it, are the responsibility of a national public body created to that effect by the Decree establishing the Park. Local interests must be represented in this public body.

The powers of the national authorities are equally predominant on Nature Reserves: the Act of 10 July 1976 on Nature Conservation provides that after a procedure of preliminary considerations, a public inquiry is held and local authorities consulted. The Minister for the Environment proceeds to further consultation at national level and the designation is then made by decree.

Nature Reserves are all administered and managed by the State, although the Act permits their management by a public body created for that purpose (as in the case of National Parks).

Since 1987 (Decree No 77-1295 of 25 November 1977), the *Commissaire de la République* may, by *Arrêté*, protect certain habitats (e.g. wetlands) under certain conditions. Such *Arrêtés de biotopes* may also prohibit certain activities (e.g. spraying of pesticides).

The Nature Conservation Act (1964: 822) of **Sweden**[5] provides that nature conservation is the responsibility of both national and local authorities. County administration must actively promote nature conservation; the National Environment Protection Board is responsible for the national supervision of nature conservation.

The Nature Conservation Ordinance (3 June 1976) implements this basic premise by determining the roles of the Board and the County Administrations under the Act. Thus, regulations concerning the administration of National Parks are to be made by the Board after consulting the County Administration, while regulations of activities within Reserves are to be issued by the County Administration after consultation with the Board! Of course, this is not the only provision of the Ordinance, which proceeds to a detailed division of competence betwee the two levels of government on matters covered by the Act.

At Government level, responsibility for environmental questions is vested, to a large extent, in the Ministry of Agriculture. The National Environment Protection Board is the central administrative authority in the environmental sector. In the field of conservation, the Board exercises mainly advisory and planning functions, as the County Administrations are the main decision-making bodies in this respect; the Planning Departments of the County Administrations have nature conservation sections, working in close cooperation with the Board.

In the **United Kingdom**[6], the responsibility to declare and manage the network of National Nature Reserves (NNRs) is exercised by the Nature Conservancy Council (NCC), an independent Council funded through the Department of the Environment. The aim of the NNRs is to protect, in perpetuity and through appropriate control and management, the most important areas of natural or semi-natural vegetation. It is achieved by the purchase of freeholdings of land, the negotiations of leases with owners, and the negotiation of formal agreements with owners and occupiers on mutually acceptable management. Powers to establish Marine Nature Reserves were created by the Wildlife and Countryside Act of 1981. The NCC also plays a role on these, although they are designated by order made by the Secretary of State for the Environment in England or the appropriate Secretary of State in Scotland and Wales, on the advice of NCC.

In the **United States**[7], in addition to protected areas created and managed at state level, several types of protected areas exist and are managed at federal level. The key to this power is federal ownership of the land, a factor which is not surprising in a country where approximately one-third of the land is owned by the federal government.

National Parks are established by an Act of Congress, and are managed by the National Parks Service of the Department of the Interior, along with many other types of areas which form part of the National Parks System (e.g. national wild rivers, national preserves). Several other federal schemes or programmes which, directly or indirectly, permit the protection of habitat at federal level exist: they all are based on federal government ownership or on powers granted by Congress to the federal administration to acquire land. The National Wildlife Refuge System is one of them, administered since 1966 by the U.S. Fish and Wildlife Service of the Department of the Interior. The authority to establish such refuges and to acquire land for them stems from various federal acts, most notably the Migratory Birds Convention Act of 1929. It requires the consent of the state legislature concerned prior to the acquisition of land by the federal government for the purposes of the Act.

Another important scheme is the National Wilderness Preservation System, created by the Wilderness Act of 1964. Although the purpose of the wilderness area is the preservation of the wilderness character of large tracts of land rather than habitat protection, Wilderness Areas play an important role in that regard. There is no single federal agency in charge of the system. The agency which administers the area at the time of its inclusion into the system by Act of Congress retains jurisdiction over it thereafter.

Germany[8], another Federal State, has a completely different system. The Federal Nature Conservation Act (consolidated and newly published on 2 March 1987) provides for six kinds of protected areas and defines their purposes as well as very broadly defined prohibitions in relation to each type. None of these provisions, however, are directly applicable, with the exception of a duty on the part of the *Land* to consult the Federal Ministry concerned when National Parks are designed. Article 4 of the Act, based on the constitutional situation, provides that these provisions "represent a framework for the adoption of complementary legal provisions by the various *Länder*".

The German *Länder* thus have a large degree of autonomy in the legislative implementation of this framework, and full freedom with regard to the modalities of its implementation. From the point of view of jurisdiction, it may generally be said that *Länder* have empowered their higher Nature Conservation authorities (districts) with the authority to designate *Naturschutzgebiete*, while *Lands-*

chaftsschutzgebiete, Naturdenkmale and *Landschaftsbestanteile* are generally designated by the lower conservation authorities (districts or communes).

As a result of the constitutional situation, even National Parks are, in Germany, established by the *Länder*. They merely have an obligation to consult with the Federal authorities with regard to the designation of such Parks (Art. 12(4) of the Act).

Austria[9] is yet another case which is characterized by the absence of a general or special legislative prerogative of the Federation on nature conservation. Protected areas fall entirely under the jurisdiction of the *Länder*. As a result of this situation, the legal instruments of the various *Länder* are even more varied than is the case in Germany. All of them have legislative provisions regarding protected areas, but their type vary from *Land* to *Land*; the powers to designate them generally lies with the government of the *Land*. Nature conservation authorities in charge of implementation are usually the district authorities (*Bezirksverwaltungsbehörden*) and in case where more than one district is concerned, the authorities of the *Land*.

General protection of certain habitats

Part of this Conference will consider the techniques which are now used to achieve wetland protection outside classical protected areas. We shall not attempt here to consider the details of such techniques, but concentrate on questions of jurisdiction and level of decisions.

Suffice it therefore to say that some legislation now provides for varying degrees of protection of certain habitats in a general manner. Such mechanisms, in many instances, provide for a permit system with regard to activities which may affect the habitats considered. Wetlands usually are specifically covered by such protection.

In **Denmark**[10] the Nature Protection Act, in its present form, provides general protection for larger wetlands. Under these provisions, all changes in the wetland types covered (public water courses, private water courses broader than 1.5 m, bogs and moors largers than 5,000 sq. m, salt marshes and salt meadows larger than 3 ha, heath over 5 ha) are subject to the permission of the County Councils (and in the Greater Copenhagen area, the Greater Copenhagen Council). The decisions made by the County Councils may be appealed to the National Forest and Nature Protection Agency, an agency within the Ministry of the Environment. Appeals may be made by Nature Conservation Associations as well as by anyone directly affected by the decision.

Austria, Germany, Luxembourg, Spain and the U.S.A., to name but a few, also have provisions providing for a general protection of wetlands (sometimes, but not always, along with the "protection" of other habitat types).

In **Luxembourg**, the Minister concerned with water and forestry (as the minister having jurisdiction over nature conservation) is entitled to grant exemptions to these protection measures, and may do so only on public interest grounds (Nature Conservation Act, Art. 14).

The situation in **Spain** is somewhat unclear without a knowledge of the practice. The Water Act (23/1985) provides that Drainage Basin Agencies and the department responsible for the environment shall coordinate their action in order to secure effective protection of wetlands of natural or scenic interest (Art. 103(4)). Drainage Basin Agencies are also empowered "in the light of favourable advice from organs competent in environmental matters" to promote the drainage of any wetlands considered unwholesome or where such drainage is otherwise deemed to be in the public interest (Art. 103(6)).

A Drainage Basin Agency is a public law body with corporate status distinct of that from the State, reporting for administrative purposes to the Ministers of Public Works and Town Planning. It has full operational autonomy pursuant to the Water Act. However, a Drainage Basin Agency is only appointed for drainage basins which extend beyond the territory of a single Autonomous Community (Art. 19). It is thus unclear whether the general protection given to wetlands by the Act only applies in cases where basins extend beyond the territory of one Autonomous Community.

In federal systems, the situation is again completely different.

In the **United States**[11], the powers of the Federal Government outside federally-owned lands are severely restricted by the Constitution to matters related to its navigation or commerce clauses.

The history and evolution of section 404 of the Federal Water Pollution Control Act (submitting the filling, etc. of wetlands to a permit system) is a classical example of the possibility for the federal jurisdiction to "nibble" its way through constitutional restrictions. The bare bones of this process may be summarized as follows (details—perhaps important ones from a legal point-of-view—are omitted from this brief account).

The authority of the federal government over certain waters in the United States was first based on a Supreme Court decision holding that the constitutional right to regulate commerce necessarily involved the regulation of navigation (1824). The concept of navigable waters was first defined by the Supreme Court as those waters "navigable in fact", i.e. "used or susceptible of being used, in their ordinary condition, as highways for commerce" (1870). The Congressional authority under the "Commerce Clause" was next considered by the Supreme Court to "necessarily include the power to keep [navigable waters] open and free from any obstruction to their navigation ... and to remove such obstruction" (1875). This evaluation was consolidated by the enactment of the River and Harbour Act of 1899, prohibiting unauthorized obstruction or alteration of any navigable waters of the United States. Such activities (broadly defined to cover excavation or dredging and filling) could only take place if authorized by the Secretary of War! The same Act also prohibited discharges into tributaries of navigable waters and refuse disposal on land, if these activities might affect navigable waters (1899). The authority to authorize activities under Article 10 of the 1899 Act was delegated to the Army Corps of Engineers, a branch of the U.S. Army established in 1802. The Supreme Court thereafter created the concept of indelible navigability—to the effect that a waterway used in interstate commerce retains this "title" in spite of subsequent alterations (1921).

The next step was to include in the purview of federal jurisdiction waters in which all reasonable improvements might make them suitable for navigation in interstate commerce (1940).

The Federal Water Pollution Control Act was enacted in 1972; section 301 of the Act prohibited discharges of pollutants (including dredged soil) from a point source in U.S. waters without a permit. Section 404 confirmed the Corps of Engineers as the permit-issuing authority for dredge and fill activities—with the veto powers retained by the Environmental Protection Agency. The definition of navigable water given by this Act is, however, substantially broader than that of the 1899 Act, as the term is defined as "waters of the United States including the Territorial Seas".

It took some time, and litigation, for the Corps to accept this expansion of jurisdiction, as it was only in 1975 that it published regulations taking into consideration this expansion, followed by new regulations in 1977 which finally referred (as in the 1972 Act) to waters of the United States (and adjacent wetlands); the criterion of the high-water mark to establish the shoreward limit of "navigable waters" was also abandoned and replaced by criteria related to species indicators. This interpretation was not altered by the revision of Section 404 by the Clear Water Act of 1977.

However, the story will never end—in 1985 the Supreme Court upheld expansive federal regulation of private development and affirmed the jurisdiction of the Corps of Engineers under Section 404 of the Clear Water Act over wetlands subject to infrequent flooding (United States v. Riverside Bayview Homes Inc.)[12].

In addition to developments at federal level, some 25 U.S. states have enacted wetland regulatory statutes; other papers submitted to this Conference will discuss their substance. We will only note here that statutes dealing with coastal wetlands usually designate a state resource or a state water agency as the implementing agency, while statutes dealing with inland wetlands usually provide for local government to perform implementation and enforcement functions[13].

In Germany, it is only recently that the framework competence of the federation has been used in relation to habitat protection; this has been accomplished by amending the Nature Conservation Act in December 1986. The Article concerned is not directly applicable. German *Länder* must adapt their legislation to reflect this new requirement within a period of two years after the entry into force of the Act (1 January 1987).

It is to be noted that a few *Länder* already have legislation on this subject—the Bavarian Nature Conservation Act (No. 16/1973 as amended)—empowers the State Ministry responsible for nature protection (as the highest nature conservation authority) to make regulations for the protection of certain types of habitats. The role of the lower nature conservation authorities (districts) in implementing this provision is predominant.

The Nature Conservation Act of Baden-Württemberg of 24 October 1975 (as amended) contains similar provisions; it also prohibits to cut or otherwise damage reed areas during the period 1 March to 30 September, but provides for numerous exemptions. The lower nature conservation authorities (districts) of the same *Land* may grant subsidies for habitat protection from funds provided by the higher nature conservation authorities, i.e. the *Regierungspräsident* (*Landschaftspflegerrichtlinien* 25 March 1983).

Austria has no federal measures on habitat protection because of lack of competence in the field of nature conservation, as mentioned earlier in this paper[14]. The legislation of the various *Länder* is, however, in full evolution in this regard and increasingly includes measures to that effect (e.g. Vorarlberg, Kärnten, Oberösterreich). Whenever a permit procedure is foreseen, the permit-issuing authorities are the district (Bezirk) authorities. The Nature Conservation Act of Kärnten (No. 54/1986) provides also (Art. 58) that where more than one district is concerned, the competent authority shall be the nature conservation authority of the *Land*.

An explanatory note to the Kärnten Act points out that the district authorities are generally competent in this *Land* as first instance authorities—as a competence of the *Land* in the first instance would preclude the possibility of an appeal.

Planning instruments

Virtually all countries have physical planning legislation, albeit at various stage of development. This type of legislation as a rule gives local authorities the possibility of designating zones for the protection of elements of the natural environment.

This process may take place independently, or separately, from nature conservation considerations and planning. Increasingly, however, the involvement of nature conservation authorities in the planning process makes planning instruments a powerful means of achieving the goals of conservation.

This paper will concentrate on only a few examples where this integration process is taking place.

In **Denmark**[15], although the overall planning system and its functioning is determined by the government, the regional and local authorities play a central role in its implementation. An important feature is also the systematic planning for nature conservation and the integration of that planning in the physical planning system.

In the process leading to the establishment of locally binding physical planning instruments, the National Forest and Nature Protection Agency of the Ministry of the Environment twice plays an important role: first, at the outset, by the development of guidelines that the County Councils should take into consideration in the preparation of the plan. These will not only concern sites of national importance (e.g. because of international commitments), but may also address local conservation requirements, such as protection of wetlands which, because of their small size, would not be covered by the general protection mentioned earlier in this paper. Second, the plans adopted must be approved by the Ministry of the Environment of which the National Forest and Nature Protection Agency is a part; the Agency advises the Minister as to the acceptability of the plan from a conservation point-of-view, and virtually exercises the power of veto at that level.

Once approved, the plan is binding. Should it contain elements which are against the general protection given to wetlands by the Nature Conservation Act, there is little that can be done. The authorization to proceed to action has still to be obtained from the County Council, and may be appealed; but as the plan is binding for the administration all that it can do in such a case is to negotiate the ways in which the plan will be implemented.

This clearly shows the importance of nature conservation inventories and mapping, providing the means for the conservation authorities to measure planning schemes against conservation requirements.

In **Germany,** Section 2 of the Nature Conservation Act deals with "Landscape Planning", a concept which might better be conveyed by the terms "Nature Conservation Planning"[16]. Landscape or nature conservation planning takes place at three levels:

1. The programme, which is mandated by the federal Nature Conservation Act (Art. 5) and is to be developed for the territory of a *Land* as a whole;

2. The master plans, which are mandated by the same Article for parts of a *Land*; and

3. The landscape plan, which is a local planning instrument.

Articles 5 and 6 of the Federal Conservation Act, which are the basis for this planning, are not directly applicable. Article 7, however, is directly applicable: it requires cooperation between the *Länder* in cases where the natural situation mandates transboundary planning, and also in cases where cooperation is necessary in order not to hamper the aims of conservation in Germany as a whole.

As to level 1: the frame programme concept has been interpreted differently in the various *Länder*. In only some of them have they been fully integrated in the general planning process (Bavaria, Northrhine-Westphalia, Hessia). The programme, viewed as the ecological input into the development plans of a *Land*, is usually adopted by Act of the Government of the *Land* as a whole, but is prepared by the authority of the Land responsible for Nature and Environmental Conservation (see Bavaria, Baden-Württemberg). Its content is fairly general and focuses on aims, rather than concrete measures. In *Länder* which have integrated them in the development planning process these plans only bind the planning authorities.

As to level 2 (planning at regional level): the lack of sufficient guidance on the content of the plans by the federation has been much criticized. It has been pointed out that the content and character of general conservation planning has been entirely left to the decision of the *Land*; some *Länder* (e.g. Hessia) have alleviated this by determining the content of this frame plan in their legislation. For example, the Conservation Act of Hessia, 19 September 1980, distinguishes:

● Areas, such as protected areas, where impairment should be prevented;

● areas which should remain free from development (as a consequence of their value for the conservation of biological diversity);

● areas which are especially valuable for recreation, etc.

The authorities responsible for this planning level are usually those responsible for regional planning within a *Land*. In Bavaria, for instance, the plans are prepared on the basis of drafts elaborated by the higher nature conservation authorities, adopted by the regional planning authorities. Their binding character results from a decision of the State Ministry for Planning and the Environment. The plans, as the programme, are binding on the administration, not on the citizen.

Level 3—the nature conservation plan—is a local planning instrument. The plan consists of an inventory of the situation of the natural environment on the one hand, and also contains an outline of the goals and of the measures needed to achieve these goals.

The jurisdictional aspects, procedure, and binding character of this plan depend on the *Land* considered, and several situations are possible:

- the plan is not integrated with the local physical planning instrument and is only valid for the areas where the latter is not applicable (*Aussenbereich*)—this is the case in Northrhine-Westphalia, where the plans are prepared by the lower national conservation authorities (district or *Kreis*);

- the plan is to be integrated into the local planning instruments (e.g. Rheinland-Pfalz); in this case, the communes usually have jurisdiction for elaborating the nature conservation plan;

- the plan has normative character (Berlin, Bremen, Hamburg, Northrhine-Westfalia) and thus is directly binding, along with others.

Many more examples of linkages between planning instruments and wetland conservation could be given, including resourceful legal constructions to overcome or alleviate difficult jurisdictional situations. Let us conclude this part of the paper by pointing out yet another case, which includes the conclusion of agreements between two levels of governments, taking the **Northwest Territories of Canada** as an example[17].

An agreement on land-use planning was signed in 1983 between the Canadian Federal Government and the Government of the Northwest Territories. The land-use programme which resulted is carried out by both the federal and territorial governments and involves representatives of indigenous peoples. Management of the programme is operated jointly by the Minister for Renewable Resources of the Northwest Territories and the Minister of Indian and Northern Affairs of Canada. A Planning Commission has been created, which reports directly to both Ministers; its function is to supervise the elaboration of several land-use plans.

To ensure that conservation interests are taken into consideration, the Northwest Territories Department of Renewable Resources has embarked on two projects: one on the identification of Wildlife Conservation Areas and another on the identification of Important Wetlands.

It is important to note that the Government of the Northwest Territories has jurisdiction over game conservation in the Territory (Section 13 of the Northwest Territory Act). The Commissioner of the Territory thus administers the Wildlife Act and regulations made under it. Under this legislation, the Commissioner may divide the Territories into Wildlife Management Units and may designate areas for special management purposes within these units. The designation as a Wildlife Conservation Area is designed to protect important habitats. The strangeness of the situation is that the administration and management of these areas is the responsibility of the Federal Department of Indian and Northern Affairs, under the Territorial Lands Act and Territorial Land-Use Regulations.

This split responsibility has led to the adoption of a further agreement between the Federal Government and the Government of the Northwest Territories in the form of a "Memorandum of Understanding respecting Wildlife Conservation Areas" (1985). This memorandum sets the stage for cooperation between the two levels of governments for identification, designation and management of the areas.

Meanwhile the Department of Renewable Resources reviews the possibilities for obtaining a larger degree of control with regard to the management of these areas and envisages further negotiations with the federal government.

Conclusions

Can conclusions be drawn with regard to the level of decision-making related to wetland protection from this mass of varying situations and the corresponding jurisdictional puzzle?

The true pessimists among us will say that there is only one answer: the variety of jurisdictional responses, created to a large extent by historical and constitutional situations, do not allow us to ascertain any trend or make any recommendation.

The quasi-pessimists will conclude that certain patterns are ascertainable, and conclusions warranted, perhaps forgetting that their level of generality did not require an examination of the situation in the first place. Such conclusions are:

1. In countries with predominantly decentralized forms of government, the central or federal authorities have limited legislative or implementation powers—if any—regarding wetland protection. Two have been described; a restricted legislative jurisdiction with full implementation powers at central/federal level (U.S.A.), and a broader-frame legislative jurisdiction with little or no implementation powers (Germany).

2. In the same countries, it is at the state/provincial/regional level that most of the legislative authority lies. In countries with predominantly centralized forms of government, this question is not significant.

3. With regard to implementation powers, a difference in trend may perhaps be ascertained: a greater role is played by lower levels of governments in the implementation of protection mechanisms in federal, decentralized systems than in centralized systems.

4. This, however, is only true for the two first mechanisms of protections (protected areas, general controls) but not for planning controls, where the role of local authorities is as important in centralized systems as in decentralized systems.

The optimists will conclude that this question is of no great importance, as it does not play a significant role in the protection of wetlands in the field. To this point, two provisos: the power of local governments[18] in implementation should not go unchecked and their decision-making powers should be balanced by supervisory powers of higher authorities—local governments are too close to local interests to have a final say in development and conservation matters[19]. Similarly, or by contrast, central authorities should not be empowered to take decisions single-handedly. They are too far from local concerns to be able to always do so wisely. In between these extremes is the golden rule—thinking nationally, acting locally, supervising regionally!

Thus, optimists will conclude that the level of jurisdiction, albeit important, is not the key factor in conservation.

The key factors are the powers themselves, at whichever level they are applied. In this paper three types of conservation powers have been envisaged:

- the power to establish protected areas;

- the power to control the degradation of certain types of habitats;

- the power to participate in the planning process and play a significant role in the elaboration of planning instruments.

There are other powers which, if not specific to wetlands, play a decisive role in the conservation of wetlands. One of them is the power of nature conservation authorities to act as guardians of the natural environment through rules concerning its damage, providing, *inter alia*;

- that avoidable damage should be prevented;

- that unavoidable damage is to be compensated;

- that damage which cannot be compensated is to be prohibited.

Other techniques include the duty of government authorities to have regard to conservation interests, and/or to consult conservation authorities[20]; other powers will be discussed in the course of this Conference.

It is in this direction that modern conservation legislation is heading; whether the conservation battle will be lost or won depends more on the availability of these powers than on the level at which they are to be exercised.

Notes

1. Nowicki, Peter L. et Nowicki-Caupin, N. 1982, *La gestion du patronomie naturel: recherche sur les politiques de la conservation de la nature dans l'optique de la décentralisation en France—Bilan de 10 pays;* this is the only study known to the authors which attempts to compare the institutional situation in various countries.

2. There are many other examples not dealt with in this report; interested readers may wish to consult Bates, C.M. 1983, *Environmental Law in Australia*, Butterworth; National Water and Soil Conservation Association (New Zealand) 1983, *Wetlands: A Diminishing Resource (A Report for the Environmental Council)*, Wellington.

3. Koester, Veit 1984, Conservation Legislation and General Protection of Biotopes in an International Perspective, *EPL* Vol. 12, No. 4, May 1984.

4. Prieur, Michel 1984, *Droit de l'environnement*, Dalloz, Paris, p. 304 *et seq*; p. 530 *et seq*.

5. National Swedish Environmental Protection Board 1984, *Environment Protection in Sweden*.

6. Nature Conservancy Council 1984, *Nature Conservation in Great Britain*; Bigham, D.A. 1973, *The Law and Administration relating to Protection of the Environment*, Oyez Publications,

Appendix: Données statistiques (voir Note 19)

Pays	Surface (sq. km.)	Populations (millions)	Densité (habitants/sq. km.)	Découpage administratif
France	551 607	50	91	22 régions, 95 départements, environs 36 000 communes
Belgique	30 513	9.6	315	
Canada	9 205 000	23.291	2.5	10 provinces + Yukon + Territoires du Nord-Ouest
Québec	1 358 000	6.283	4.6	4 500 municipalités environ
Espagne	504 741	36.615	72	17 régions (2 fonctionnent sous le statut autonome, 2 viennent de l'adopter par référendum; les autres doivent l'acquérir avant le 1/02/83, 50 provinces, 8 655 communes
Grande Bretagne	227 463	54.4	239	Angleterre + Pays de Galles: 8 régions, 46 comtés, 332 districts, 7 000 paroisses
Italie	301 262	55	183	20 régions, 95 provinces, 8 074 communes
Pays-Bas	36 175	13.7	379	11 provinces, 810 communes
R.F.A.	248 600	62	249	11 Länder, 25 Regierungbezirke, 235 Kreise, 8 421 communes
Suède	449 800	8.5	19	24 départements, 23 communes de Conseil Général (dont le territoire coïncide avec celui des départements), 297 kommuns
Suisse	41 293	6.37	154	26 cantons (209 districts judiciaires), 3 050 communes

London. Although this publication has in many aspects unfortunately become out of date, it remains very interesting for those wishing to understand the basis of environmental controls in the U.K.

7. Bean, Michael J. 1983, *The Evolution of National Wildlife Law*, Praeger.

8. Soell, Hermann, Naturschutz- und Landschaftspflegerecht (1982, 1987), In *Grundzüge des Umweltrechts*, Erich Schmidt Verlag, Berlin, 1982, p. 481 and 1987 revision (in print); see also Lorz, Albert 1985, *Naturschutzrecht*, Verlag C.H. Beck, München.

9. Soell, Hermann 1984, Nature Conservation Law in Austria—A View from the Outside, *EPL* 13, p. 57.

10. See Note 3.

11. Myhrum, Christopher B. 1979, Federal protection of wetlands through legal process, *Boston College Environmental Affairs Law Review*, Vol. 7, No. 4, p. 567.

12. Kimmel, Jeffrey J. 1986, *A Review of the Supreme Court's 1985 term: an expansion of Federal and State Oversight in Environmental Law*, American Bar Association (Fall 1986); United States v. Riverside Bayview Homes, Inc. (106 S. ct. 455 (1985) is dealt with in detail in: De Voe, Curt 1986, Army Corps of Engineers jurisdiction over wetlands under Section 404 of the Clear Water Act, *Ecology Law Quarterly*, Vol. 13 No. 3, p. 579.

13. Kusler, Jon A. 1983, *Our National Wetland Heritage—A Protection Guidebook*, Environmental Law Institute, Washington, D.C.

14. See Note 9.

15. See Note 3.

16. See Note 8.

17. The Information on the Northwest Territories is derived from: Gray, P.A., Livingston, R., Fergueson. R.S. and Annas, R. 1986, *Management of Wildlife Conservation Areas and Important Wetlands in the Northwest Teritories, Canada*, Department of Renewable Resources, Government of the Northwest Territories, Canada.

18. Deutsche Rat für Landespflege 1980, *Analyse und Fortentwicklung des neuen Naturschutzrechts in der Bundesrepublik Deutschland*; the Council notes a tendancy in State legislation to delegate powers to lower conservation authorities and is critical of this trend.

19. The study mentioned under Note 1 contains a table illustrating the number of authorities involved in conservation decision-making. This is reproduced on the previous page as an appendix to this paper; especially interesting is the number of local authorities (districts, communes) involved.

20. Water Space Amenity Commission (1980), *Conservation and Land Drainage Guidelines*, London.

Aires protégées et zones humides

JEAN UNTERMAIER
Professeur à l'Université Jean Moulin Lyon III, Lyon, France

Le thème "Aires protégées et zones humides" regroupe de multiples questions[1]. S'il est inscrit à la Conférence, c'est qu'il paraissait indispensable de déterminer dans quelle mesure les zones humides bénéficient d'une protection particulière du type parc naturel ou réserve. De plus, il est tout aussi nécessaire de s'interroger sur l'efficacité de ces institutions au regard des problèmes spécifiques que posent la conservation et la gestion des zones humides et de réfléchir aux moyens de combler en ce domaine les lacunes de nos législations respectives.

Dans le questionnaire, l'expression "aire naturelle protégée" revêt une signification très large. Désignant un "territoire soumis à un régime juridique spécifique dans un but de protection de la nature"[2], elle s'applique à des institutions[3] aussi différentes qu'une réserve naturelle ou une zone simplement déclarée inconstructible par un document d'urbanisme. Ces institutions sont répandues dans le monde entier, mais les définitions varient beaucoup selon les Etats, ce qui rend difficile la confrontation des données. De fait, la seule définition à valeur universelle, établie par l'Union internationale pour la conservation de la nature et de ses ressources, ne concernant que les parcs nationaux[4], le questionnaire s'est prudemment contenté de fournir des exemples. C'est dire que, pareillement, une très grande prudence s'impose dans l'interprétation des réponses.

Ces incertitudes et l'extrême diversité des aires naturelles protégées n'excluent cependant pas les comparaisons et les regroupements. La classification proposée, imparfaite mais, semble-t-il, acceptable en tant que base de discussion, conduit à distinguer entre trois types d'aires ou d'institutions de protection.

1. Les institutions de protection à vocation générale se caractérisent par

   (a) leur objectif, exclusivement ou prioritairement attaché à la conservation de la nature dans son ensemble, c'est-à-dire des milieux naturels, de la faune et de la flore sauvages et des relations qui les concernent;

   (b) un régime de protection en principe contraignant, se traduisant par des restrictions sérieuses à l'exercice des activités susceptibles d'affecter les écosystèmes ou les paysages. Ces restrictions peuvent impliquer, entre autres, un système d'autorisation, voire des interdictions pures et simples.

   (c) une structure administrative chargée de l'application des mesures de conservation et de la gestion de la zone.

Les aires naturelles de ce type sont essentiellement, pour reprendre la terminologie de l'UICN, les parcs nationaux et réserves analogues.

2. Les institutions de protection à but particulier sont illustrées notamment par les réserves cynégétiques ou piscicoles, les réserves botaniques et peut-être serait-il possible d'y ajouter les sites préservés en raison surtout de leur beauté ou de leur caractère pittoresque[5]. Dans ces lieux assimilés à des monuments naturels ou érigés en réserves, la réglementation s'avère plus ou moins contraignante et si certains d'entre eux, à l'instar des grandes réserves de chasse, disposent d'un organe de gestion, ce n'est pas toujours le cas. Leur spécificité est ailleurs et réside dans le fait qu'ils s'attachent seulement à la préservation d'un aspect ou d'un élément du territoire considéré.

3. Les institutions indirectes de protection, enfin, ne méritent pas vraiment le qualificatif d'institutions, même dans l'acception la plus étendue. Il s'agit en réalité d'une simple réglementation particulière de l'utilisation du sol dans une périmètre déterminé. Les règles en question résultent, soit de la législation en matière d'urbanisme ou d'aménagement du territoire, soit d'un statut spécial dérogeant au droit commun de la propriété. Ainsi, dans les pays qui admettent que les lacs, les fleuves navigables ou le littoral font partie du domaine public de l'Etat, ceux-ci bénéficient d'une protection particulière. Bien sûr, la conservation de la nature n'est pas la finalité des protections de ce type, lesquelles ne sont d'ailleurs pas toujours d'une efficacité convaincante. Il n'empêche qu'il est intéressant que le bord de la mer soit inaliénable[6] ou qu'un document d'urbanisme interdise la construction dans une zone inondable.

On remarquera que la présente classification n'englobe pas des institutions telles que les parcs régionaux français ou les espaces dont la sauvegarde n'est assurée que par des recommandations sans portée juridique.

Cette exclusion procède peut-être d'un choix arbitraire, choix qu'au surplus d'aucuns jugeront rétrograde, s'il est vrai que dans de nombreux Etats, on s'efforce de privilégier des mécanismes de protection non contraignants. Elle s'impose néanmoins si l'on veut garder à la notion d'aire protégée un minimum de consistance juridique.

Quelle que soit leur situation administrative, et plus précisément la catégorie à laquelle se rattachent les zones humides bénéficiant d'une protection particulière, toutes posent deux séries de problèmes: problèmes d'organisation et de gestion d'abord, de réglementation ensuite, ce qui conduit le juriste à se pencher sur le régime, ou si l'on préfère, les modalités de la protection.

La situation juridique des zones humides protégées

Elle a été appréhendée à travers les réponses au questionnaire, complétées—et heureusement, confirmées pour l'essentiel—par l'analyse du statut des zones d'importance internationale inscrites sur la liste prévue à la Convention de Ramsar[7], ainsi que par diverses sources concernant les législations nationales[8].

On ne saurait dissimuler, au plan méthodologique, les lacunes et les riques d'erreurs d'une telle démarche. Indépendamment de l'absence dans certains Etats de travaux scientifiques en droit de l'environnement, voire du moindre traitement de l'information en ce domaine, l'échantillon de référence semble un peu limité. Les réponses au questionnaire se rapportent en effet à dix-huit pays et seuls quatorze des tableaux annexés à la question 3-3 ont été remplis[9]. De plus, les concepts retenus tant pour opérer une classification juridique des zones humides protégées que pour interpréter les résultats s'avèrent sans doute discutables et il conviendra effectivement de les discuter[10].

Pour l'essentiel, nous avons tenté à partir des réponses à la question 3-3 de mesurer l'effort accompli par les Etats pour protéger ces zones, puis de déterminer comment se répartissait cet effort en fonction des types de milieux aquatiques (tableau 1) et des différentes institutions de protection (tableau 2). C'était là une banale affaire de pourcentages, en l'occurrence pourcentages du nombre de pays consultés, et dont l'addition a permis de calculer un coefficient de protection écologique[11], et un coefficient de protection juridique[12].

Au total, les données recueillies doivent être comprises comme de simples indications qu'il s'agira évidemment de compléter, vraisemblablement de corriger, et qui permettront—peut-être—de formuler des hypothèses et des propositions. Ces données concernent, d'une part, les milieux protégés, d'autre part, les formes de protection.

Les milieux protégés

(a) *Il n'est aucune catégorie de zone humide qui ne bénéficie d'une protection dans au moins deux des Etats consultés* (tableau 1). En revanche, les protections sont réparties de manière assez inégalitaire dans la mesure où certaines zones paraissent mieux et plus souvent protégées que d'autres. Ces milieux privilégiés sont, dans l'ordre, les lacs et les marais de l'intérieur.

Toutefois, il est plus significatif de relever que la protection semble se porter prioritairement sur des milieux présentant un intérêt à la fois écologique et paysager ou récréatif. Tel est effectivement le cas des lacs, le coefficient de protection écologique révélant par ailleurs que les cours d'eau et les étangs figurent eux aussi dans le groupe le plus favorisé[13] avec les plans d'eau artificiels où l'on pratique intensément toutes sortes de sports et d'activités aquatiques. Quant à la seconde place des marais de l'intérieur, elle s'expliquerait assez facilement par leur exceptionnelle valeur écologique. S'il existe des milieux naturels à sauvegarder, pourrait-on dire, ce sont ceux-là.

(b) *A l'inverse, les prairies submersibles et les milieux inondables dans leur ensemble paraissent nettement moins bien traités par le droit.* Il en est de même des tourbières[14] et des zones littorales. De fait, avec un C.P.E. de 230,1, la protection des marais côtiers s'avère inférieure à celle des marais de l'intérieur (350,1) et toujours selon l'échelle des C.P.E., les espaces du type vasières, prés salés, salines se situent à peu près au niveau des milieux inondables.

(c) Compte tenu de l'exceptionnelle qualité de certains milieux quelque peu délaissés par les institutions de protection, *ces disparités ne s'expliquent*

Nombre d'Etats
(en pourcentage)

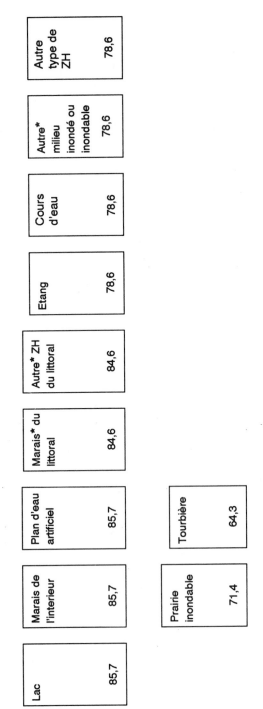

Lac	Marais de l'interieur	Plan d'eau artificiel	Marais* du littoral	Autre* ZH du littoral	Etang	Cours d'eau	Autre* milieu inondé ou inondable	Autre type de ZH
85,7	85,7	85,7	84,6	84,6	78,6	78,6	78,6	78,6

Prairie inondable	Tourbière
71,4	64,3

* Zones dont le pourcentage de protection par pays varie si l'on exclut les protections résultant du droit de l'urbanisme.

Tableau 1

L'effort de protection des Etats en fonction des catégories de zones humides

Tableau 2

Aires naturelles protégées et zones humides

	Lac	Marais de l'intérieur	Cours d'eau	Etang	Plan d'eau artificiel	Tourbière	Marais du littoral	Autre[3] milieu inondé ou inondable	Prairie inondable	Autre[2] ZH littorale	Autre type de ZH Mangrove[1]	Coefficient de protection juridique
Réserve naturelle	71.4	85.7	78.6	71.4	50	64.3	61.5	50	50	53.9	42.9	679.7
Parc national	57.1	64.3	57.1	57.1	42.9	57.1	46.2	42.9	50	38.5	42.9	556
Zone protégée par des documents d'urbanisme ou d'aménagement du territoire	50	42.9	42.9	35.7	42.9	42.9	30.1	42.9	28.6	46.2	28.6	434.4
Réserve cynégétique	35.7	42.9	35.7	50	35.7	28.6	23	28.6	21.4	23	21.4	346
Réserve halieutique	42.9	14.3	35.7	35.7	28.6	7.1	15.4	7.1	7.1	15.4	14.3	223.6
Site ou monument naturel	28.6	35.7	21.4	21.4	14.3	28.6	7.7	21.4	21.4	7.7	14.3	222.5
Autre aire naturelle protégée	28.6	14.3	28.6	28.6	35.7	14.3	15.4	14.3	14.3	7.7	14.3	216.1
Parc régional	35.7	28.6	28.6	28.6	21.4	21.4	15.4	7.1	14.3	7.7	7.1	215.9
Autre réserve à but particulier	28.6	21.4	14.3	14.3	28.6	7.1	15.4	7.1	7.1	0	7.1	146
Coefficient de protection écologique	378.6	350.1	342.9	342.8	300.1	271.4	230.1	221.4	214.2	200.1	192.9	

1. Protégées dans deux pays par des documents d'urbanisme et aux Philippines, par des réserves à but particulier;
2. Par exemple, vasière, pré salé, saline;   3. Par exemple, forêt riveraine, plan d'eau temporaire ou épisodique.

évidemment pas par des considérations écologiques. Sans doute faut-il plutôt incriminer les obstacles auxquels se heurtent les efforts de conservation s'agissant de territoires où s'exercent des activités relativement importantes au point de vue économique. En règle générale, l'agriculture est déjà plus intense dans les plaines alluviales que dans les marais, cependant que le littoral, par rapport aux zones humides de l'intérieur, est presque systématiquement l'objet d'exploitations plus lourdes financièrement, de convoitises plus âpres, où s'affrontent des intérêts et des groupes plus puissants.

Une autre explication, qui est aussi une question posée à la communauté scientifique, mérite réflexion. Les milieux les mieux protégés ne sont-ils pas également les plus spectaculaires, déjà pour le public, mais surtout aux yeux de l'écologue et plus encore aux jumelles de l'ornithologue, dont on sait le rôle qu'il a joué dans le monde entier ou presque, au service de la conservation de la nature? C'est en tout cas ce que l'on pourrait déduire de la médiocre situation juridique des tourbières et des plaines alluviales, infiniment moins attrayantes que les immenses vasières couvertes de Limicoles migrateurs ou que les grandes roselières avec leurs colonies d'Ardéidés.

Les formes de protection

(a) En ce domaine, le traitement des réponses au questionnaire s'annonce plus délicat encore, en raison des incertitudes, évoquées plus haut, qui pèsent sur la définition des aires naturelles protégées à travers le monde. De surcroît, il n'est par rare de rencontrer des zones où se superposent plusieurs régimes de protection, à l'instar de la Camargue, inscrite par la France dans la liste Ramsar et qui cumule, entre autres, le statut de parc naturel régional et celui de réserve naturelle en y ajoutant le bénéfice de règles d'urbanisme et des dispositions applicables au domaine public maritime. Or, aucune indication n'avait été donnée aux destinataires du questionnaire, sur la façon de traiter de telles situations.

Nonobstant ces sources supplémentaires d'ambiguïtés, les réponses offrent à la réflexion, quelques matéraux fiables et d'un intérêt non négligeable.

(b) Les institutions de protection à vocation générale sont de loin les plus utilisées en faveur des zones humides. Ainsi, dans l'échantillon observé, *tous les Etats recourent aux réserves naturelles et presque tous (92,9%) aux parcs nationaux.*

De l'analyse par catégorie de zones des chiffres du tableau 2, il ressort que les parcs nationaux sont un peu moins utilisés pour la sauvegarde des plans d'eau artificiels et des zones humides littorales (46,1 % pour l'ensemble de celles-ci). On serait tenté de trouver là l'expression d'une certaine logique institutionnelle: d'un côté, les parcs nationaux sont des parcs naturels, dont ils constituent en quelque sorte le prototype. Dès lors, les espaces qu'ils préservent doivent répondre à certaines exigences "d'authenticité" auxquelles tous les lacs de barrage ne peuvent prétendre. D'un autre côté, il existe actuellement peu de parcs marins, pour des raisons qui ne sont sans doute pas sans relations avec l'histoire même des parcs nationaux qui, de Yellowstone au parc Kruger ou au

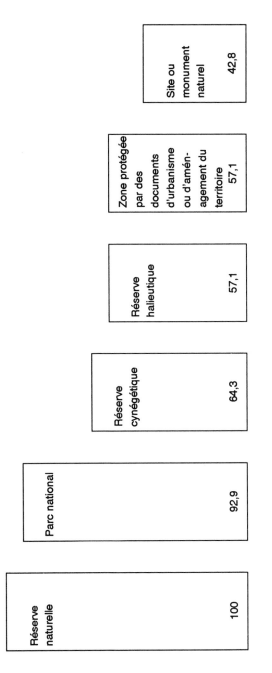

Nombre d'Etats
(en pourcentage)

Réserve naturelle	Parc national	Réserve cynégétique	Réserve halieutique	Zone protégée par des documents d'urbanisme ou d'aménagement du territoire	Site ou monument naturel
100	92,9	64,3	57,1	57,1	42,8

Tableau 3

Les institutions de protection des zones humides

Pourcentage des pays consultés appliquant tel type de protection aux zones humides

Gran Paradiso italien, ont d'abord été conçus pour les grand arbres, la grande faune et les grands paysages de montagne.

Les réserves cynégétiques constituent également une formule couramment employée, par environ deux-tiers des Etats. Il conviendrait de vérifier si ce phénomène concerne spécialement les zones humides ou s'il montre au contraire que ces réserves, certes limitées dans leurs effets mais plutôt faciles à mettre en place, font l'objet d'une utilisation très générale. Si toutefois la première interprétation se trouvait confirmée, on pourrait l'expliquer par l'exceptionnel intérêt d'une majorité de zones humides pour la chasse des oiseaux d'eau[15].

(c) Parmi *les instruments les moins employés*, la législation relative aux sites et aux monuments naturels (42,8% des états consultés) est supplantée par les mécanismes issus du droit de l'urbanisme (57,1%). On serait tenté de voir là une manifestation supplémentaire du discrédit culturel qui affecte, un peu partout, les marais, vasières ou autres milieux traditionnellement inquiétants ou repoussants, alors que le caractère "monumental" d'un paysage de montagne est plus volontiers admis[16].

(d) *Ces résultats appellent diverses observations ou remarques complémentaires.*

En premier lieu, l'analyse du statut des zones inscrites sur la liste de la Convention de Ramsar (tableau 4) confirme la prépondérance des institutions à vocation générale. Il est logique, en effet, que "l'importance internationale" des zones en question se traduise par une protection forte. De fait, les réserves naturelles conservent ici la première place, cependant que les parcs nationaux régressent (mais au troisième rang), supplantés par les "autres aires naturelles protégées"[17]. Les réserves cynégétiques sont elles aussi moins bien classées que dans le questionnaire: sans doute sous-estimées (cf. supra, note 16), elles ne peuvent de toute manière se substituer à un parc national ou à une réserve naturelle pour garantir la pérennité de zones prestigieuses et de vastes dimensions.

Il convient de noter également que 41 zones de la Convention de Ramsar (soit 14,5%) ne semblent pas bénéficier d'une protection spéciale. Dans la mesure où ce chiffre est fiable[18], il suscite maintes interrogations et pose en particulier le problème de l'intérêt en soi, pour la conservation de zones humides, d'un statut particulier. D'un autre côté, il est indéniable que la Convention se présente comme un instrument de protection dynamique, l'inscription sur la liste constituant une incitation à doter d'un régime protecteur des sites qui en sont jusqu'à présent dépourvus.

Enfin, il est apparu intéressant d'apprécier l'effort des Etats consultés en faveur de la conservation des zones humides, en ne prenant plus en compte les territoires protégés uniquement par des règles d'urbanisme ou d'utilisation des sols. Contrairement à ce que l'on pouvait a priori escompter du fait que ce type de protection, somme toute faible, est infiniment plus facile à mettre en oeuvre qu'une réserve quelconque, les résultats ne varient guère. Cela tend à prouver qu'une majorité d'Etats qui protègent efficacement leurs zones humides au moyen d'institutions spécifiques, ont également une bonne ou assez bonne législation en matière d'urbanisme.

Au demeurant, cette dernière s'avère plus utilisée que la plupart des autres formes de conservation pour la sauvegarde des zones inondables, dont elle constitue assez fréquemment la seule protection.

Gestion des zones humides protégées et choix d'une forme de protection

Le document préparatoire—qui ne pouvait entrer dans trop de détails—ne contient aucune rubrique relative aux modalités de gestion des zones humides protégées. Cette question n'en est pas moins importante et la confrontation de monographies et d'expériences nationales devrait permettre ultérieurement de la traiter sous une forme synthétique.

Cependant, les indications du tableau 3-3 permettent déjà d'aborder le problème fondamental: "Quel est le type d'institution convenant le mieux aux zones humides?"

Les données du problème

Dans nombre de pays, de grandes zones humides bénéficient d'une protection forte, parc national ou réserve naturelle. D'autres, parfois dans ces mêmes pays, ne disposent que du statut plus modeste de réserve à but particulier, essentiellement réserve de chasse. Il en est enfin qui sont simplement protégées par des dispositions d'urbanisme ou, d'une façon générale, par une réglementation de l'utilisation des sols.

Le choix de la formule la plus appropriée dépend de multiples paramètres, notamment de la superficie et de l'intérêt écologique de l'aire considérée. De même qu'il est ni souhaitable, ni possible de recourir à un marteau-pilon pour écraser une noisette, le parc national ne constitue pas, sauf exception, l'instrument adéquat s'agissant d'un étang de quelques hectares.

Dans le cas des zones humides importantes par leur étendue et leur valeur biologique, les réserves cynégétiques donnent fréquemment de bons résultats, à condition qu'elles bénéficient d'un minimum de pérennité et surtout, qu'elles soient assorties d'une protection complémentaire du troisième type, réglementation d'urbanisme et/ou domanialité publique. Ainsi le réseau de réserves de chasse maritime, mis en place dans le cadre de la loi française du 24 octobre 1968, joue un rôle considérable dans la préservation de milieux littoraux prestigieux et, pour l'avifaune, d'étapes le long de l'axe de migration atlantique.

Toutefois, le recours à une institution générale présente pour les grandes zones, indépendamment de la qualité de la protection (laquelle peut-être de toute façon aussi rigoureuse dans une réserve de chasse) des avantages substantiels au point de vue de leur gestion.

Tableau 4

Situation juridique des 358 sites inscrits sur la liste de la Convention Ramsar

Pays avec nombre de sites inscrits	parc national	parc régional	réserve naturelle	réserve cynégétitique	réserve halieutique	réserve à but particulier	site ou monument naturel	autre aire naturelle protégée	pas de protection spéciale
Afrique du Sud (6)			5					1	
Algérie (2)									2
Allemagne RDA (8)			6						2
Allemagne RFA (20)	2		15				2		1
Australie (27)	6	1	10			1	1	3	5
Austriche (5)			5						
Belgique (6)			4				1		1
Bulgarie (5)[1]	2		2						
Canada (16)	2		5		1	6			2
Chili (1)						1			
Danemark (25)			12			2		1[2]	
Espagne (3)	2					1			
Finlande (10)			9			1			
France (1)		1							
Gabon (3)	1		2						
Grande-Bretagne (30)			19				11[3]		
Grèce (10)	1			3				6	
Hongrie (8)	2		3			1	2		
Inde (2)	1					1			
Iran (18)[4]	3		4			2			9
Irlande (10)			5				5		
Islande (1)			1						
Italie (40)	4		8	6	2	2	3		15
Japon (2)			1				1		
Jordanie (1)			1						
Maroc (4)						1			3
Mauritanie (1)	1								
Mexique (2)			1				1		
Nouvelle Zélande (2)			1				1		
Norvège (14)			9			4		1	
Pakistan (9)			3					5	1
Pays-Bas (13)	5		5			1	1		1
Pologne (4)			4						
Portugal (2)			2						

Pays avec nombre de sites inscrits	parc national	parc régional	réserve naturelle	réserve cynégét-itique	réserve halieutique	réserve à but particulier	site ou monument naturel	autre aire naturelle protégée	pas de protection spéciale
Sénégal (4)[1]	2		2						
Surinam (1)			1						
Suède (21)	2		14		1				4
Suisse (2)								2	
Tunisie (1)[1]	1								
U.R.S.S. (12)								12	
Uruguay (1)[1]	1								
U.S.A. (4)	3			1					
Yougoslavie (2)		1	1						
Total	41	3	161	9	3	26	19	44	52
Pourcentage (43 Etats, 358 sites)	11,5%	0,8%	45%	2,5%	0,8%	7,3%	5,3%	12,3%	14,5%

Les chiffres indiquent pour chaque pays et chaque forme de protection le nombre de zones concernées.

Notes—1: dont 1 réserve de biosphère et site UNESCO; 2: NC.A; 3: SSSIs; 4: dont 4 réserves de biosphères.

Les avantages des institutions à vocation générale

(a) Plus que les autres milieux naturels, les zones humides exigent, en raison justement de la présence de l'eau, *un système de gestion relativement complexe.* Même dans une aire restreinte, l'eau est en effet presque toujours l'objet d'usages contradictoires. Dans les régions d'étangs, par exemple, les pisciculteurs souhaitent en principe un niveau d'eau le plus élevé possible, afin d'éviter les mauvaises surprises (oxygénation insuffisante) en période de sécheresse. Cette exigence correspond en particulier à des berges verticales et celles des étangs de pisciculture sont souvent recreusées en ce sens. De plus, les pisciculteurs ne tiennent pas à voir trop se développer la végétation palustre. A l'inverse, les chasseurs (rejoints ici par les naturalistes) préféreront de beaucoup des étangs aux bords en pente douce avec cariçaies et roselières.

Il n'est pas rare non plus de rencontrer des usages du même type, interdépendants et néanmoins conflictuels à l'occasion. L'exemple du Marais poitevin, dans l'ouest de la France, est à cet égard significatif. Ensemble de

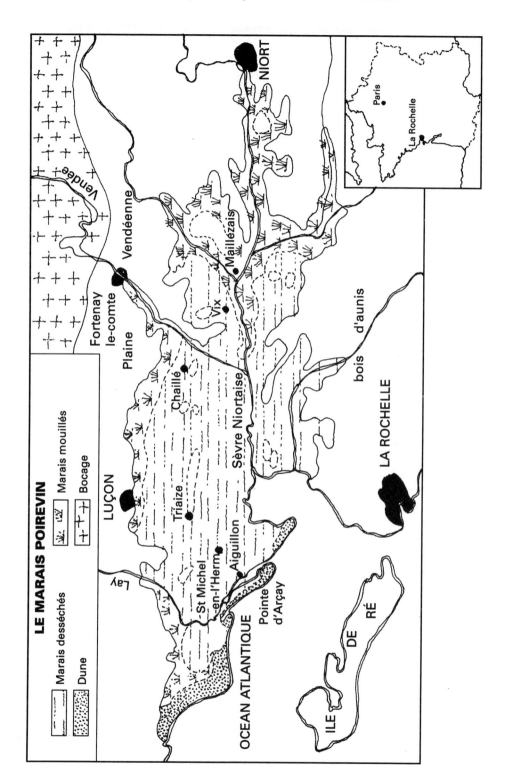

LE MARAIS POIREVIN

quelque 300.000 hectares, il se compose de deux entités "socio-écologiques". Au nord et en amont, les marais mouillés sont constitués de prairies naturelles pour l'essentiel, de petits bois et de "mottes"[19] et, périodiquement inondés, ils servent de champ d'expansion au moment des crues. Les marais desséchés, au sud, sont protégés des inondations venues de l'amont par des endiguements réalisés à partir du XVIIè siècle. Ils évacuent leurs eaux à la mer par de grands émissaires: Lay, Sèvre niortaise, canal de Luçon. En période sèche, ils prélèvent de l'eau dans les marais mouillés. L'interdépendance est ici manifeste.

Les conflits ne le sont pas moins. Ils apparaissent avec la coexistence dans les marais mouillés aussi bien que dans les marais desséchés, de deux types d'agriculture. L'agriculture extensive, fondée sur l'élevage, s'accommode parfaitement des crues et d'un niveau maximum de l'eau. Dans les marais mouillés, les crues favorisent la production herbagère et même dans les marais desséchés, les agriculteurs ont intérêt à ce que l'eau reste le plus longtemps possible dans les fossés qui, en été, servent d'abreuvoir et de clôture. En revanche, pour l'agriculture intensive, qui repose sur la culture des céréales, les crues constituent l'ennemi. Les céréaliers redoutent en particulier les crues tardives, car elles peuvent empêcher de semer à temps, et les crues persistantes qui ont des effets négatifs sur les sols du fait de phénomènes de tassement[20].

(b) Pour de multiples raisons, il est souhaitable que les intérêts et les groupes qui existent—et le cas échéant s'affrontent—dans un territoire protégé puissent dialoguer de façon institutionnelle. Dans le cas contraire, il est à redouter en effet que ces forces n'agissent hors du cadre administratif, et le plus souvent dans le désordre et sans contrôle.

En règle générale, les structures permettant aux uns et aux autres de s'exprimer ne manquent pas. Il existe ainsi des syndicats d'agriculteurs, des commissions des digues, des associations de propriétaires, etc., mais elles ont été habituellement conçues et fonctionnent de manière univoque. Mises en place pour défendre une catégorie déterminée d'intérêts (par exemple, l'agriculture céréalière), elles se révèlent parfaitement ignorantes des préoccupations des autres parties et surtout, incapables de prendre en considération les exigences de la protection de la nature. D'où l'importance de la présence, dans une institution de protection, de scientifiques siégeant avec les porte-parole des groupes de pression.

La véritable représentation, celle qui en tout cas peut convenir à la gestion des milieux naturels, revêt un sens plus matériel qu'administratif. La représentation ainsi comprise correspond à un processus qui se rapproche du mécanisme d'étude d'impact, car elle permet de comprendre toute la portée, toutes les incidences de l'activité en cause. Et en particulier, les incidences d'ordre écologique. Dans le cas, par exemple, d'un groupe tel que les éleveurs utilisant un ensemble de prairies inondables, la représentation habituelle, administrative donc, se traduit par un représentant au sein de l'institution qui parlera au nom des éleveurs, expliquant que le cheptel devrait passer, mettons de 200 vaches à 250, ou l'inverse.

Or la représentation doit garantir non seulement l'expression des éleveurs—"composante" essentielle de l'agrosystème—et de leur volonté, mais également de mesurer l'impact écologique de cette dernière. La représentation concrète d'un groupe d'éleveurs, ce n'est donc pas un éleveur mais un éleveur plus un écologue. Et réciproquement!

Ces observations, corroborées a contrario par l'histoire des grandes zones humides, histoire que ponctuent d'innombrables affrontements et maints échecs en matière de protection, sont des arguments en faveur d'institutions étoffées et bien structurées. De ce point de vue, les parcs nationaux et les réserves naturelles sont dotées d'un organe délibérant où peuvent se cotoyer des fonctionnaires de l'Etat, des élus locaux, des délégués des catégories socio-professionnelles ainsi que des personnalités scientifiques. Le cas échéant, des structures consultatives spécialisées—conseil scientifiques et aussi commissions diverses: de la chasse, de la pêche, de la gestion hydraulique—sont à même d'assurer, en fonction des circonstances et des caractéristiques spécifiques du territoire en cause, une sur-représentation des intérêts les plus importants, et d'offrir un cadre à des débats plus approfondis. C'est en ce sens que les grandes institutions paraissent irremplaçables.

La réglementation des zones humides protégées

Il s'agit là encore de questions que le document préparatoire, strictement maintenu dans des proportions raisonnables, n'a pas abordées. Ces questions, il faut néanmoins les poser. Elles se rapportent d'abord aux modalités de la protection et à sa pérennité. De plus, les zones humides sont particulièrement concernées par la maîtrise des activités extérieures à l'aire protégée.

Les activités interdites, réglementées ou libres

La discussion pourrait aborder plus précisément les projets suivants:

(a) Le cas des aménagements agricoles, des travaux susceptibles d'affecter le régime des eaux et plus généralement, risquant de menacer l'équilibre des écosystèmes aquatiques.

(b) Les procédures applicables à de telles activités, dans l'hypothèse où elles ne sont pas prohibées.

L'effectivité et la pérennité des règles de protection

(a) La portée des dérogations et les risques d'évasion réglementaire[21].

(b) Les mécanismes de suppression ou de modification des limites du parc, et de révision de son statut. Trop souples, ils peuvent priver de toute portée réelle le régime de protection le plus ambitieux[22].

Inversement de nombreux Etats, écartant le principe du parallélisme des formes et des compétences, prévoient une procédure de suppression ou de réduction d'emprise des protections, plus difficile à mettre en oeuvre que la procédure d'élaboration.

Le problème de la maîtrise des activités extérieures à la zone

(a) Les zones humides protégées sont souvent menacées par des activités ou aménagements extérieurs à la zone, en raison des relations étroites qui caractérisent les usages ou les vocations de l'eau dans un même bassin hydrographique. Les dommages écologiques infligés il y a quelques années aux Everglades ou aux marismas du Guadalquivir par des équipements touristiques lourds, réalisés pourtant en dehors du parc (respectivement dans le environs de Miami et de Séville), démontrent les limites des protections ponctuelles. Pour réduire l'impact des perturbations externes, il conviendrait de développer territorialement le régime de protection. En ce sens, l'article 3.1 de la Convention de Ramsar dispose que les Parties doivent "élaborer et appliquer leurs plans d'aménagement de façon à favoriser la conservation des zones humides inscrites sur la liste". Le principe est donc posé de la nécessité d'une préservation de ces zones tant en ce qui concerne les causes de dégradation directe qu'à l'encontre des agressions extérieures résultant par exemple d'une modification du régime hydrique ou de pollutions.

(b) Il reste alors à déterminer les moyens permettant d'atteindre ce résultat[23]. Pour l'essentiel, ceux qui viennent à l'esprit, soit tentent de limiter les activités étrangères nuisibles, soit visent à renforcer institutionnellement les capacités de résistance de la zone protégée.

   1. Parmi les instruments de la première catégorie, C. de Klemm mentionnne les "zones tampons" dans lesquelles certaines activités seraient spécialement réglementées. Malheureusement, les obstacles à la mise en place de tels mécanismes ne manquent pas. Dans certains pays, où le moindre projet de conservation rencontre presque systématiquement de vives résistances, l'édiction d'un régime de protection venant s'ajouter aux contraintes d'un parc national ou d'une réserve, paraît très aléatoire. De plus, la superficie de la zone tampon risque fort de se révéler insuffisante, pour de semblables raisons.

   Les "institutions tampons", comme l'expression ne l'indique pas, tendent également à limiter ou à interdire certaines activités dans la zone de captation des eaux du parc. Il est concevable en l'occurrence de transposer aux parties protégées des techniques éprouvées comme les périmètres de protection des captages d'eau destinée à l'alimentation humaine ou les zones spéciales d'aménagement des eaux. A l'intérieur de ces zones caractérisées par les risques élevés de pollution, l'autorité administrative dispose d'importants pouvoirs pour interdire, réglementer ou suspendre les activités dangereuses.

   2. Les solutions de type institutionnel consistent, par exemple, à doter l'autorité de gestion d'un parc ou d'une réserve analogue de pouvoirs à l'extérieur du parc. Un tel système paraît a priori acceptable mais il se

heurte à des difficultés juridiques dans les Etats qui ont du principe de spécialité des collectivités locales ou des établissements publics une conception stricte.

Il n'est pas inconcevable enfin d'imaginer des parcs naturels à capacité étendue, auxquels seraient conférés des compétences en matière d'aménagement régional. Intégrés à tous les processus de décisions concernant directement ou indirectement les écosystèmes qu'ils ont pour mission de préserver, ils pourraient prendre, empêcher ou en tout cas se prononcer sur des mesures à caractère économique, social ou culturel pouvant avoir des incidences écologiques.

D'aucuns verront en de telles réformes un progrès décisif. D'un autre côté, la nature même de ces "super-parcs" laisse perplexe dans la mesure où ils ne se distinguent plus guère des institutions administratives "ordinaires" à compétence territoriale. Leur apparition ne marquerait-elle pas la fin des régimes particuliers de protection, privés de la spécificité qui constituait leur raison d'être? Et à ce terme et pour des raisons identiques, la fin du droit de l'environnment?

Notes

1. Il fait l'objet, dans le document préparatoire de la Conférence de Lyon, des questions 3-3-1 et 3-3-2.

2. Document préparatoire de la Conférence de Lyon, Annexe I, Définitions, p. 13 (version française).

3. Dans le document préparatoire comme dans le présent rapport, le terme "institution" désigne aussi bien une institution au sens strict du mot—organe, autorité—qu'un simple phénomène, une entité appréhendée par le droit et caractérisée par un régime déterminé. En ce sens, la famille, le mariage ou les parcs nationaux sont des institutions juridiques.

    Cette conception extensive de l'institution a pu entraîner quelque doute à propos de la question 3-3-1. "Certaines institutions de protection des milieux naturels concernent-elles des zones humides?" Tout le monde y a répondu "oui", peut-être en se référant parfois au sens étroit du mot institution. En fait, cette possible ambiguïté n'est guère gênante dans la mesure où la question suivante et le tableau qui l'accompagne ont montré qu'effectivement tous les Etats utilisaient au moins une institution de protection (cette fois au sens large englobant parcs et réserves) pour sauvegarder les zones humides.

4. Définition adoptée par l'Assemblée générale à Delhi en 1969. Quant aux "réserves analogues", la Commission des parcs nationaux en a énoncé certains critères en fonction de paramètres écologiques.

5. Voir, par exemple, la loi française du 2 mai 1930 qui a pour objet de réorganiser la protection des monuments naturels et des sites de caractère artistique, historique, scientifique, légendaire ou pittoresque.

6. Tel est le cas en France des dépendances du domaine public.

7. UICN 1987, *Directory of Wetlands of International Importance*, Ramsar Regina Conference, Gland et Cambridge.

8. En particulier: C. de Klemm 1984, *La conservation des zones humides: techniques juridiques et problèmes d'aménagement*, Rapport UICN pour la 2è Conférence des Parties à la Convention de Ramsar, Groningen (Pays-Bas), ronéotypé, 31 p.

Rapports nationaux en vue de la Conférence sur les problèmes juridiques de protection des zones humides (Lyon, septembre 1987): Braks, G.J.M. (Ministre néerlandais de l'Agriculture et des Pêcheries) 1987, *The Implementation of the Wetlands Convention in the Netherlands*, septembre 1987, ronéotypé, 22 pp.; Mekouar, Mohamed Ali 1987, *Les zones humides en droit marocain*, août 1987, ronéotypé, 12 p.; Tolentino, Amado S. Jr., *Legal aspects of mangroves protection*, ronéotypé, 15 pp.

9. Il est vrai que le questionnaire représentait un exercice redoutable et le responsable scientifique de la Conférence tient à remercier une nouvelle fois ceux qui n'ont pas hésité à s'y livrer.

10. Le caractère trop restreint de l'échantillon n'a pas permis de dégager des données significatives sur les formes de protection des zones humides en fonction de considérations géopolitiques. En revanche, l'examen de cas nationaux devrait apporter sur ce point d'utiles indications.

11. Le coefficient de protection écologique est déterminé pour chaque type de zone humide, par la somme des pays de l'échantillon (en pourcentages) accordant une protection à cette zone.

12. Pour chaque type d'aire protégée, la somme des pays de l'échantillon (en pourcentages) utilisant cette forme de protection au profit des zones humides.

13. Dans le plupart des cas, l'intérêt de leur protection se trouve renforcé par leur vocation piscicole.

14. Situées au dernier rang dans le tableau 1, leur position s'améliore un peu (6è rang) si l'on se fonde sur les coefficients de protection écologique.

15. En ce sens, on ne sera pas surpris par la moindre utilisation des réserves cynégétiques pour la protection des tourbières, ni par le fait que l'institution obtienne ses meilleurs résultats avec les étangs et les marais de l'intérieur. Dans le même ordre d'idées, il n'est guère étonnant que les réserves halieutiques aient moins de succès que les réserves de chasse, dès lors qu'elles sont par hypothèse inapplicables aux zones ne disposant pas en permanence d'une importante surface d'eau libre (tourbières, milieux inondables, marais, etc. ...).

16. Le tableau 2 contient néanmoins un détail troublant. On y lit en effet que la législation sur les sites s'applique aux lacs dans 28,6% des Etats consultés, alors que ce chiffre atteint 35,7% dans le cas des marais de l'intérieur. Il faut admettre jusqu'à preuve du contraire, que ces données aberrantes résultent d'une sous-estimation du nombre de lacs classés au titre des monuments naturels, cette forme de protection n'étant pas toujours mentionnée dans le questionnaire lorsqu'elle se combine avec une protection "plus forte", du type parc national.

    Il reste que plusieurs Etats (dont la France), disposent d'une législation sur les monuments naturels applicable, par référence à la notion de site scientifique, à des zones d'intérêt écologique.

17. Ce qui n'est pas très significatif compte tenu du caractère hétéroclite de cette catégorie.

18. Cf. Untermaier, Jean 1984, La protection implicite de la nature, Le cas du Val de Saône et de la Dombes, In La Saône, Trévoux, Ed. *Patrimoine des Pays de l'Ain*, Trévoux, pp. 17-25.

19. Ilots artificiels dont le niveau a été rehaussé. Insubmersibles, les mottes sont occupées par des jardins et des vergers.

20. Cf. sur ce point, Billaud, Jean-Paul 1984, *Marais poitevin*, Ed. L'Harmattan, p. 112.

21. L'évasion, à la différence de la fraude ou de la violation de la loi, est l'art d'éluder la règle de droit ou d'en écarter les effets sans la transgresser directement. Ce phénomène est souvent aggravé par l'imprécision des termes employés par le législateur. Ainsi la loi française du 2 mai 1930 sur les sites soumet à autorisation, dans les sites classés (ou à déclaration, quatre mois à l'avance, dans les sites simplement inscrits à l'inventaire), les travaux susceptibles de modifier l'aspect des lieux, à l'exception toutefois des travaux d'entretien normal ou d'exploitation courante. Or, l'interprétation de l'expression exploitation courante n'est pas évidente et certains n'ont pas hésité à soutenir que dans le cas d'une zone humide protégée, le drainage constituait

un acte d'exploitation courante. Et c'est pour cette raison (et quelques autres, il est vrai …), qu'à une quinzaine de kilomètres au nord-est de Lyon, le marais des Echets, site prestigieux de plusieurs centaines d'hectares, a été transformé en champ de maïs.

22. Toutefois, une rigidité excessive favorise les illégalités et l'inapplication du droit.

23. Cf. de Klemm, Cyrille 1984, *La conservation des zones humides, Techniques juridiques et problèmes d'aménagement*, Rapport UICN à la Conférence des Parties à la Convention de Ramsar, Groningen, 7–12 mai 1984, Doc. C2.10, p. 22.

La protection des zones humides en dehors des aires protégées

CYRILLE DE KLEMM

Expert Consultant auprès l'UICN, Paris, France

Introduction

La création d'aires protégées, c'est-à-dire de zones géographiquement délimitées ayant fait l'objet d'un acte juridique de classement, comme par exemple des réserves naturelles, aussi indispensables qu'elles soient pour préserver des biotopes d'intérêt majeur, ne suffira jamais en soi à assurer une conservation suffisante des zones humides. Etant donné les difficultés considérables, tant financières que politiques, qu'entraînent l'acquisition par l'Etat ou le classement de terrains appartenant à des propriétaires privés à des fins de conservation de la nature, ces procédures ne pourront en général être utilisées que d'une manière exceptionnelle.

L'objet de cette présentation est de passer en revue les méthodes qui ont été adoptées par certains pays pour accorder aux zones humides un statut général de protection. La préservation des eaux contre la pollution, l'eutrophisation ou les dépôts acides, et, d'une manière générale, les règles relatives à la police des eaux, qui, de toute évidence, jouent un rôle capital dans la préservation des zones humides, mériteraient en elles-mêmes un examen approfondi qui ne peut être envisagé dans le cadre de cette étude nécessairement limitée. Elles ne seront donc pas traitées ici. Il en sera de même des mesures d'incitation ou de désincitation, financières ou fiscales, à la protection ou à la destruction des zones humides, qui doivent être examinées au cours d'un autre exposé présenté à cette conférence.

Les textes instaurant des régimes de protection obligatoire

Les régimes d'application générale

Certaines législations, de plus en plus nombreuses, accordent une protection générale à certains types de milieux naturels ou semi-naturels comme, par exemple, les forêts, les landes à bruyères, les pelouses sèches, et à différents types de zones humides, en particulier les tourbières, les forêts alluviales et les marais. Tout changement d'affectation est alors généralement interdit sans autorisation. C'est probablement le Danemark qui a été parmi les premiers à se doter d'une législation de ce type. Aux termes de la loi de 1969 sur la protection de la nature, amendée en 1978 et en 1983[1], toute modification de l'équilibre des lacs, tourbières, prés salés, habitats côtiers et cours d'eau, est soumise, au-dessus d'un certain seuil, à une autorisation des autorités de protection de la nature. On envisage d'ajouter à cette liste les prairies humides, dans un avenir proche. Ce texte s'applique à toutes les activités potentiellement destructrices, y compris les activités agricoles.

Au Luxembourg, la loi du 11 août 1982 sur la protection de la nature et des ressources naturelles interdit la destruction des mares, marécages, et roselières. En Autriche, des dispositions de même type figurent dans la législation adoptée récemment par plusieurs Länder. Ainsi, en Haute Austriche, la loi sur la protection de la nature et du paysage du 19 mai 1982 soumet à l'autorisation des autorités de protection de la nature l'assèchement ou le boisement des marais ou tourbières, le drainage de toutes les zones humides de plus de 5 ha, le comblement des mares et le défrichement des forêts alluviales. En Carinthie, depuis la loi du 3 juin 1986, il est interdit de drainer, combler ou détruire les marais, tourbières, roselières et forêts alluviales. Des dérogations sont possibles dans certains cas.

En Suisse, la loi fédérale sur la protection de la nature et du paysage du 1er juillet 1966 et ses amendements du 7 octobre 1983 énoncent qu'il y aura lieu de protéger tout particulièrement les rives, les roselières et les marais. Cette disposition nécessite une législation d'application au niveau cantonal. Ainsi, la loi du canton de Fribourg[2] prévoit la protection des rives des lacs et des cours d'eau ainsi que celles des étangs, des marais et des tourbières. En outre, la législation fédérale sur la pêche (loi sur la pêche du 14 décembre 1973) soumet à autorisation le drainage et l'irrigation des terrains agricoles.

En Allemagne fédérale, les amendements du 10 décembre 1986 à la loi fédérale sur la protection de la nature du 20 décembre 1976 (art. 20 c) posent une interdiction de principe pour toute action pouvant conduire à la destruction, ou à une altération importante ou durable, de certains types de biotopes dont les tourbières, marais, roselières, prairies humides, rives à l'état naturel des cours d'eau, forêts alluviales et marécageuses, prés salés et vasières. L'application de cette disposition est laissée aux Länder qui devront adopter une législation appropriée.

Aux Etats-Unis, la compétence en matière de protection des zones humides appartient aux Etats, sauf en ce qui concerne les eaux navigables. Une interprétation extensive de ce terme par le Congrès et par la jurisprudence a permis de soumettre à autorisation des autorités fédérales compétentes—il s'agit en l'espèce du Corps du Génie militaire—le déversement de substances de toute nature dans la quasi-totalité des eaux intérieures ou côtières (art. 404 du Water Pollution Act de 1972). Ce texte ne s'applique qu'à l'apport de substances et ne vise donc pas le drainage, le dragage ou l'extraction de matériaux à condition qu'aucun déversement n'en soit une conséquence. En outre, certains états, encore relativement peu nombreux, se sont maintenant dotés d'une législation spécifique en matière de protection des zones humides, notamment de celles qui sont situées dans les régions côtières ou riveraines des Grands Lacs (lois des états de Massachusets, Connecticut, Rhode Island, Minnesota, Michigan, New Hamphire, New York pour les zones humides intérieures et côtières; lois de états de New Jersey, Caroline du Nord, Virginie, Géorgie, Delaware, Maine, Wisconsin, Floride et Californie pour les zones côtières seulement)[3].

Certains pays règlementent certaines activitées particulières pouvant affecter certains types de zones humides. Ainsi, au Venezuela, un règlement du 5 juin 1972 interdit de couper des arbres, de déverser des matériaux, de draguer et de construire des installations sur pilotis dans les mangroves. En Suède, un amendement de 1986 à la loi sur la conservation de la nature de 1964 soumet à autorisation le creusement de nouveaux fossés ainsi que l'approfondissement de fossés existants ou leur remplacement par des canalisations de drainage. L'effet de cette mesure est d'empêcher la diminution du nombre des fossés et des petites mares dans les régions rurales. Dans la Région wallonne en Belgique, un amendement de 1984 à la loi nationale sur la conservation de la nature du 12 juillet 1973 interdit de creuser de nouveaux fossés de drainage dans les zones classées en zones naturelles dans les plans de secteur.

Enfin, une loi récente d'Australie du Sud (Native Vegetation Management Act du 19 septembre 1985) dont la portée est plus générale mais qui ne manquera pas d'avoir une influence profonde sur la préservation des zones humides, soumet à autorisation tout défrichement ou élimination de la végétation indigène[4].

A ces textes, il convient d'ajouter certaines lois qui posent le principe de la protection des zones humides sans en établir les modalités. Ces dernières doivent faire l'objet de règlements d'application qui ne semblent pas encore avoir été pris. Il s'agit, en particulier, des lois françaises du 9 janvier 1985 sur la montagne et du 3 janvier 1986 sur le littoral. La première prévoit que des prescriptions particulières, établies par décret en Conseil d'Etat, pourront désigner les espaces, paysages ou milieux les plus remarquables et définir les modalités de leur préservation. Parmi ces milieux figurent les lacs, tourbières et marais. La seconde précise qu'un décret fixera la liste des espaces et milieux à préserver qui comporteront, entre autres, les parties naturelles des estuaires, les rias, les marais, les vasières, les zones humides et milieux temporairement immergés ainsi que les zones de repos, de nidification et de gagnage de l'avifaune et, dans les départements d'outre-mer, les récifs coraliens, les lagons et les mangroves. Ces deux textes sont ambigüs, peut-être volontairement, en ce qu'il n'apparaît pas clairement si l'on entend accorder une protection générale à certains types de zones naturelles ou s'il s'agit de sites géographiquement délimités qui s'apparenteraient alors plus à des réserves.

En Espagne, la nouvelle loi des eaux du 2 août 1985, en son article 103, prévoit un régime d'autorisation pour toutes les activités affectant les marais. Les agences de bassin pourront prendre l'initiative de faire classer des marais en zones d'intérêt spécial pour la conservation (art. 103 de la loi).

Il faut citer aussi la loi du 13 juin 1985 de la Généralité de Catalogne sur les espaces naturels, qui dans son article 11 prévoit que toutes les zones humides devront être préservées des activités susceptibles de provoquer leur régression ou leur dégradation, par des règles établies à cet effet par les administrations compétentes.

Il convient, enfin, de mentionner le rôle que peuvent jouer, même si ce n'est pas leur objet premier, les législations relatives à la police des eaux pour la préservation des zones humides. Lorsque tout captage ou dérivation d'eaux superficielles ou souterraines est soumis à autorisation, l'Administration dispose d'un mécanisme efficace pour prévenir le drainage des zones humides. Ainsi, en

Nouvelle Zélande, où il n'existe aucune disposition particulière relative à la protection des zones humides en tant que telles, à l'exception de la possibilité de désigner des cours d'eau protégés, la législation sur les eaux (Water and Soil Conservation Act de 1967) donne à la Couronne le droit exclusif d'utiliser les eaux naturelles. Ce droit peut évidemment être concédé, mais l'Administration dispose d'un pouvoir discrétionnaire pour accorder ou refuser une concession et le rejet d'une demande n'ouvre aucun droit à indemnisation. Il a ainsi été jugé[5] que la loi permettait d'accorder une protection réelle aux zones humides dans la mesure où le refus d'accorder un droit de drainage (assimilé à une dérivation) était justifié par l'importance écologique de l'espace concerné (il s'agissait d'une demande d'octroi d'un droit de drainage pour convertir 172 ha de marais en pâturage permanent).

Les régimes applicables à certains espaces particuliers

Il s'agit, en général, d'espaces dont la protection est jugée prioritaire mais que l'on ne désire par nécessairement classer en réserve naturelle.

L'exemple le plus connu est celui des sites d'intérêt scientifique particulier (Sites of Special Scientific Interest) ou SSSI en Grande Bretagne[6]. Les SSSI sont désignés par le Nature Conservancy Council (NCC), qui est l'administration compétente en matière de conservation du milieu naturel, en fonction de critères exclusivement scientifiques. Cette désignation a des effets juridiques. Les propriétaires sont informés par le NCC des activités susceptibles de porter atteinte à la valeur scientifique des sites. Lorsqu'ils désirent entreprendre l'une de ces activités, ces derniers doivent le notifier préalablement au NCC. Celui-ci peut alors proposer une acquisition à l'amiable ou une convention de gestion assortie d'une indemnisation. A défaut d'accord des propriétaires, le NCC peut, au terme d'un certain délai, procéder à une expropriation. Les infractions à la législation concernant les SSSI sont pénalement sanctionnables. Un autre effet de la désignation d'un SSSI consiste en la possibilité, dans certains cas, de refuser des subventions agricoles lorsque les travaux envisagés, de l'avis du NCC, auraient pour effet une dégradation de la faune ou de la flore. Le NCC doit alors obligatoirement proposer au propriétaire une convention de gestion et une indemnisation. Au 31 mars 1986, il y avait 4.842 SSSI couvrant 1.430.000 ha[7].

En Finlande, des décisions récentes du Conseil des Ministres établissent des règles relatives à la préservation des deux types de zones humides les plus importants du pays: les tourbières et les lacs ou baies eutrophes. Ces décisions sont accompagnées d'un programme d'action qui doit être mis en oeuvre par les autorités chargées de la protection de la nature. Toutes les autres administrations se voient interdire de prendre des mesures pouvant porter atteinte aux sites figurant sur une liste. Ces décisions ne lient que l'Administration et ne sont donc pas opposables aux propriétaires privés. Ceux-ci sont, cependant, informés et savent qu'au cas où un site inscrit sur la liste serait menacé, il peut faire l'objet d'une expropriation[8]. Un projet de loi est en cours d'élaboration dans le but de soumettre à autorisation les activités susceptibles de porter atteinte à l'habitat d'espèces protégées.

En Suisse, à la suite d'un projet de construction d'une place d'armes militaire dans la zone marécageuse de Rothenthurm en Suisse centrale, une initiative populaire a été lancée en 1983 en vue d'amender la Constitution en y ajoutant un article interdisant de modifier les marais et sites marécageux d'une beauté particulière et présentant un intérêt national. Le Conseil fédéral a répondu par un contre-projet qui, sans nécessiter de réforme constitutionelle, donnerait une protection accrue à tous les types de milieux naturels et pas seulement aux marais[9]. Si ce projet est adopté, les biotopes d'importance nationale seront désignés par le Conseil fédéral, mais ce seront les cantons qui devront prendre les mesures de protection nécessaires. A défaut, ces mesures seront prises par la Confédération. Pour les biotopes d'importance régionale ou locale, la désignation sera faite par les cantons. Le financement des mesures de protection et d'entretien des biotopes d'importance nationale sera assuré, en principe, par la Confédération. Les cantons assumeront les dépenses encourues pour la protection des biotopes d'importance régionale ou locale. La Confédération pourra y contribuer par des subventions. Le système fonctionnera, autant que possible, sur la base d'accords conclus avec les propriétaires fonciers. Ces accords établiront les méthodes d'agriculture et de sylviculture traditionnelles les mieux adaptées à la préservation des espaces considérés. Les propriétaires pourront être indemnisés. Les cantons pourront ordonner des restrictions permanentes au droit de propriété en cas de nécessité. Pour les sites d'importance nationale, des inventaires établis selon des critères scientifiques valables pour tout le pays sont en voie d'élaboration pour les bas-marais et les prairies humides. Ils sont d'ores et déjà achevés pour les zones alluviales et les hauts-marais.

Le fonctionnement des régimes de protection obligatoire

Inventaire et définition des espaces concernés

Il est indispensable, pour une application effective de la législation, que les propriétaires intéressés et l'Administration elle-même, sachent avec précision quels sont les espaces auxquels les mesures de protection sont applicables. Il faudrait donc, en principe, procéder à des inventaires, informer les propriétaires des inscriptions à l'inventaire et, pour éviter des difficultés éventuelles en cas de transmission des biens, procéder à des mesures de publicité foncière.

Lorsqu'il s'agit d'espaces qui ont été choisis pour leur intérêt particulier, comme les SSSI britanniques ou les futurs biotopes d'importance nationale en Suisse, ces inventaires ont été réalisés ou sont en cours et ils ont été ou seront notifiés aux propriétaires. Mais lorsqu'il s'agit d'un régime de protection s'appliquant à tous les espaces appartenant à une même catégorie, par exemple les tourbières ou les marais, la situation est plus complexe. Idéalement, il conviendrait également dans ce cas de procéder à des inventaires. C'est par exemple ce qui se fait aux Etats-Unis au niveau fédéral, ainsi que dans plusieurs autres pays. Mais il s'agit là d'opérations de longue haleine. A défaut d'inventaires, ou en attendant leur achèvement, une définition juridique des milieux protégés est indispensable. La plupart des textes se contentent cependant d'établir la liste de ces milieux en utilisant des termes courants tels que marais, tourbière, roselière, sans les définir plus avant. Dans certains cas, des définitions plus précises sont fournies par la législation elle-même ou dans les règlements ou circulaires d'application. Il en est ainsi, par exemple, au Danemark où plusieurs circulaires exposent en détail les caractères écologiques des milieux considérés. Aux Etats-Unis, la plupart des états définissent les zones humides en fonction de la présence d'espèces végétales aquatiques nommément désignées. Dans certains cas, les définitions se fondent sur la présence d'eau pendant une partie de l'année ou sur la saturation du sol.

Dans tous ces cas, en l'absence de notifications, impossibles sans inventaires, ce sera au propriétaire ou à l'exploitant de s'assurer qu'un espace ne répond pas à la définition légale des milieux protégés avant d'engager des travaux susceptibles de modifier l'état des lieux. Plus les définitions sont imprécises, plus il y aura de risque de contentieux.

L'octroi des autorisations

Selon les législations, il peut exister, soit un régime d'interdiction des activités susceptibles de porter atteinte aux milieux protégés, assorti de possibilités de dérogations, soit un régime d'autorisation préalable pour ces activités. En pratique, cela semble revenir au même.

L'octroi des autorisations, ou le cas échéant des dérogations, repose le plus souvent sur un pouvoir discrétionnaire de l'administration compétente, donc sans recours possible. Les autorisations seront accordées ou refusées au cas par cas ou sur la base de critères établis par l'administration elle-même. Ainsi au Danemark, on ne donne pas d'autoritations pour les activités pouvant affecter un site protégé au titre de la Convention de Ramsar ou de la Directive communautaire sur la protection des oiseaux.

Un certain nombre de textes prévoient, cependant, des cas de compétence liée, la loi fixant elle-même les circonstances dans lesquelles les autorisations doivent être refusées. C'est ainsi que la loi du Luxembourg du 20 août 1982 prévoit expressément que les autorisations seront refusées lorsque les projets du requérant constituent un danger pour la conservation de la faune, de la flore et du milieu naturel en général. De même aux Etats-Unis, les autorisations délivrées par le Corps du Génie militaire pour les déversements de substances dans les eaux sous compétence fédérale ne peuvent être accordées que pour des raisons d'intérêt public et à condition que les avantages découlant du projet contrebalancent les dommages causés aux zones humides concernées. Dans l'état de Rhode Island, la loi établit clairement que l'autorisation doit être refusée lorsque les travaux envisagés auront vraisemblablement pour conséquence de diminuer les effets modérateurs d'une zone humide sur les inondations, la capacité de recharge de la nappe phréatique, la qualité des eaux, l'élimination des polluants ou encore le caractère naturel d'une zone humide exceptionnelle ou importante pour la vie sauvage, notamment si elle constitue l'habitat d'espèces endémiques ou menacées[10].

Mais même lorsque, comme dans le cas de Rhode Island, la loi donne à l'autorité compétente des indications précises sur les chefs de refus d'autorisations, la part de pouvoir discrétionnaire reste relativement grande puisqu'il s'agira le plus souvent pour la dite autorité de porter un jugement de valeur sur l'importance des intérêts publics en présence ainsi que sur les effets éventuels de l'opération projetée. Dans tous les cas donc, il devra être procédé à un bilan.

Ce dernier est d'ailleurs souvent expressément prévu par les textes. Il en est ainsi, par exemple, dans la loi fédérale américaine précitée ou encore dans la loi du Land autrichien de Carinthie de 1986. Cette dernière précise que des dérogations à l'interdiction de détruire des zones humides pourront être accordées lorsque l'intérêt public de l'activité projetée est plus important que celui de la sauvegarde de la zone concernée.

Les législations prévoient, en général, que lorsqu'une autorisation est accordée, elle peut être assortie de conditions visant à minimiser l'impact de l'opération sur le milieu naturel. Dans certains cas, les textes prévoient aussi la possibilité d'imposer une compensation au requérant. Ainsi l'article 18.1 ter de la loi fédérale suisse sur la protection de la nature et du paysage du 1er juillet 1966, amendée en 1983, précise que "si tous les intérêts pris en compte, il est impossible d'éviter des atteintes d'ordre technique aux biotopes dignes de protection, l'auteur de l'atteinte doit veiller à prendre des mesures particulières pour en assurer la meilleure protection possible, la reconstitution ou, à défaut, le remplacement adéquat".

Le pouvoir discrétionnaire de l'Administration n'est pas sans limites dans la mesure où il est, en général, soumis au contrôle du juge. Encore faut-il pour qu'une association de protection de la nature puisse exercer un recours contre une décision présumée illégale, que ce droit de recourir lui soit reconnu par la loi ou la jurisprudence, ce qui est encore loin d'être le cas partout. Lorsque ce droit existe, la tâche du tribunal consiste à effectuer un nouveau bilan qui se substitue alors à celui de l'Administration. C'est ainsi que certaines décisions autorisant la destruction de zones humides ont été annulées par les tribunaux, après que ceux-ci aient fait pencher la balance dans le sens de l'intérêt public de la préservation. Un exemple intéressant est celui d'un arrêt du Tribunal fédéral suisse du 6 décembre 1983[11], rendu à propos de la construction d'une centrale hydro-électrique sur l'Aar, qui annule l'autorisation accordée par les autorités cantonales aux motifs que l'intérêt public prédominant était celui de la sauvegarde du paysage constitué par ce cours d'eau dans son état présent dans la région considérée. La présence de quatre espèces d'oiseaux protégés par la Convention de Berne sur la conservation de la vie sauvage en Europe a également été prise en considération.

Les limites des mesures de protection

Les textes établissent en général des seuils en-deçà desquels la législation ne s'applique pas. Ils soustraient également souvent certaines activités des champs d'application de la législation. Enfin, ils se préoccupent rarement de la gestion des espaces concernés.

(a) Les seuils

La plupart des textes fixent des seuils, par exemple des seuils de superficie. La législation ne s'applique alors qu'aux espaces dépassant une certaine surface, les autres ne bénéficiant d'aucune protection. Ainsi au Danemark, seuls les lacs de plus de 0,1 ha, les marais et tourbières de plus de 0,5 ha et les prés salés de plus de 3 ha, sont soumis au régime de l'autorisation préalable pour les aménagements les concernant. L'existence de ces seuils s'explique en général par des considérations d'ordre pratique. On ne peut tout protéger et s'il fallait une autorisation pour tout, l'Administration serait vite débordée. Il n'en reste pas moins que la destruction d'un grand nombre d'espaces naturels de petite dimension peut avoir un effet cumulatif très grave sur le paysage et la préservation de la vie sauvage. En outre, certaines espèces sont inféodées à des biotopes de faible surface. C'est ainsi que l'on s'est aperçu au Danemark que plusieurs espèces d'amphibiens étaient en régression en conséquence de la destruction de petites mares qui ne sont pas protégées par la législation.

(b) Les activités exemptées d'autorisation

La plupart des législations accordant une protection à certains types d'espaces naturels ne s'appliquent pas aux activités agricoles et sylvicoles. Etant donné que les améliorations foncières sont responsables de la disparition de la grande majorité des zones humides, les dérogations générales établies en faveur de ces activités risquent de faire perdre à la législation une très grande partie de son efficacité. La situation évolue lentement. Au Danemark, la loi s'applique aux activités agricoles et ne semble pas s'être heurtée à l'opposition des milieux ruraux. Dans certains états des Etats-Unis, par exemple le Rhode Island et le Wisconsin, une autorisation est toujours requise quel que soit l'objet des travaux. La loi de 1986 du Land de Carinthie en Autriche s'applique aussi aux activités agricoles pour ce qui est des zones humides.

La gestion des espaces préservés

Beaucoup d'espaces naturels que l'on désire conserver, notamment en Europe, ne sont en fait que semi-naturels dans la mesure où la végétation qui y croît ne constitue qu'une étape intermédiaire de la succession naturelle. Livrés à eux-mêmes, ils s'embroussaillent et se boisent. En ce qui concerne les zones humides, cela peut être le cas des marais et des tourbières. Il faut donc entretenir ces espaces en les fauchant à certaines dates ou en y pratiquant l'élevage extensif. Or, la plupart des textes accordant une protection générale aux zones humides ne prévoient pas de mesures de gestion. Les espaces que l'on s'efforce de protéger risquent donc de disparaître à plus ou moins long terme.

Dans le nouveau projet d'amendement à la loi fédérale suisse sur la protection de la nature et du paysage, le principe de la nécessité d'une agriculture et d'une sylviculture adaptées à l'objectif de la préservation des biotopes d'importance nationale, régionale ou locale se trouve maintenant clairement posé. C'est aux propriétaires qu'il appartient de procéder à une gestion écologique de ces biotopes. A défaut, ils devront en tolérer l'exploitation par des tiers. On trouve d'ailleurs déjà des règles allant dans le même sens dans la législation du canton de Zürich. La législation d'urbanisme de ce canton (*Planungs- und Baugesetz* du 7 septembre 1975 et son règlement d'application, *Natur- und Landschaftsschutzverordnung* du 20 juillet 1977) prévoit expressément, en effet, la prise de mesures d'entretien et de gestion pour les biotopes protégés. Ces mesures doivent notamment concerner la prévention de l'embroussaillement et le maintien de l'alimentation en eau des zones humides. Au besoin, un plan de gestion devra être établi. Au cas où les mesures prescrites dépasseraient immodérément celles qui découlent de l'obligation légale du propriétaire d'entretenir son terrain, l'entretien sera pris en charge par la commune. Le propriétaire ne peut s'y opposer.

Indemnisation et conventions de gestion

Le refus d'une autorisation ou l'octroi d'une autorisation subordonnée à des conditions contraignantes ne donnent en général pas lieu à indemnisation. Il semble, en effet, que l'on considère que la préservation des espaces naturels étant d'intérêt général, les propriétaires ont une obligation sociale de les préserver semblable à celle à laquelle ils sont soumis en matière de construction par la législation d'urbanisme. Cette interprétation semble prévaloir lorsque le régime de l'autorisation préalable s'applique à tous les espaces d'un certain type et que tous les propriétaires de ces espaces sont placés, a priori, sur un pied d'égalité. Ainsi, ni la législation danoise, ni celle des états des Etats-Unis où des mesures de protection générale des zones humides sont en vigueur, ni d'ailleurs la législation fédérale américaine, ne prévoient d'indemnisation. Les tribunaux américains ont d'ailleurs jugé que, dans la mesure où le propriétaire ne se trouvait pas privé de certains usages de son fonds, il n'y avait pas de prise de la propriété par l'Etat (taking) et donc que les droits constitutionnels des propriétaires n'avaient pas été lésés[12]. Il faut évidemment, également, que les limitations au droit de propriété aient été édictées dans l'intérêt public.

Certains textes, cependant, prévoient bel et bien une indemnisation. C'est le cas, par exemple, de la loi d'Australie du Sud qui soumet à autorisation tout défrichement de la végétation indigène. L'indemnité, qui est payée une fois pour toutes, ne porte que sur les terres agricoles acquises antérieurement à la loi et seulement sur 87,5% de leur surface. Lorsque le régime de protection s'applique à des espaces géographiquement délimités figurant sur une liste, comme c'est le cas par exemple des SSSI britanniques, une indemnisation est généralement due si une autorisation est refusée. En Grande-Bretagne, il peut s'agir d'une indemnité annuelle. Le projet d'amendement à la loi fédérale suisse sur la protection de la nature et du paysage prévoit également l'indemnisation des propriétaires fonciers "qui, dans l'intérêt de la protection souhaitée, limitent leur exploitation actuelle, renoncent à une possibilité d'exploitation concevable ou assurent une prestation sans avantage lucratif immédiat". Cette disposition concerne tous les biotopes désignés comme ayant une importance nationale, régionale ou locale.

Le paiement d'indemnités est en général lié à la conclusion de conventions de gestion. Il en est ainsi pour les SSSI et les zones couvertes de végétation indigène en Australie du Sud. Le projet de loi fédérale suisse prévoit également des accords avec les propriétaires. Les conventions de gestion contiennent non seulement des obligations de ne pas faire, mais souvent également des obligations de faire. L'indemnité correspond alors à une compensation pour la moins value du terrain et à une rémunération pour les activités rendues obligatoires par la convention. Lorsqu'une indemnité annuelle est versée à un propriétaire pour qu'il s'abstienne simplement de certaines actions (qu'il n'avait peut-être nulle intention d'entreprendre), ce qui semble être assez fréquemment le cas en Grande-Bretagne, on peut se demander si cela ne pose pas un problème de moralité de l'institution et s'il ne vaudrait pas mieux payer une fois pour toutes une indemnité correspondant à la perte de valeur du terrain assortie d'une servitude perpétuelle, suivant le fonds en quelque main qu'il se trouve, interdisant les activités susceptibles de porter atteinte au milieu protégé. Bien entendu, une indemnisation en contre-partie d'une obligation de faire sera toujours justifiable.

Conclusion

Il est difficile de se faire une opinion sur l'efficacité des régimes de protection générale applicables à tous les espaces d'un même type, comme par exemple celui qui est établi par la législation danoise. Il semble que les autorisations soient assez facilement accordées. Toute statistique, cependant, serait illusoire car elle ne pourrait pas prendre en compte les cas où aucune demande n'a été formulée, son auteur éventuel sachant parfaitement qu'elle n'aurait aucune chance d'aboutir. En outre, les régimes d'autorisation préalable font souvent une part importante à la négociation. Une demande a priori inacceptable pourra se trouver modifiée sur les conseils de l'Administration ou l'autorisation sera assortie de conditions qui rendront les effets de l'opération beaucoup moins destructeurs. Le succès du système repose donc en partie sur la compétence technique de l'Administration elle-même, ses effectifs et ses moyens, d'autant plus que l'octroi d'une autorisation ne met pas en général un terme à la procédure. Lorsqu'il y a des conditions imposées, il faut évidemment en assurer le suivi et intervenir si elles ne sont pas respectées. Il faut aussi excercer une surveillance générale sur tous les espaces dont l'altération est soumise à autorisation et faire cesser le trouble si des activités ont été entreprises illicitement. Il faut également des sanctions suffisamment dissuasives et pouvoir faire ordonner la remise en état des espaces dégradés sans autorisation dans la mesure où cela est encore possible. Enfin, les associations de protection de la nature doivent pouvoir exercer des recours en annulation contre les décisions d'octroi d'autorisation.

L'expérience montre que ces conditions ne sont pas toujours remplies. Ainsi, dix ans après son adoption, la loi du Rhode Island était encore mal appliquée. De nombreux travaux continuaient à être exécutés sans qu'aucune autorisation n'ait été demandée. Certes, l'Administration peut ordonner l'interruption des travaux et la remise en état des lieux et saisir les tribunaux. Mais l'amende encourue est faible (1000 dollars) et la remise en état impossible ou peu souhaitable. Il ne reste plus alors qu'à régulariser l'opération en accordant une autorisation a posteriori[13].

L'existence d'une réglementation soumettant à autorisation la destruction ou l'altération de certains types d'espaces naturels, et le même raisonnement s'applique aux SSSI britanniques, doit être considérée comme une mesure conservatoire donnant à l'Administration le pouvoir de s'opposer aux travaux qu'elle estimerait inopportuns. Dès lors, cependant, qu'une autorisation a été refusée ou a été accordée sous certaines conditions, la protection devient ponctuelle et l'on assiste à la création en fait sinon en droit d'un véritable réseau d'aires protégées dont l'établissement est simplement différé jusqu'au moment où une menace particulière en justifie la création.

Les pays qui ont instauré des régimes de protection générale applicables à certains types d'espaces naturels sont en nombre croissant, ce qui semble indiquer que ces régimes sont promis à un certain avenir. A défaut, ou en complément, d'autres mesures seront, en général, également nécessaires. Il s'agit d'abord de l'élimination des obstacles juridiques qui s'opposent à la protection de ces espaces, comme par exemple l'existence de textes rendant le drainage obligatoire. Un exemple récent est celui de l'Espagne dont la nouvelle loi des eaux du 2 août 1985 abroge la législation antérieure qui favorisait les assèchements. Vient ensuite l'élimination des subventions et avantages fiscaux accordés pour la destruction de milieux naturels, et notamment de zones humides. L'exemple le plus spectaculaire du type de mesures qui peuvent être prises à cet effet, est constitué par certaines dispositions du Food Security Act américain de 1985 qui suppriment toutes les aides fédérales, y compris le bénéfice du soutien des prix, aux exploitants qui auront converti des zones humides en terres agricoles.

Il faut enfin souligner le rôle que peuvent avoir les mesures de protection volontaire, en particulier lorsqu'elles sont accompagnées d'incitations financières ou fiscales. L'adoption par le Conseil de la CEE le 12 mars 1985 d'un règlement autorisant les Etats membres à subventionner, dans des zones qualifées sensibles du point de vue de l'environnement, l'usage de pratiques agricoles compatibles avec la nécessité de conserver le milieu naturel, constitue déjà un pas important dans ce sens[14]. Au Royaume-Uni, cette disposition a déjà permis la désignation de certaines de ces zones, dont plusieurs sont des régions de marais. Un nombre important d'exploitants agricoles ont fait savoir aux autorités compétentes qu'ils désiraient bénéficier des aides prévues par la législation adoptée à cet effet. Ils percevront, selon les cas, de 30 à 200 livres par hectare, s'ils se conforment à certaines conditions de gestion[15].

Notes

1. Loi sur la conservation de la nature du 18 juin 1969 (no. 314), amendée par les lois du 7 juin 1972 (no. 284), du 26 juin 1975, (no. 297), du 24 mai 1978 (no. 219) et du 25 mai 1983 (no. 208). Sur le système danois de protection générale de certains types d'espaces naturels voir Koester, V. 1984, Conservation, Legislation and General Protection of Biotopes in an International Perspective, *Environment Policy and Law*, Vol. 12, no. 4, mars 1984, pp. 106–116.

2. Arrêté concernant la protection de la faune et de la flore fribourgeoises du 12 mars 1973.

3. Kusler, Jon A. 1983, *Our National Wetland Heritage: A Protection Guidebook*, Environmental Law Institute, p. 83.

4. Sur la genèse et le contenu de ce texte, voir Fowler, R.J. 1986, Vegetation Clearance Controls in South Australia: A Change of Course, *Environmental and Planning Law Journal*, Vol. 3, no. 1, mars 1986, pp. 48–66.

5. The Conservation of Wetlands in New Zealand, *Environmental and Planning Law Journal*, Vol. 3, no. 1. L'arrêt cité a été rendu par la Court of Appeal of New Zealand. Auckland Acclimatisation Society v. Commr. of Crown Land (31 juillet, 1er août et 23 août 1985) (11 NZTPA, p. 33).

6. Le régime des SSSI est établi par le Wildlife and Countryside Act, 1981 et ses amendements du 26 juin 1985.

7. Nature Conservancy Council, *12th Report, 1 April 1985–31 March 1986*, p. 82. Ce rapport mentionne également le cas où des dommages ont été causés à des SSSI.

8. Rapport de la Finlande à la troisième réunion de la Conférence des Parties à la Convention de Ramsar, Regina, Canada, mai 1987.

9. Message du Conseil fédéral du 11 septembre 1985 à l'Assemblée fédérale de la Confédération suisse.

10. Fresh Water Wetlands Act du 16 juillet 1971, Rhode Island General Laws: 2-1-7 à 2-1-24.

11. Arrêts du Tribunal fédéral suisse rendus en 1983, *Recueil officiel*, Vol. 108.3, p. 214.

12. Voir en particulier un arrêt de la Cour Suprême du Wisconsin: Just v. Marinette County, 56 Wis. 2d 7, 201 N.W. 2d 761 (1972) cité par Kustler, Jon A. 1983, *Our National Wetland Heritage*, Environmental Law Institute, pp. 83 et 91.

13. Bryan, Tood A. 1981, The Rhode Island Fresh Water Wetlands Program, In *Selected Proceedings of the Midwest Conference on Wetlands Values and Management*, Brandt Richardson, Ed., St. Paul, Minnesota, pp. 603–611.

14. Règlement du Conseil no. 787/85 du 12 mars 1985 concernant l'amélioration de l'efficacité des structures de l'agriculture (art. 19), J.O.C.E. no. L. 93 du 30 mars 1983, p. 1.

15. *Countryside Commission News*, no. 27, juin-juillet 1987, p. 8.

Control of Activities Harmful to Wetlands and of their Use in the United States

DONALD W. STEVER
Sidley and Austin, New York, U.S.A.

Introduction

The United States, because of the large size and topographical diversity of its land mass, contains a very wide diversity of wetland types. In general, the eastern half of the country contains by far the greatest acreage of wetlands, owing to the aridity of the western areas.

From the Gulf of Mexico area as far north as southern Georgia, the east coast wetlands are predominantly of mangroves. To the north, various *Spartina* communities dominate, with *Spartina alterniflora* predominant throughout the areas of lesser tidal fluctuation, and *Spartina patens* communities predominant in the most northerly areas, where tidal fluctuation is the greatest[1]. Since most of the west coast rises steeply from the ocean, opportunities for the development of significant saltwater wetland systems are rare, though speciation is no different than in the east.

Freshwater wetlands vary in species composition with climatic change. Cypress and Tupelo communities in the deep south give way to cattail and red maple communities in middle latitudes to sedges in the northerly areas. There are a number of unique arid area wetland systems in the western areas. Examples are prairie potholes and playa lakes.

The diversity and distribution of wetlands have contributed to shaping the legal framework within which wetlands are addressed by the law. However, the more significant factors are the historical context in which wetland protection laws developed in the United States, and the constitutional and structural framework within which they are positioned.

The constitutional framework

In general terms, the Constitution of the United States prescribes certain powers exclusively to the national government—the "federal government"—and provides that governmental powers not given to that government are left to the individual state governments[2]. The federal government's authority over activities undertaken in wetlands is premised either on the navigation clause of the Constitution[3], or the commerce clause[4]. Under the former, federal jurisdiction is exclusive, and under the latter, federal jurisdiction is exclusive if either the Congress decrees it to be so or in the absence of such a legislative determination, coexistent federal and state legal regulation would be inconsistent or otherwise overly burdensome[5]. In general, regulation of wetlands has been viewed as not pre-empted by the federal government, and thus individual states are free to impose their own regulatory laws in addition to those of the federal government.

A similar pattern exists in most states for the sharing of power between state and local (city, county, town) governments, although the source of the power-sharing is the state's constitution, and relates to the degree of "home rule" given to local governments.

A second level of the framework are those provisions of the United States Constitution designed to protect individual liberty and property from governmental interference[6]. Since most of the wetland acreage in the United States (at least in the east) is in private ownership, those provisions, particularly the Fifth Amendment due process[7] and just compensation[8] clauses, impose constraints that have shaped the development of the law. Governmental protection of wetlands has had to be structured so as to provide opportunities for hearings, and to limit outright prohibitions to those matters clearly related to public purposes, which do not deprive the owner of all use of the property[9].

A final structural constraint is the nature of the ownership of wetland areas as either public or privately owned resources. This is a complex issue of U.S. law, whose origins include early English common law doctrines for the original 13 east coast states, French and Spanish civil law for Florida, Lousiana and California, and the statehood statutes enacted during the 19th Century as each of the western states were created by Act of Congress. For coastal wetlands, the predominant pattern is that public (usually state) ownership extends from the sea floor upland to the mean high tide line[10]. For freshwater wetlands, in some states the public owns the bed of streams and lakes up to the high water line, and in others the beds are subject to private ownership. There are many variations.

Historical development of laws relating to wetlands in the United States

The earliest laws affecting wetlands in the United States related not to the protection of wetlands, but to regulating the use of tidal wetlands as an agricultural resource of the colonial era. Thus, one finds statutes in the original 13 English colonies[11] establishing property rights to "salt hay" (predominantly *Spartina patens*), seaweed and rockweed. The early regulatory statutes were intended to protect these proprietary rights.

From the 1930s to the mid 1960s, fear of malaria produced statutes designed to authorize the ditching and draining of coastal wetlands as a way to control mosquitoes[12]. Some states, such as Florida, also maintained until the 1950s aggressive progammes to encourage the filling-in of wetlands for the purpose of building development or access to waterways. These and similar laws in many other states required a deed from the Governor or some other designated state official prior to filling in or dredging lands in public ownership[13].

Acting primarily in the interest of protecting navigation, Congress in 1899 adopted a series of statutes that, 70 years later, inadvertently became the first federal wetland protection laws. Section 9, 10 and 13 of the River and Harbor Act of 1899[14] required (a) a special act of Congress in order to create a dike spanning navigable waterways, and (b) a permit from the Secretary of the Army before filling, dredging, placing a structure in or otherwise altering the navigable capacity of a navigable waterway[15]. Beginning about 1969, reacting to citizen pressure, the Army Corps of Engineers[16] began to require persons seeking to dredge canals in the coastal regions of Florida to obtain permits under §10 of the statute[17].

At about the same time, several individual states began to regulate activities that impacted wetland areas. Among the earliest of these statutes was New Hampshire's Revised Statutes Chapter 483A. Under this law, any person placing fill, excavating, or building a structure in either a tidal wetland or a freshwater wetland was required to obtain a permit from a state governmental agency[18].

Whereas the River and Harbor Act's jurisdiction was premised upon the navigability of the water body in question, and thus was severely limited in terms of the scope of the activities that could be regulated under it[19], state statutes, based as they were on the general power to regulate harmful private conduct, defined their jurisdictional reach in much broader terms. For example, the New Hampshire statute reached conduct in any area where "freshwater stands or flows", and in coastal areas up to 3.5 feet above the mean high tide line, where peat substrate occurred, or where any of a number of listed salt-tolerant plant species existed[20]. Unfortunately, the state laws were (and still are) not consistent in defining those areas or activities subject to regulation[21], and thus the pattern of regulation is confusing and not in any sense uniformly protective.

In 1972, Congress adopted the Federal Water Pollution Control Act (FWPCA), a sweeping federalization of the control of water pollution[22]. One section of the FWPCA, §404[23], created a new federal permit programme affecting the discharge of "dredged or fill material" into "waters of the United States"[24]. The legislative history of the FWPCA made it clear that Congress intended the jurisdictional reach of the statute to be much broader than "navigable waters"—that jurisdiction should be as broad as possible within the confines of federal government jurisdiction under the commerce clause of the Constitution[25]. In essence, this statute has been held by the Supreme Court of the United States to be applicable to wetland areas that form the border of or are in reasonable proximity to water bodies, even though there is no apparent surface connection[26].

The Federal Wetland Regulatory Program under Section 404 of the Federal Water Pollution Countrol Act

Jurisdiction and the overall regulatory scheme

Precise definition of those areas and activities that are subject to §404 jurisdiction is contained in the implementing rules of the Corps of Engineers, which reflect the determinations on the subject made by the U.S. Environmental Protection Agency (EPA)[27]. EPA is given authority to establish by regulation (rule) the substantive criteria that must be employed by the Corps of Engineers in issuing permits[28]. Under those regulations, any placement of materials of any sort into any of the following types of areas requires a permit from the Corps of Engineers[29]:

(a) Coastal wetlands, mud flats, swamps, and similar areas that are periodically inundated by saline or brackish waters and that are normally characterized by a prevalence of salt or brackish water vegetation capable of growth or reproduction;

(b) Freshwater wetlands, meaning those that are periodically inundated and which are normally characterized by a prevalence of vegetation that is typically adapted for survival and reproduction in saturated soil conditions; and

(c) Certain isolated wetlands that are not connected to any other aquatic system (though this jurisdiction is limited and exercised only on a case-by-case basis).[30]

In practice, whether an area falls within the regulatory definition of "wetland" is determined in the field by means of a four part analysis. First, it is determined whether there is a presence of wetland "indicator" species[31]. Next, it is determined whether the indicator species are "prevalent". If the prevalent indicator species are of the type that must live in saturated conditions[32], the inquiry ends, and the area is deemed subject to federal jurisdiction. If, however, the prevalent species are only adapted to (e.g. tolerant of) saturated conditions[33], then a further analysis, involving looking at the soil characteristics and hydrology is necessary before the final determination can be made[34].

Some wetland areas are only cyclically inundated. Nevertheless, they are subject to regulatory control if they otherwise meet the jurisdictional test, and so permits may be required for depositing fill or building structures even if at the time the activity is accomplished the area is dry[35].

Even though an area is a wetland for §404 purposes, not every activity that might harm it requires a permit. The statute addresses only the "discharge of dredged or fill material". These terms are given precise definition in the statute and implementing rules, and are significant limitations on jurisdiction. Dredging and excavation, for example, are not subject to regulatory control under the law, though inadvertent placement of dredged spoil on the adjacent wetland areas is subject to it[36]. The placement of harmful chemicals, such as pesticides, on wetlands, is also not covered, though such activity may be controlled under other provisions of law[37].

In spite of this limitation, the term "discharge of dredged or fill material" is given very broad interpretation, including any placement of material that has the effect of replacing an aquatic area with dry land, or of changing the bottom elevation of a water body[38]. Building a structure, even on piles, falls within the jurisdiction of the statute[39].

It is the responsibility of the individual landowner or other person contemplating work in a wetland area to seek a permit. Failure to do so exposes that person to monetary penalties[40] and the potential that any work done without a permit will have to be removed, and the disturbed area restored[41].

Substantive criteria

The Corps of Engineers permit progamme, which was developed initially under the River and Harbor Act of 1899, was administered using a very general standard for permit issuance. The Corps applied what has become known as the "public interest review" standard, under which the decision-maker would weigh all relevant factors surrounding a given permit application and determine whether the activity is, on balance, in the public interest[42].

A new substantive standard was mandated by section 404(b) of the FWPCA, which requires the U.S. Environmental Protection Agency to issue substantive guidelines that are to be based solely on environmental impact criteria, which must be applied by the Corps of Engineers in deciding whether or not to issue permits. Those guidelines, which were issued in final form in 1980, require in general that the applicant demonstrate affirmatively that (a) there is no practical alternative that would have a lesser impact, (b) there will be no significant adverse impacts resulting from the project[43], (c) all reasonable impact mitigation techniques are being employed, and (d) the activity will not result in a violation of any other law[44]. For projects that are not "water dependent", EPA has construed its guidelines to require an affirmative showing that there is no upland (non-wetland) alternative for the type of use being proposed[45].

Each of the §404(b)(1) Guidelines factors are subject to refinement and interpretation, some of which are provided within the text of the EPA regulation itself, and others must await development on a case-by-case application of the factors. In general, however, the approach to analysis under the Guidelines focuses on three elements: the nature of the material being discharged into the wetland (its source and composition), the nature of the discharge activity, and the characteristics of the wetland area into which the material is being discharged.

One area of contention has been the extent to which mitigation measures may be used to justify issuance of a permit that would destroy all or a portion of the wetland an applicant seeks to fill. The Corps of Engineers, until 1986, was generally willing to consider a wide range of mitigation measures. For example, an applicant might propose to fill a naturally-occurring wetland area and in mitigation create an artificial wetland elsewhere. The use of this device was curtailed somewhat in 1986 when EPA exercised its statutory right to veto a permit issued by the Corps of Engineers[46], ruling that under its guidelines, destruction of a high quality, productive natural wetland area could not be mitigated by creation of an artificial wetland[47]. The Corps of Engineers permit regulations apply the "public interest review" standard to §404 permits, though the EPA guidelines are also applied and are deemed controlling. Under the approach used by the Corps, a project that fails the guidelines analysis may not be permitted and a project that is acceptable under the guidelines may still be denied a permit on the basis of general public interest factors. There is no statutory authority for this two-fold approach, though it has not been challenged to date.

The permit issuance process

The permit issuance process itself is interesting, and somewhat complex. It is a peculiar product of the American traditions of "due process of law" and citizen participation in governmental decision-making[48].

After receipt of an application seeking a permit to alter a wetland area, the Corps of Engineers must issue public notice of the application and invite written comments on it from the general public. In the case of large projects, the Corps will hold an informal "hearing", generally held in a public auditorium in the vicinity of the proposed activity, at which time oral statements regarding the proposal are accepted.

The Corps of Engineers is also required to comply with two other procedural statutes in connection with its role as permit issuer. Under the National Environmental Policy Act of 1969, it must decide whether the activity is potentially significant enough to require it to prepare a formal Environmental Impact Statement (EIS)[49]. If an EIS must be prepared, the amount of time it will take for the permit to be processed is significantly lengthened. Another ancillary procedural statute is the Fish and Wildlife Coordination Act, which requires the Corps, as permitting authority, to consult with the federal wildlife management agencies regarding the applicability of laws under their jurisdiction to the project, and in general the effect of the activity on federally protected species on federal sanctuaries[50]. If any coordinating agency objects to the permit, it can force the decision to be moved up to a higher administrative level of the Corps, and ultimately force a negotiation between the Secretary of the Army and the head of the coordinating agency's Department before the permit can be issued.

Citizens are given the right to participate fully in the permitting process, and have the right to seek judicial review of a decision to issue a permit[51]. Significant citizen participation ordinarily occurs only in large, controversial projects. Citizens have successfully blocked a number of very large fill projects by raising issues during the administrative process, and subsequently challenging the permit if it is subsequently issued or is issued without restrictive conditions sought by the citizens[52].

Judicial review and enforcement

Another feature of American administrative law jurisprudence is the right of access to the judicial branch of government[53] of one who has "standing" to seek such review, who is dissatisfied with an administrative action. The notions of "standing" are often difficult for non-U.S. lawyers to understand. Essentially, the federal courts only have jurisdiction to hear "cases or controversies" between separate parties, and are powerless to render advisory opinions. This constitutional limitation has given rise to the concept of "standing to sue", which requires any plaintiff in a federal court to show that he or she has a sufficient real interest in the subject matter to present an actual case or controversy. Standing can, however, be granted as a statutory right, and the FWPCA's judicial review provisions grant standing to any "person" who has participated in the administrative process. Clearly a permit applicant is one such person. Another might be an opponent to the project who submitted comments during the permit process.

Under ordinary circumstances, judicial review of the grant or denial of a permit does not provide the challenging party with a trial *de novo*. The court will review the administrative record of the Corps of Engineers and determine whether the administrative action was "arbitrary and capricious" or an "abuse of administrative discretion". Nevertheless, occasionally a judge will elicit additional facts, particularly if what is being challenged is the government's threshold jurisdiction over the activity.

Enforcement ordinarily occurs when a private citizen places fill in a wetland area without seeking a permit, or exceeds the scope of a permit issued for the activity. As discussed above most enforcement actions are civil in nature, although the FWPCA does provide that knowing and wilful violations may result in criminal charges, with fines or prison terms resulting.

State and local control of wetland alteration

The federal statute covering wetland alteration does not pre-empt individual states or local governments from legislating with respect to the same activity[54]. States may protect wetland areas either by seeking delegation of the federal permit programme from the Corps of Engineers[55], or simply regulate wetland alteration activity by means of a parallel state law-based programme.

As mentioned at the outset of this paper, a number of states have chosen to protect wetland areas, though the means by which they have done so varies. The jurisdictional definition of areas subject to protection varies[56], as does the procedure by which regulation is carried out[57]. In some states, wetland protection is principally the function of a state agency[58], while in others there is a shared jurisdiction between a state agency and local governments[59].

Since there is no federal pre-emption of state or local laws governing wetland-altering activities, there is a great potential for multiple layers of redundant legal regulation. The EPA and the Army Corps of Engineers have sought to limit this phenomenon by essentially ceding jurisdiction on small projects to states with reasonably complete regulatory programmes[60]. The FWPCA provides for formal delegation of the federal jurisdiction to states with equivalent programmes.

Private property rights and wetland regulation

Since most wetland areas in the United States are held in private ownership, a recurrent issue raised by landowners who desire to fill or dredge the areas and are denied permits to do so is a claim that a "Fifth Amendment Taking" has been made[61]. Such a claim is premised on the theory that if a government-imposed restriction on the use of private property is sufficiently severe that it effectively destroys all reasonable use of the property, then the government has "taken" the property from the owner, and must compensate the owner for the lost value under the eminent domain clause of the Fifth Amendment to the U.S. Constitution[62].

Since there is considerable reluctance on the part of the government (indeed, probably not enough money in the government treasury) to protect wetlands by purchase, this legal issue is one of great significance.

The law has not yet clarified just how far the government can restrict private use of a wetland area without overstepping the constitutional limit of land-use restriction without compensation, but the indications are that at least the Federal courts (including the United States Supreme Court) will countenance a very significant degree of restriction, indeed almost to the point of complete destruction of economic value, without finding that a taking of the property has occurred. Nevertheless, the potential for an award of damage tends to encourage the granting of permits that might, without the presence of such concern, be denied.

Conclusion

Laws designed to protect wetland areas have existed in the United States for over 20 years. It has only been within the last 10 years, however, that sophisticated approaches to wetland protection have been undertaken. In spite of procedural and other legal impediments to complete protection of wetlands, significant gains have been made in the United States to arrest the rapid elimination of wetland areas, particularly in coastal areas, that was occurring before the inception of regulatory controls. Nevertheless, it is likely that only obviously significant wetlands will be kept free of negative impact due to building development over the long term. Problems remain with methodologies for determining wetland significance, particularly the role they play in primary production related to food chains, and in terms of habitat significance and groundwater recharge.

Coastal wetlands are under enormous pressure for development, driven by the potential for huge profits from the residental development of coastal areas. Such pressures push at the political basis of the wetland regulatory programmes.

Notes

1. Tidal fluctuations vary from a few vertical inches in southern Florida to over nine feet in northeastern Maine.

2. See U.S. Constitution, Articles I and IV and the Tenth Amendment.

3. Article I, section 8.

4. Article I, section 8. This clause has been interpreted by the Supreme Court to provide authority to the federal government to regulate commerce which may affect interstate commerce. See e.g. Katzenbach v. McClung, 379 U.S. 294 (1964); Wickard v. Fulburn, 317 U.S. III (1942).

5. See, Cooley v. Board of Wardens, 53 U.S. 299 (1852).

6. These are contained in the so-called "Bill of Rights", the first ten amendments to the Constitution, adopted coterminously with adoption of the basic text.

7. The due process clause, which is applicable directly to the federal government and derivatively to state and local governments because of the Fourteenth Amendment, essentially prohibits summary governmental intrusion on private citizens, thus requiring opportunities for hearings prior to restrictive measures being taken, and access to the judiciary to redress grievances against action by government agencies. Access to the judiciary is significant because of the independence of the judiciary under the Constitution.

8. The relevant part of Amendment V states, "nor shall private property be taken for public use without the payment of just compensation therefor". This provision, part of the so-called eminent domain clause, is derived from a provision of the English Magna Carta that was originally designed to prevent the King from confiscating crops or houses for the purpose of feeding or housing troops without paying the owner compensation. Under the United States Constitution, the provision is at the same time a source of authority for the government to seize property for any public purpose, and a requirement that if it does so it must compensate the private owner for the lost value. Although normally applicable to acts of governmental possession, such as the construction of a highway or park, this provision has been interpreted to require compensation where a legal prohibition or limitation on the use of property renders it useless to the owner. See, James Patrick Bollan, *et ex.* v. California Coastal Commission. 483 U.S. 825, 107 S.Ct. 3141 (1987), and Penn Central Transportation Co. v. City of New York, 438 U.S. 104 (1978).

9. See, e.g. Jentgen v. United States, 657 F.2d 1210 (Ct. Cl. 1981), for a discussion of this principle.

10. Thus in the southern states, since most of the coastal wetlands are of the type that lie below m.l.w., they were, unless ceded away by the state legislature, historically public resources. In the northern states, however, this was not the case, since most of the area of *Spartina patens* wetlands from New Jersey northward lies above m.h.w.

11. Maine (originally a part of Massachusetts), Massachusetts, New Hampshire, Rhode Island, Connecticut, New York, New Jersey, Delaware, Virginia, South Carolina, North Carolina, Georgia, Maryland (Pennsylvania had no saline water).

12. Not only was this effort destructive of wetlands, it was ineffective for the control of mosquitoes.

13. See e.g. New Hampshire Rev. Stat. Ann. §483.

14. 33 U.S.C. §§ 403, 404, 406.

15. "Navigable waters" in this context are those "subject to the ebb and flow of the tides" or those on which commercial navigation has actually taken place, or on which such navigation is feasible. See The Daniel Ball, 77 U.S. (10 Wall) 557 (1870); United States v. Appalachian Electric Power Co., 311 U.S. 377 (1940); and Minnehaha Creek Watershed District v. Hoffman, 597 F.2d 617 (8th Cir. Ct. App. 1979) (examples of court decisions interpreting the Constitutional principle of navigable waters).

16. Though part of the military establishment, the Corps of Engineers has historically played a role in non-military affairs, as the governmental agency chiefly responsible for maintaining harbor depth by dredging, and as one of the two agencies that construct government-owned dams. Jurisdiction over waters rests with the Civil Works unit of the Corps.

17. In doing so, the Corps began to seek to control activities undertaken in areas that were not normally viewed by the public as "navigable". The activity led to lawsuits challenging the Corps' jurisdiction. See United States v. Holland, 373 F.Supp. 665 (M.D. Fla., 1974), in which a federal court concluded that an area inundated by the tides 50 times each year was sufficiently "navigable" to vest regulatory jurisdiction in the Corps.

18. Unlike the earlier state statutes, this one was not premised upon a riparian or littoral owner expanding his property into public waters. Rather, it was straightforwardly a "police power" statute, intended to regulate private conduct in the interest of promoting the general welfare of the community at large.

19. Many wetlands are not part of navigable waters, as that term has been defined by the Supreme Court and other federal courts interpreting the scope of the navigation clause of the Constitution.

20. N.H. RSA §483-A: 1.

21. There are two predominant approaches. A number of states define regulatory jurisdiction in terms of the presence of wetland indicator species of plants. Others, however, rely on the type of soil found on the site.

22. Public Law 92-500. Prior to that time, regulation of water pollution was predominantly within the domain of the individual state governments. Following significant amendments in 1977 (unrelated to wetlands), this statute became known as the "Clean Water Act".

23. 33 U.S.C. §1344.

24. The statute actually makes reference in its text to "navigable waters", but defines that term to mean "all waters of the United States". See §502.

25. The Commerce Clause, Article I, §8, gives to the federal government the power to regulate "commerce among the states". Two hundred years of Supreme Court interpretation of this clause essentially produced a doctrine that federal authority extended to any activity that even remotely could have an effect on or deal with interstate commerce. For a detailed discussion of this, see Stever, D.W. 1987, Water (Chapter 12 of Novick *et al.*, *Law of Environmental Protection*, Clark Boardman).

26. See United States v. Riverside Bayview Homes, 474 U.S. 121 (1985).

27. Although the Corps of Engineers was given permit-issuing authority under §404, EPA has overall substantive control of the statute, and its view of the jurisdiction has been ruled predominant by the Attorney General of the United States. See 43 Op. Atty. Gen. 15 (1979).

28. Congress could, of course, have simply given EPA the authority to issue permits itself. That it did not do so is apparently due to a perception that the Corps of Engineers could handle the permit issuance more easily, since it had already established a permit programme under the River and Harbor Act of 1899. It did not, however, trust the Corps to fashion adequate substantive criteria, and thus made the Corps of Engineers subservient to EPA in this regard.

29. Certain activities are exempt, or are deemed permitted for administrative convenience. Examples include minor filling associated with residential house construction, and power line stream crossings.

30. See 40 CFR Part 320. Most wetlands are contiguous or adjacent to water bodies. However, some wetlands are "perched", that is they are self-standing and not part of another system. These are made subject to jurisdiction on a case by case basis.

31. These are plants that are normally associated with wetlands, that are "typically adapted for life in saturated soil conditions". Lists of such species are maintained by the Corps of Engineers, EPA, and the U.S. Fish and Wildlife Service (a unit of the Department of the Interior).

32. Obligate hydrophyte species.

33. Facultative hydrophyte species.

34. See 33 CFR §323.3(c). This approach was found to be consistent with the FWPCA's intent in Avoyelles Sportsmen's League v. Alexander, 511 F.Supp. 278 (W.D.La. 1981), affirmed on other grounds 715 F.2d 897 (5th Cir. Ct. App. 1983).

35. See United States v. Phelps Dodge Corp., 391 F.Supp. 1181 (D. Ariz. 1975).

36. Dredging of navigable waters (a significantly narrower class of areas) is subject to control under §10 of the River and Harbor Act of 1899.

37. The water pollution discharge sections of the FWPCA provide potential control, as do the Toxic Substances Control Act and the Federal Insecticide, Fungicide and Rodenticide Act.

38. See 40 CFR §122.2; Avoyelles Sportsmen's League v. Alexander, 715 F.2d 897 (5th Cir. 1983) [holding that placing slash from trees cut in area in windrows as part of a land clearing operation is subject to jurisdiction]. Certain activities are, however, exempt. Those are discharges that are incidental to normal farming and silvicultural activities.

39. The Corps of Engineers has, for administrative convenience, deemed certain types of activities clearly falling within the statutory jurisdiction, not subject to individual permits. Very small projects, such as utility line stream crossings, where some minor filling is involved, are deemed to have a permit (called a nationwide permit or general permit).

40. Originally, the statute required that the government bring a lawsuit against the person concerned and seek a levy of penalties (up to $10,000 per day) from the court. In 1987, the FWPCA was amended to provide for administrative levy of penalties by the Corps of Engineers. Under the amended provision, the recipient of a penalty determination may seek a hearing before the Corps, and ultimately appeal the levy to a federal court.

41. The "restoration" remedy was established in a series of enforcement lawsuits brought by the government against land developers in the mid-1970s. In order to secure an order requiring restoration, the government must demonstrate that the remedy is environmentally sound, is achievable as a practical matter, and bears an equitable relationship to the magnitude of the violation. See United States v. Weismann, 489 F.Supp. 1331 (M.D. Fla. 1980).

42. 33 CFR §320.4. Public interest factors include the impact on the aquatic ecosystem, the impact on navigation, the extent to which public access to waters is enhanced or impeded, and the impact on endangered or threatened species of wildlife and flora. The extent to which environmental impacts that are associated with the overall project of which the wetland permit is a part are "relevant" has been a hotly contested issue, because such impacts have been held by several courts necessary to disclose in connection with the environmental impact analysis required of the Corps by the national Environmental Policy Act of 1969 (NEPA), 42 U.S.C. sec. 4321 *et seq.*

43. Whether a given set of impacts is "significant", of course, involves value judgments, and a determination of significance includes policy as well as scientific judgment. The first issue is whether the wetland at issue is itself significant, and then whether the degree of degradation that will result if the permit is granted is significant to the wetland. Varying approaches to this determination have been tried.

44. 40 CFR §320.10.

45. This is a significant interpretation, since EPA made it clear that a showing by the applicant that it does not have access to an upland site for its project is not enough. What must be shown is that no upland sites are available for the type of use proposed.

46. Section 404(c) of the FWPCA gives EPA the power to veto a permit issued by the Corps if EPA concludes that the permit is inconsistent with the substantive Guidelines.

47. Attleboro Mall ("Sweden's Swamp") Decision. EPA suggested, however, that mitigation might be acceptable where the wetland at issue was of lower value. Similar reasoning has been articulated by a court, in National Audubon Society v. Hartz Mountain Development Corporation, 14 Env. Law. Reptr. 20724 (D.N.J. 1983).

48. Another aspect of citizen participation is the "citizen suit". The degree of public participation in environmental decision-making in the U.S. is one of the most unique aspects of the nation's legal system.

49. NEPA, as this statute is called, requires a formal deliberative study to be done of "major federal action significantly affecting the quality of the human environment". Permit issuance is a "federal action", and the scope and nature of the activity for which a permit is sought determines whether the action is sufficiently "major" or "impact-producing" to trigger the obligation to do a formal study. A determination not to produce an EIS, called a "negative declaration", must be accompanied by a formal "finding no significant impact" ("FONSI"). Guidelines for compliance with NEPA are issued by the Council on Environmental Quality, a branch of the Office of the President of the United States.

50. The two agencies involved are (a) the U.S. Fish and Wildlife Service, a unit of the Department of the Interior, which administers the federal wildlife refuge system, and has jurisdiction over a

number of federal wildlife protection laws, including the Endangered Species Act, and the Migratory Bird Treaty Act, and (b) the National Marine Fisheries Service, a part of the Department of Commerce, which is responsible for administering various marine mammal and fishery protection laws and treaty obligations.

51. The applicant may seek review of denial of his application.

52. Frequently the challenge raises statutory claims that are only ancillary to the substantive §404 issues. Most often raised is non-compliance with the National Environmental Policy Act, where the citizen litigant claims that the Corps failed to write an adequate Environmental Impact Statement prior to acting on the permit application. Such a claim effectively killed the $100 million "Westway" highway project in New York City, which was to be constructed partly on fill placed in the Hudson River.

53. Under the U.S. Constitution, the judiciary is independent from the executive and legislative arms of the government.

54. The pre-emption doctrine is another U.S. Constitution-derived one, which holds certain types of regulatory action by the national government to be exclusive. In the case of water pollution control, the FWPCA specifically allows states to employ more restrictive laws.

55. Section 404(4) of the FWPCA provides that EPA may, if it deems a state to have an equivalent programme, delegate to the state the permit issuance functions that would otherwise be exercised by the Corps of Engineers. One environmental disadvantage of such delegation is that the states are not subject to the National Environmental Policy Act (it applies only to federal agencies), and thus once the permit programme is delegated, no more Environmental Impact Statements will be required. This is not as significant a problem as it may at first seem, however, since the §404(b)(1) Guidelines, to which the states must adhere, require a reasonably thorough analysis.

56. Some states define protected areas by vegetative indicators, some by soil types, others by reference to the presence of surface water.

57. Several states actually map areas subject to protection and classify them according to their perceived value. New York, for example, protects only wetland complexes greater than 12 acres in size, and maps the areas that qualify, classifying them as either Class 1, Class 2 or Class 3 wetlands. Class 1 wetlands are subject to more stringent substantive permit requirements than the other two. Other states simply define the areas subject to jurisdiction in general terms, and place the burden on individual developers to determine the need for a permit.

The classification of wetlands by function and value is, of course, highly subjective.

58. E.g. New Jersey, Maine, New Hampshire.

59. In New York, for example, the state Department of Environmental Conservation exercises jurisdiction over inland wetland complexes of 12 acres or more, and all tidal wetlands, leaving protection of smaller inland complexes to local governments (towns, cities, villages), which are not required to exercise regulatory jurisdiction, but may do so if they wish to undertake such activity. In California, counties, which are geographically large units of local government, exercise most of the regulatory juridisction, except in coastal areas, where regional "coastal commissions" have exclusive jurisdiction under the California Coastal Act.

60. Typically, there will be a "general permit" authorizing activities involving less than 10 acres of inland wetlands or less than 1 acre of tidal wetlands.

61. See Note 8, above.

62. The source of this theory is a 1922 opinion of the United States Supreme Court, in a case called Pennsylvania Coal Company v. Mahon, 260 U.S. 393 (1922).

Fiscal and Financial Factors in the Conservation of Wetlands: Response to the Questionnaire

MALCOLM J. FORSTER
University of Southampton, U.K.*

Tax and public finance represent a complex and specialized area of law and practice and one which is somewhat remote from the everyday experience of those engaged in wetland conservation. Perhaps for this reason, the responses to the enquiries on the questionnaire which related to these matters were answered with a degree of abstraction and with a lack of detail that was markedly higher than was apparent in responses to other parts of the questionnaire. In many cases, the information provided for each country was vestigial and therefore only the broadest outline of the comparative position can be attempted.

The general scheme of taxation of land and its impact on wetland conservation

Although most countries from which responses to the questionnaire were received possess some form of land taxation, opinions varied as to whether or not this taxation system contributed to the conservation of wetlands or encouraged their conversion to agriculture or other uses. On the whole, however, it was the opinion of those responding that tax systems at present, in a wide range of countries, tended to favour the conversion rather than the conservation of wetlands. This is usually the result of a land improvement and development policy, which employs agricultural production or the value of such production as a yardstick by which to measure the utility of land-use.

Almost all countries from which responses were received possess some kind of land-tax, although this naturally takes many forms. In most cases, it was thought that the operation of this tax tended to prejudice the retention of wetlands in their natural condition. In Morocco, there is a agricultural tax whose purpose is to promote agricultural production, and in many other countries, such as Canada, there is an in-built bias in the tax structure towards the use of land for agriculture.

A particularly threatening feature of the system of land taxation in a number of countries is a positive attempt to discriminate in fiscal terms against owners of land

Now Head, International Division, Environment Group, Freshfields, London

who permit their property to lie fallow, to remain "unimproved" in its natural state, or who fail to maximize its productive value in agricultural or other terms. Compared to land under cultivation, such land is subject to unfavourable tax treatment—in Chile, for example. Much the same is true in Portugal. In the Philippines, there is at present a general tax based upon land values, but there is a proposal to introduce a new system of taxation which would penalize owners whose land stands "idle"; however, this reform has yet to be implemented. In the Netherlands, the tax structure also bears unfavourably upon unused lands and, although the impact of taxation is mitigated by allowable deductions, the overall effect is still unfavourable, as these deductions are limited in extent.

In a number of countries, although there is no such explicit discrimination spelt out in the law, there are other provisions which, although more indirect, have an equally powerful effect in stimulating the conversion of wetlands into other uses. Thus, in Czechoslovakia, there is an agricultural tax which on the surface does not appear to differentiate between cultivated and uncultivated land. This should, however, be read together with another provision which obliges any person or enterprise wishing to use land in a rural area for investment or any other non-rural purpose to reclaim an acreage equal to that dedicated to such purpose from land which is abandoned or uncultivated. Similarly, in Morocco, there is no unfavourable treatment expressly imposed upon land lying fallow, yet land which has been distributed cannot be repossessed, provided those to whom it has been allocated make it productive. If "productive" in this context means yielding a certain amount of traditional agricultural produce, then this provision amounts to a clear incentive to convert wetlands, which on the whole would not offer great potential in this sense, into land on which such crops or livestock could be raised.

Not all countries from which responses were received make such a distinction in their general land taxation law, between land in cultivation and land which is allowed to remain in its natural state. Thus, the Greek law places no additional tax burden on uncultivated land, nor are such lands treated with any particular severity in Sweden. A number of countries operate a land taxation system which is based upon some assessment of the value, either capital or productive, of land. Such a valuation may be based upon actual income received by the owner or on some sort of notional value, but no examples were reported of systems of this type under which the owner is taxed on the bases of wilful default, i.e. upon what should have been received had the land been used in such a manner as to derive the maximum possible economic benefit from it. Thus, in Switzerland, landowners are subject, in addition to a land tax, to an income tax based upon the produce of their land. The taxable sum is calculated by reference to the area of land in cultivation, a specified amount of produce being assumed to have been derived from each square metre in cultivation, and tax is payable on this amount of produce at the appropriate rate.

A number of common law countries, such as New Zealand and the United Kingdom, have a type of land taxation which takes as its basis a notional rental value of the land in question, although, in the nature in things, the assessment is invariably somewhat out of line with the actual rental value on the estate market. On the face of it, systems such as these should operate in such a way as to favour the retention of wetlands and other "non-productive" lands in their natural state.

In principle, a tax structure which bases assessment to tax on the amount which the owner might confidently expect to receive by way of rent for the land on the open market ought to do little to encourage such owners to "improve" their wetlands, if the result would simply be to increase the tax base upon which they are to be assessed. In fact, such an evaluation is somewhat of an over-simplification. It predicates, for example, the enjoyment by the tax-paying landowner of sufficient income from other sources to enable him to forego the post-tax element of the income to be derived from improving the land. In many countries, farming communities display a somewhat marginal economic perform-ance and it is necessary for farmers to extract every iota of benefit which can be derived from their land. Thus, the security offered to wetlands by an assessment system based upon rental value is an illusory one, even in highly developed economies. Even there, other factors may outweigh it, as has been the case until very recently in many of the countries of the European Community, where subsidies altogether unreflective of world market forces have sheltered farm production and stimulated the conversion into arable land of wetlands which would otherwise have remained untouched.

A second limitation of such systems may be that even the limited benefit which it confers in the conservation of wetlands in their natural state is confined to land which is kept in hand by the landowner. Clearly, if land is let at a certain rental value, the lessee will be obliged to seek to produce an income from the land in excess of the rent paid for it. Thus, where the assessment of the annual value of the land is based upon an actual, rather than a notional, rent, much of the theoretical impetus of the system for the conservation of wetlands disappears. Few wetlands will actually be leased to tenants who do not seek to gain from the exploitation of the holding by grazing or otherwise. (An obvious exception lies in the leasing of such lands by conservation bodies. Where such bodies lease wetlands of low rental value under such a tax system, the potential tax benefits available are maximized).

These factors, however, only apply with any force when there is complete equality of treatment of all the types of land subject to the assessment system, and where there is no distortion of the effects by attempts to favour land employed in certain uses. Such a pure system is indeed a rarity, as almost invariably national law seeks to promote certain types of land-use, particularly agriculture and forestry, by modifying the tax system in order to favour them. Thus, even where apparently non-disciminatory systems exist, it is not true to say that wetlands are treated no less favourably than other uses of land. In many such countries, certain preferred uses may benefit from tax burdens which, although they may be calculated on the same capital or rental value, are levied at a lower rate than that generally applicable or which are mitigated by special exemptions or relief.

Thus, it is common to find that, even where the basis of taxation of all land is roughly or exactly uniform, special treatment produces a distortion. A widespread example is the levying of land taxes on agricultural land at a rate of tax lower than that applicable to other property. Where this is done, even though the basis of assessment is the same for farmland as for wetlands, the amount of tax actually paid by the landowner on farmland is substantially lower than on an equal acreage of land put to other uses. While a landowner may be prepared to renounce such a benefit in respect of, for example, garden or park land from which he derives a recreational benefit or of land which he devotes to an industrial or commercial use with a high enough yield to offset the loss of the preferential rate, he would be unlikely to do so in respect of a unproductive wetland which, if converted, would not only produce an income for him, but would produce one which is treated for taxation purposes more favourably than almost any other.

It should be noted that in some tax systems this effect is so pronounced as to make the investment of substantial sums in the conversion of even the least promising wetlands not only feasible, but positively attractive. In the United Kingdom, for example, the encouragement of forestry by fiscal means formerly reached a level of sophistication which must approach the ideal. There were two bases upon which the landowner might be taxed on his forestry operations—on the profits which accrued to him from the forest during the taxable period or on a notional sum equivalent to one-third of the annual value of the land (itself calculated on the rent which the owner would receive for the land in its natural and unimproved state and ignoring the value of the trees planted upon it). An owner selected which of these methods of assessment he wished to adopt and, once he had done so, the election was irrevocable. The election, however, only bound the original owner and new owners could make a new election. Thus, a wise owner would, while the trees were growing and producing no income, elect to be taxed upon the profits deriving from the forestry operation. As soon as the trees were ready for felling, he would arrange for the land to be transferred to a company or other legal entity which he controlled and this new owner would then elect to be taxed on the notional annual value, reaping a substantial gain treated extremely favourably for tax purposes. When taken together with many other benefits conferred on forestry by the British tax system, this device made large-scale investment in forestry an almost standard element in tax-planning for wealthy clients. The result in ecological terms caused widespread concern in the United Kingdom and has since been addressed by a radical revision of fiscal treatment of forestry.

The favourable tax treatment of activities inimical to the conservation of wetlands in their natural state

In addition to the indirect threat to the conservation of wetlands posed by differential treatment within the same tax framework of competing uses, many countries actively mount a direct attack on wetland conservation by positively encouraging activities to harm wetlands, by applying direct fiscal or financial advantages to those activities. Most prominent among these advantages are the benefits conferred on those conducting drainage operations, and these benefits may take the form of subsidies or even the privilege of raising special taxes or charges.

The conferral upon those carrying out drainage operations of a power of levying charges on those benefitting by the operation is somewhat rare, but it does exist in some countries from which replies were received. Among such jurisdictions are Quebec in Canada, the Netherlands and New Zealand. The most usual form in which they occur is that of a charge levied by a water authority, part of whose responsibility is for drainage and flood control. In the United Kingdom, inland drainage boards have the power (although it does not appear to be widely exercised) to raise a special drainage charge on agricultural occupiers. In this form, it may be suspected that this device is rather more widespread than the answers to the questionnaires suggest, as such authorities are not uncommon and they frequently are empowered to levy charges for their services.

If is clear, however, that in the majority of the jurisdictions for which replies were received drainage schemes and other activities which are detrimental to wetland conservation receive a significant level of subvention and state aid.

Thus, for example, the Canadian National Department of Regional Development makes subsidies available for land drainage operations, particularly where these are conducted for the purpose of producing hydro-electric power, or for transport or public utility developments. Loans on specially favourable terms and other forms of tax incentives are also available for these operations. Furthermore, similar advantages are available in Canada from provincial, state and local government bodies. Thus, in Quebec, these forms of subvention are available for flood control projects. Similarly, in the Netherlands, aid is available from the central government, from the governments of the individual provinces, from other public authorities and from international sources, including the EC. This aid takes the form of subsidies, loans on specially favourable terms, project support and development assistance. A similar situation exists in New Zealand, where subsidies and special loans are available from the state and from certain public authorities. Technical assistance and substantial tax concessions are made available by the national government in the Philippines, where international support is also given to drainage projects. State aid of one sort or another is also available in Spain and in Sweden. In Switzerland also, special subsidies may be available from federal, cantonal and local authority sources. In the United Kingdom, the national government, local governments, water authorities and inland drainage boards may make grants or subsidies for drainage operations.

In every jurisdiction from which a questionnaire reply was received, the balance of opinion seems to be that the tax system, on the whole, favours the conversion of wetlands into agricultural or other uses.

Consequently, it is important to consider, in outline, what devices may be available in order to use the tax or public finance system of a particular country in such a manner as to redress the balance somewhat in this respect.

Taxation and public finance as an instrument for wetland conservation

It is by no means established that taxation is an effective method of influencing public behaviour. Even quite punitive tax burdens (such as those imposed in some jurisdictions upon tobacco products) have failed to make much impact on the socially undesirable conduct which they are intended to diminish or discourage. The tobacco example is perhaps a little unjust as it addresses a deep-seated personal course of conduct for which there is perhaps no parallel in the field of wetland conservation, but the point should not altogether be lost. Tobacco duties are an exception, because they represent an occasion when legislatures have felt politically strong enough to impose a penal rate of taxation. In few other areas, even in that of effluent charges related to pollution of water (for example), has such political confidence been felt. It is, in practical terms, hard to envisage such an aggressive tax policy towards wetland depletion.

Thus, the influence which the tax or public finance system will bring to bear is likely to be gentler, more in the nature of pursuasion and inducement than compulsion. There are two basic methods by which this may be achieved—by the provision of tax incentives or by the imposition of disincentives—"the carrot or the stick".

Incentives—"the carrot"

The use of tax-saving devices in environmental controls has centred around the use of incentive systems. These have operated largely in the field of pollution control and have usually manifested themselves as methods of setting off capital expenditure on pollution abatement equipment against income produced by the polluting activity. Although subject to a number of shortcomings from the pollution control standpoint, they are widespread and confer some significant ecological benefit. In a number of jurisdictions, they have been extended to soil and water conservation projects, so that a farmer who, for example, terraces his land to avoid soil erosion, may deduct the cost of that operation from his taxable income from his farming operations (and, in some jurisdictions, from income from other sources).

There are some features of wetland conservation which make these traditional types of incentive less appropriate than in the pollution control setting. Pollution abatement incentives, which allow the setting-off of capital expenditure against trading profits, normally envisage both substantial outlay and an income sufficiently large to make the offset attractive enough to stimulate the expenditure. Although these elements may be present in wetland conservation, this is by no means certain. No major expenditure may be required and the available income against which the allowance may be set may not be sufficient to result in an actual gain to the taxpayer large enough to justify the retention of the wetland, even if all other agricultural income is available for relief. In some jurisdictions, the potential for such relief is further limited by excluding non-agricultural income from reduction, and many countries have restrictions on the use of tax losses made from "hobby-farming". Whatever the value of these restrictions from the taxation point of view, they seriously hamper the usefulness of tax deductions for wetland conservation, which would perhaps benefit markedly if taxpayers were encouraged to employ income generated outside agriculture for conserving wetlands. In industrialized countries, at least, the type of taxpayer who "hobby-farms" normally does so because of the amenity value of living in rural areas, and is thus likely to be favourably disposed towards retention of the wetland in its present state.

In addition to these traditional types of incentive, national laws are increasingly conferring direct grants and other cash benefits for the conservation of certain landscape features, including wetlands. A notable recent example is the decision of the European Community to encourage Member States to introduce national schemes to promote the introduction and continuance in environmentally sensitive areas of agricultural practices which are compatible with the special features of those areas. In particular, these measures include aids and subsidies which require the lessening of the intensification of farming in these areas.

Some national laws, while not making such aid generally available, encourage the negotiation of private agreements with landowners, by which the latter accept certain restrictions on their use of land in return for cash payments from the public purse. These management agreements usually involve a public agency, but they are nonetheless private contracts. The obligations placed upon the landowner may include the retention or management of wetlands on his land. This device is widely used in the United Kingdom, the United States, Sweden, Switzerland and other jurisdictions.

Nonetheless, it remains a major problem that in most taxation systems the incentives for converting wetlands into other uses outweigh those available for conservation of wetlands.

Disincentives—"the stick"

An entirely different fiscal device is the imposition of disincentive burdens upon courses of action inimical to wetland conservation. These devices vary somewhat in the jurisdiction in which they occur. They may, as in the United Kingdom, take the form of a provision that certain agricultural subsidies may be refused if they are likely to be applied in a manner which is likely to be detrimental to wildlife or other features. In the United States, the Food Security Act of 1985 has introduced a rather more draconian system by which any farmer who plants a crop on soil which is highly susceptible to erosion or an a drained wetland will forfeit his eligibility to a wide range of federal agricultural support payments, including some (such as loans for the construction of barns) which are not directly connected with the production of the crop concerned and can thus be seen to be penal in character.

The Legal Protection of Wetlands in Poland

JERZY SOMMER

Professor, Research Group on Environmental Law, Institute of State and Law, Polish Academy of Sciences, Warsaw

It is very difficult to outline the legal protection of wetlands in Poland in a comprehensive way because there is no systematic regulation of these areas as such. The Polish language (both common and legal) does not have an equivalent for the English word "wetlands". The protection of wetlands is regulated by many other Acts which do not directly regulate wetlands. They regulate either the protection of the environment, the conservation of nature, the management of certain natural resources or the competence of state bodies. The legal instruments used are general in character, aiming at the protection of the environment or the rational use of natural resources.

The obligation to protect wetlands is comprised of general legal notions whose meaning is vague. One finds such expressions as: "the protection of the ecological balance", "the ensurance of rational use of water, agriculture or forest land". Very seldom do we have a direct regulation on certain kinds of wetlands.

These obligations to protect wetlands are formulated in statutes or regulations. The legal methods used to specify these duties are administrative decisions, court decisions, land-use plans, supervision and inspection, fees and fines. The procedural matters are, as a rule, regulated in the code of administrative procedure. This code ensures the judicial review of administrative decisions. It also gives social organizations the legal possibility of influencing the decision-making process. The social organizations also have a legal possibility of influencing the process whereby the acts and plans are created.

Under these regulations, wetlands, or certain kinds of wetlands, may be protected, but there is no compulsion to protect them. It depends on the knowledge, determination and ability of the participants in the decision-making process.

Generally speaking, the legal protection of wetlands is primarily comprised of three bodies of law:

1. Conservation of nature law;

2. Protection and management of water law;

3. Protection of agricultural and forest land law.

The conservation of nature is regulated by the 1949 Act on the Conservation of Nature (Dz.U. nr. 25 poz. 180) and the 1980 Act on the Protection of the Environment (Dz.U. nr. 3 poz. 6 and Dz.U. of 1983 nr. 44 poz 201). Conservation of nature is covered by three kinds of legal instruments on: (a) special protected areas, (b) protection of animal and plant species, and (c) the protection of natural monuments. This last category has little relevance to wetlands.

Any territory which has value from the point of view of public interest may be recognized as a special protected area. The concept of public interest is broad and also covers the ecological value of an area. According to the 1949 Act, an area may be protected as a National Park or as a Nature Reserve.

A National Park should comprise an area not less than 500 ha and should possess great natural values, not changed significantly by the activity of man. A National Park is created by the order of the Council of Ministers, which specifies the rules of management and restrictions for the park. These restrictions are generally defined in Section 18 of the Act.

A Nature Reserve is created by an order of the Minister for the Protection of the Environment. This order specifies the rules of management and the restrictions for the reserve. National Parks and Nature Reserves are created to preserve ecosystems in their original form.

Our legal system can create two other forms of protected areas: Landscape Parks and Areas of Protected Landscape. These areas are created by an order of the Regional People's Council on the basis of the 1983 Act on the People's Councils. The contents of an order are, to a certain degree, defined by the 1980 Act on the Protection of the Environment. It is expected that a future Act on the Conservation of Nature (which is in preparation) will define more precisely the form and content of the protection of these areas.

The protection of nature in Landscape Parks and Areas of Protected Landscape is weaker than in National Parks and Nature Reserves. The reasons for this are obvious. The character of the areas protected as National Parks or Nature Reserves is different from the character of the areas protected as Landscape Parks or as Areas of Protected Landscape. Also, the aim of protection is different. But these forms together ought to create the condition for preserving the ecological balance in the country as a whole. This endeavour was recently strengthened by the 1984 Act on Town and Country Planning. By now we have 14 National Parks comprising 122,718 ha and 747 Nature Reserves comprising 74,442 ha. By 1982 there were 11 Landscape Parks comprising 340,532 ha. It is planned that eventually the areas of protected landscapes will comprise 20% of the territory of the country and that all these areas together will comprise no less than 30% of the country.

For the protection of wetlands, the Fishing Reserves created under the Act of 1985 on Inland Water Fishing are also of value (Dz.U. nr. 21 poz. 91). Their aim is to protect water areas for fish culture. I think that this approach is of great importance for the protection of wetlands because it does not conflict, but aids the fulfilment of other ecological goals.

Also important for the protection of wetlands are the protection of animal and plant species. These are regulated by the executive orders of the Minister of Forestry (two orders of 1983). Under protection are those species which, together with their habitats, may perish. Thus wetlands, as the habitat of certain plants and animals, are also under protection.

The law on water protection and water management is especially important for the protection of wetlands, since the extraction of water for domestic and industrial purposes has a great influence on wetlands. There may be a conflict between protection of wetlands and exploitation of water. The law ought to regulate this conflict, keeping in mind not only short-term gains but also long-term ones. It is not an easy task.

In support of short-term gains are powerful economic forces. Long-term gains are supported, sometimes, by the minority without political influence. Water management and water protection are regulated by the 1974 Act on Water Law and the 1980 Act on the Protection of Environment. The 1980 Act, in Sections 18-23, regulates the protection of water. Sections 10 and 22 are of special importance. Section 20 regulates the activities which may change the water condition in a large area. These activities must be conducted in such a manner that the ecological balance will not be disturbed. In areas of special ecological importance (not the same as the protected areas mentioned above), the State Inspection for Environmental Protection is obliged to regulate the conditions under which such activities may be carried out. Section 22 imposes the obligation to prepare an environmental impact assessment for all economic activity changing the water condition in a large area. Also, the 1974 Water Law introduced several obligations aiming at environmental protection in the process of water exploitation. The most important obligations can be found in Section 25 and Section 78 para. 3. According to Section 25, a license for a specified use of inland water ought not to be granted when the use of water may damage the environment. Section 78 para. 3 orders that the regulation of inland water ought not to damage the beauty of the landscape and the biological conditions of water environments. But these stipulations do not take the upper hand. Other aims are, in practice, prevalent. These other aims are: provision of the national economy with water of the proper quantity and quality, anti-flood protection, improvement of agricultural land by drainage and the creation of good conditions for inland water transport. As a result, many wetlands have been eliminated due to the prejudice in favour of the national economy.

One may ask the question why the provisions in favour of the environment and wetlands are not strong enough. It is impossible for me to explain it fully in this paper. This problem is worth a separate paper. However, I would like to indicate, in shortened form only, the basic reasons. One of these reasons is the state of the prevailing goals of the national economy. The main goal was the production, at any cost, of material things. In addition, the system of management of the national economy, which gave the upper hand to bureaucracy on the one hand and to heavy industries and mining on the other hand, played a role. Also, the ecological knowledge, not only of administrative officials, but also of the technicians, was insufficient. So, the biological aspects were neglected in the decision-making process. However, there are other reasons, in addition to the socio-economic factors. Some imperfections of the legal regulations also play a role. I think that the basis for these imperfections is the vagueness of the legal clauses on the protection of the environment. These clauses do not always fully specify the subjects of obligation, the contents of duties, the mode of inspection and the responsibility for non-fulfilment. This is not so much due to legal norms as to ideological proclamations. It is obvious that the legal system, for several reasons, cannot dispense with such general clauses. But their successful operation is only possible if there is a systematic judicial review of administrative decisions which provide content to these general clauses. This situation does not exist. The decisions are made by an administrative organ, with little competence in legal matters, and these decisions are very seldom subordinated to judicial review.

The protection of wetlands by the body of law aiming at the protection of agricultural and forest land is the weakest. This is regulated by the 1982 Act on the Protection of Cultivable and Forest Land (Dz.U. nr. 11 poz. 79). The aim of this regulation is to protect cultivable and forest land against two dangers: (a) appropriation for non-agricultural and forest aims; and (b) diminution of the agricultural and forest value. According to this regulation, wetlands are not agricultural or forest land but wasteland, and as such they are not protected. According to this regulation, wasteland ought to be transformed into cultivable land or forest land. There are only two exceptions; the first is peatbogs and peat, and the second is nurseries. They are treated as cultivable land and protected in the same way. In this context one can mention the 1987 Executive Order of the Council of Ministers on the Protection of Earth Surfaces. According to para. 5 of this Order, administrative bodies are obliged to formulate the biological principle for treatment of wasteland which is not assigned to agriculture or forestry. The legal instrument by which these principles becomes binding is the land-use plan.

Thus, it may be said that the protection of wetlands in Poland is strongest under the nature conservation laws and weakest under in the system of laws to protect agricultural land.

Legal Aspects of Mangroves Protection in the Philippines

AMADO S. TOLENTINO, JR

Environmental Law Consultant, National Environmental Protection Council, Quezon City, Philippines

Introduction

In the Philippines, there are many ways in which mangroves are used. Mangroves have intangible benefits for and influences on people and their environment. They are a source of food and of valuable raw materials, which are used in the production of glues, dyes, fabrics, charcoal, livestock, tannins, resins for plywood, medicines, thatching materials, alcohol, vinegar, dissolving pulp, and rayon for textile manufacture. The timber products from mangroves are good materials for shelter, railway ties, submerged foundation piles, bridges, wharves, poles, posts, etc.

From the ecological standpoint, mangroves are of paramount importance in near-shore nutrient enrichment, as breeding, feeding and nursery grounds of ecologically and economically important waterfowl, fish and shellfish species, and in shoreline stabilization and protection. In the Philippines, in particular, the most important uses of mangrove areas from the "direct economic" standpoint include aquaculture (fishponds), gathering of forest products, gathering of fish fry, and reclamation of artificial land.

The mangroves situation in the Philippines

Mangroves are an integral component of the Philippine wetlands system. Statistics show that for the 7,100 islands comprising the Philippines, freshwater lakes cover an approximate area of 114,000 hectares. Swamps and estuaries total about 527,000 hectares. Brackish ponds encompass approximately 176,000 hectares and reservoirs amount to 130,000 hectares.

Be that as it may, the country's mangrove forest reserves are facing depletion, causing extinction or near extinction of indigenous species of animals and plants, due mainly to encroachments by fishponds. The National Mangrove Committee of the Department of Environment and Natural Resources (DENR) noted that fishpond operators have asked for the release of 70,300 hectares when the hectarage available for disposal is only 67,546 hectares. The government has reserved 78,593 hectares as permanent mangrove forests but fishpond operators want to take over these critical areas.

While the depletion of mangrove areas has been attributed mainly to their conversion into fishponds, other reasons cited by the Committee for the diminishing mangrove areas are: heavy cutting of trees for firewood and for decorative purposes, the expansion of urban areas that have required land-filling of mangrove areas, clearing for salt-making, indiscriminate use of pesticides and fertilizers, dumping of mine tailings, junk, garbage, and oil spills.

The situation shows signs of an alarming rate of destruction of the Philippine mangroves. The environmental imbalance is of a disproportionate size which could lead to catastrophe—a debilitating vector to the environment, more so to man.

The legislative response to mangroves protection

There are very few legislative pronouncements and administrative announcements on mangroves. From the 1920s to the 1980s, edicts dealt with forest reservations, and mangroves were treated only as ordinary and minor forest products. Seldom do we see the enactment of policies dealing with mangroves utilization and management. On the other hand, Philippine Supreme Court decisions offered no explanations for the effective and better utilization and management of mangrove resources, for they only settled disputes and ironed out conflicting issues and controversies that arose from forest laws, rules and regulations.

By 1975, general laws, government policies and regulations on the subject of natural resources were presented. Mangroves henceforth received a measure of importance and some consideration for conservation purposes.

In 1976, an administrative regulation was enacted for the creation of a committee to study the mangroves and to prepare a national mangrove programme (Special Order No. 309). It was organized so as to develop schemes for the protection, conservation, development and utilization of the mangrove areas on all the islands of the Philippine archipelago.

During the last few years, several policies on mangrove conservation, embodied in Presidental Decrees (PD), Letters of Instruction (LOI) and Bureau of Forestry Development (BFD) Administrative Orders have been formulated to ensure a rational and environmentally-oriented development of mangrove areas.

PD 705, otherwise known as the Forestry Reform Code of the Philippines, contains specific provisions on the conservation of mangroves. It stipulates that "in brackish water fishpond development, there should be a buffer strip of at least 40 metres wide along the river banks, lakes and other bodies of water and at least 100 metres on mangrove areas facing bays on the sea to protect the shoreline from the destructive forces of the sea, wind and typhoon". In addition, PD 950 requires every leaseholder of mangrove areas to plant trees extending at least 20 metres from the edges of river banks and creeks, and any person who cuts, destroys or injures naturally growing or planted trees of any kind in these areas without authority from the government agency concerned is liable to a fine and/or imprisonment. BFD Administrative Order 74, series of 1974, on the other hand, requires that "20 or more seed trees per hectare with a diameter of 20 centimetres or larger, should be left undamaged on strategic places after cutting", to ensure successful regeneration after logging.

In order to determine which of the remaining mangrove areas of the country are needed for forestry, fishery, and other purposes, a DENR Composite Land Classification (LC) Team is zoning the mangrove areas. Based on suitability, areas are classified into permanent forest or timberland or agricultural land areas appropriate for fishpond development. Several socio-economic and ecological criteria are being considerd by the LC Team in its mangrove zoning work.

Likewise, in recognition of the important role played by forest resources in maintaining the water supply and a balanced ecosystem, preventing excessive soil erosion and runoff, and also in promoting national welfare and security, LOI 917, series of 1979, was issued. The LOI states that "mangrove forests essentially needed in foreshore marine life, including special forests which are exclusive habitats of rare and endangered Philippine flora and fauna, are declared wilderness areas". Wilderness areas or greenbelts are closed to any form of forest resource exploitation. It can be gleaned that a salient feature of LOI 917 is the consideration that mangrove forests are needed in foreshore protection and the maintenance of estuarine and marine life.

On 3 June 1980, Special Order (SO) 178 was issued creating the National Mangrove Committee and in furtherance of various pieces of legislation; Proclamations Nos. 2151 and 2152 were also issed in 1981. Proclamation No. 2151 declared certain islands and/or parts of the country as wilderness areas and "withdraws from entry, sale, settlement and exploitation of whatever nature or form of disposition wilderness areas located in the provinces of Quezon, Camarines Sur, Masbate, Cebu, Bohol, Surigao del Norte and Davao del Sur". Proclamation No. 2152, on the other hand, declared the entire province of Palawan and certain parcels of the public domain and/or parts of the country as mangrove swamp forest reserves. Other areas included in this Proclamation are Quezon, Camarines Norte, Camarines Sur, Albay, Sorsogon, Marinduque, Leyte, Cebu, Bohol, Lanao del Norte and Misamis Occidental as mangroves swamp forest reserves. These areas were withdrawn from entry, sale, settlement and/or other forms of disposition. Based on the Natural Resources Management Center aerial survey, LANDSAT data analysis and the guidelines set up for the selection of mangrove areas to be preserved, 78,593 hectares of mangrove areas are to be conserved. The term "preserved" means that no exploitation in any form except gathering of fish fry and other species to supply the needs of aquaculture is allowed, while the term "conserved" means wise utilization of the mangrove swamps and forest resources in accordance with existing forest laws and regulations.

Of great relevance to mangroves protection is PD 1586 requiring environmental impact assessment (EIA) of environmentally critical projects (like extraction of mangrove products and fishpond development projects) and projects located in environmentally critical areas (Proclamation 2146). The latter includes mangrove areas characterized by one or any combination of the following conditions: (a) with primary pristine and dense young growth; (b) adjoining the mouth of major river systems; (c) near or adjacent to traditional productive fry or fishing grounds;

(d) which act as natural buffers against shore erosion, strong winds and storm floods; and (e) on which people are dependent for their livelihood.

Other significant pieces of legislation germane to mangroves are the Fisheries Decree of 1975 (PD 704), the Marine Pollution Decree of 1976 (PD 979), the Philippine Environment Policy Decree (PD 1151) and the Philippine Environment Code (PD 1152).

Problems, issues and prospects

Recent practices reveal that the emphasis for mangrove forests has been on development, in particular, conversion of these areas into fishponds. Through the years, the mangrove issue has evolved into a question of sustainability and environmental balance. Take out one element of the ecosystem and one will have an unquantifiable and serious dilemma. Add to these the policy decisions made by the government which take into consideration only the economic and productive values of mangroves.

There is a fragmented approach to wetland research which results in too much concentration on studies of only small segments and particular habitat types. There is also a vacuum on legislation on wetlands, and this results in a piecemeal approach to wetland management.

Specific problems of the conservation and protection of mangroves call to mind the following areas of concern:

● Resource Inventory and Assessment—the understanding and knowledge of mangrove swamp distribution and the inventory of flora and fauna in mangrove forest;

● Reforestation—the development of silvicultural practices that will lead to rehabilitation of mangrove swamps;

● Pest and Disease Control—activities leading to control of pests and diseases which are affecting our mangrove forests;

● Timber Production and Utilization—activities on the proper utilization of mangrove resources, and maintenance of the timber stand;

● Species Education—activities leading to the understanding of why major mangrove species are being lost;

● Pollution—the activities leading to the development of agricultural methods that will not affect mangrove areas, at the same time increasing fishery harvests from mangrove swamps;

● Aquaculture—activities leading to the development of aquaculture methods that will not affect mangrove areas, at the same time increasing fishery harvests from mangrove swamps;

- Sedimentation—activities leading to the understanding of factors causing sedimentation on mangrove swamps and development of proper methods for sedimentation control;

- Wildlife Conservation—activities leading to inventory and preservation of the endemic flora and fauna of mangrove swamps;

- Habitat Management—activities that will effectively maintain the balance of nature within the development of a management scheme;

- Desalination—studies of the effective means of lowering the effect of salt water on mangrove lands and water which can be tapped as potential source for agricultural lands and irrigation water;

- Soil Erosion—activities that will identify causes of erosion within mangrove swamps and identify possible solutions to this phenomonon;

- Socio-Economic Impact—studies of the social and economic implications of the various activities conducted within mangrove swamps and whether or not the maintenance of virgin mangrove areas would be socially acceptable;

- Marine Productivity and Fisheries—studies regarding the productivity of mangrove swamps with respect to fisheries resources, and determining the effect of mangrove deterioration on fisheries production;

- Shoreline Protection—activities leading to an understanding of the phenomena affecting the coastline and how many destructive phenomena can be prevented;

- Species Improvement—activities which will deal with methods of developing new mangrove species which are resistant to diseases or to drastic changes of the environment;

- Non-timber Production and Utilization—activities on the proper utilization of non-timber products of mangrove swamps;

- Non-Conventional Energy Production—the utilization of mangrove forest resources for energy production and the determination of whether such activities will not destroy the mangrove ecosystem;

- Recreation—activities which will study the effect of converting portions of the mangrove swamp into recreational areas.

Particular legislation should address not only specific or partial components of wetland management but must be encompassing and comprehensive.

Sectorally, there are certain ways to minimize the rapidly growing problems which face mangrove management. The protection of the ecosystems, polders, embankments and similar structures should not be carried out indiscriminately in such areas. An unique defensive tool could be the agricultural product rice. Rice could be an ideal crop in degraded or denuded mangrove wetlands, considering the salt-tolerant rice varieties, innovative plant breeding techniques, and improved soil and water conservation techniques.

Cost benefit assessment must be emphasized in the reclamation of mangrove areas for paddy cultivation or other uses. This includes not only the socio-economic impact of the project but also, most importantly, the probable adverse effect of the conversion on the ecology of the swampland, which must be given ample thought in the assessment. Again, the principle of short- and long-term benefits and costs should be taken into consideration.

In addition, there should be a critical analysis of mangrove, or in general, wetland management. Concepts regarding wetlands should be changed to emphasize other functional values of the resources. In the proposed shift to other functional areas, a careful study or updating should be uniformly conducted so that monitoring of baseline surveys could lend some credibility to statistical configurations. In relation to the points presented, research undertakings should not be too limited to certain types of wetlands, for there is a vast array of other scientific studies which could shed some light in terms of the conservation and protection of wetlands in general.

As far as what the national government could do to minimize such degradation, a national policy should be enacted on wetland management; a national policy which has enough political will to succeed; a national policy which must answer the question: what happens in and after implementation?—for political history tends to show lack of insights in policy formulation by the bureaucratic machinery.

Lastly, what possible legal strategies may the government follow on the management of the mangrove resources of the Philippines? In this regard, two alternatives are presented. As a first alternative, the government may opt to suspend or declare a total ban on large-scale clear cutting of mangrove forest for fishponds and regulate the dumping of industrial waste in areas occupied by mangrove forest. The salient features of the strategy are: (a) the suspension should be implemented immediately; (b) the suspension should be applied to all forested areas; and (c) the suspension should continue in effect until such time as the necessary research has been evaluated and an allocation plan has been set up—a process that is estimated to last from five to seven years.

An alternative to the above five-to-seven-year suspension strategy is one that involves the proclamation of mangrove forest areas for conservation, preservation or declaration as national forest reserves. As previously mentioned, two such proclamations have been made in 1981. The two proclamations involve a combined total of 78,593 hectares (4,326 + 74,267). This area, which represents about 53% of the existing 146,139 hectares of mangrove forest, can be devoted to scientific research and educational endeavours to satisfy the ecology sector, while the remainder—67,546 hectares or 47%—can be released for fish production by fishpond development to qualified citizens to satisfy the industrial sector.

Conclusion

The foregoing is a brief sketch of the legal protection accorded mangroves in the Philippines. The subject merits special attention like research and study, as a necessary part of environment and development management in the Philippines.

The usefulness of the legal protection of mangroves will depend on its not being considered an isolated sector, but as part of the mainstream of overall national environmental management.

In the face of the problems, issues and concerns brought out above, the suggested alternatives, which are loaded with legal implications, should be seriously considered. They are meant to promote a mutually productive and long-term co-existence of artificial fisheries (aquaculture) and natural fisheries (sustenance fisheries, commercial fisheries, also fry-gathering which is still the principal source of seed fish for stocking fishponds), as well as to minimize environmental degradation of the mangrove or wetland ecosystems in general.

The conservation and preservation of mangroves in the Philippines is said to have been taken for granted in the past. The attention presently focused on wetlands is the result of increasing concern that the destructive processes underway may be irreversible and may be so fundamental as to endanger human existence. As a famous environmentalist said, when a species is wiped out or threatened, it is dangerous to human beings—because if the wildlife cannot survive it means we are creating conditions which are not conducive to life. Indeed, we are beginning to realize that man's activities against the environment are beginning to endanger the whole world.

References

An Overview/Analysis of the Present Program, Policy and Innovation Undertaken by the Government Relative to Utilization and Management of the Mangrove Resources of the Philippines, National Mangrove Committee of the Natural Resources Management Center, December 1986.

Biña, R.T., Jara, R.S., Lorenzo, E.N. and de Jesus, B.R 1979, Mangrove inventory of the Philippines using multi-sectoral data and the Image 100 System, *NRMC Resources Monogram* 2, 1–8.

F M declare Wilderness Areas, Mangroves Swamp Forest Reserves, *Bakawan Newsletter*, Vol. 1, No. 4, November 1981.

Mangroves sustain off-shore fisheries, *Bakawan Newsletter*, Vol. 1, No. 3, August 1981.

Mangroves forests: problems and management strategies, *Likas Yaman, Journal of the Natural Resources Management Forum*, Vol. 1, No. 3.

Philippine Environmental Law, Vols. I, II and III, National Environmental Protection Council, 1985.

Proceedings of the National Symposium—Workshop on Mangrove Research and Development, Parañaque, Rizal, 1977.

Proceedings of the International Workshop on Mangrove and Estuarine Area Development for the Indo-Pacific Region, Manila, 1977.

Santos, V. 1980, *Wetlands: Resources for Regional Development Planning*, Manila.

Serrano, R.C. 1978, Preserving the Philippine mangrove swamps, *Canopy* (7): 6, 7.

Umali, R.M. 1977, Present status in distribution of mangrove areas in the Philippines, *Proceedings of the National Symposium—Workshop on Mangrove Resource Development*, Parañque, Rizal.

Zamora, P.M. 1985, Conservation strategies for Philippine mangroves, *Enviroscope*, Vol. 2, No. 2.

United States: Further Remarks and Case Studies

DONALD W. STEVER

Sidley and Austin, New York, U.S.A.

Introduction

Before discussing several illustrative case studies that demonstrate the workings of the U.S. wetland protection regime, I have a few general remarks about the practical realities of wetland protection in the U.S. These observations are intended to provide the Conference with insight into the practical funtioning of the regime, whose legal and theoretical underpinnings I set forth in my other paper to this Conference (pp. 87-98).

The first thing that I want to underscore is that we have, in many states in the U.S., what is really a three-tiered regulatory system for wetlands. There may exist at the same time federal, state and local wetland regulatory programmes, each one quite different from the other. What is common to all of them, however, is the fact that their effectiveness is dependent in large measure on (a) the attitude of the agency administering the programme (i.e. is it committed to the goals of wetland protection), and (b) the number and the degree of competence of the biologists, field enforcement personnel, and ecologists employed by the agency. On the first issue, the federal programme has been handicapped for years because the administering agency, the Army Corps of Engineers (a branch of the Department of Defense) has never been comfortable with the role of regulator. The Corps, whose principal non-military function has been the building of dams east of the 100th meridian, would have preferred to have remained in its narrow niche, and as a result delayed implementation of the Section 404 programme for many years, and continues to be lax in enforcement matters.

Because field judgement calls are so significant to jurisdictional determination under the U.S. regime, the system requires a large number of skilled professionals within the wetland regulatory agencies in order for it to function well. Unfortunately, government salaries for such professionals are largely not competitive with the private sector, and thus the agencies have a difficult time attracting and retaining highly skilled professionals.

My second general observation deals with threats to wetlands that are not within the regulatory system at present, or at least are not sufficiently subject to regulatory detection and control that they are being managed effectively. The first of these, and arguably the most insidious, is the threat to wetlands posed by upstream or local non-point source pollution.

Consider the following scenario: in California there is a government-owned wetland of 10,000 acres, managed as a waterfowl preserve under the control of the U.S. Fish and Wildlife Service. The predominant upstream use of the source of water for this wetland is agricultural irrigation. Selenium salts and mercury from the agricultural return flows are causing significant bird mortality, morbidity and reproductive failure, to the point that the entire preserve is biologically stressed nearly to the point of total habitat loss. How can this happen?

The answer lies in part in the fragmentation of regulatory responsibility over wetland protection and water pollution control, and in part in the politics of American agriculture. The agency having jurisdiction over the preserve has no control over off-preserve private conduct. The wetland protection laws, moreover, address only direct activities, such as filling or draining the wetlands *per se*. Control of water pollution lies with the U.S. Environmental Protection Agency and a state environmental agency, which have regulatory jurisdiction only over point sources (i.e. pipes, etc.) discharging pollutants. Pesticide and fertilizer run-off are not currently subject to government regulation. But, one might ask, is not an irrigation return ditch a "point source"? The answer is that it is, but the political might of the agriculture lobby managed to secure an exemption from federal regulation of irrigation return discharges in the Clean Water Act. The illustration I have just given is not fictitious. It describes the fate of the Kesterson Wildlife Refuge in California.

Another source of risk is "normal" agricultural and silvicultural activity, which is exempt from regulation, at least under the federal wetland laws. Substantial acreage of wetlands are lost annually to plowing and erosion from farming and logging activities. A recent positive development on this point was the enactment of the so-called "swampbuster" provisions of the Agriculture and Soil Conservation Authorization Act of 1985. These provisions provide economic incentives to farmers to leave wetland areas intact. Nevertheless, substantial acreage of wetland are lost each year to draining for agricultural purposes, particularly in the south. Some types of activities that can result in drying of wetlands are not clearly within the regulatory system.

Case studies

Case 1

Case 1 involves a residential real estate developer in the State of New York who constructed a roadway to serve an area of a 250 acre development, and in so doing placed earth fill in about three acres of a high value (in the New York classification scheme, a "class 1 wetland") freshwater marsh without any governmental authorization. The developer's plans also proposed a development of 200 industrial lots, 30 of which would be placed on fill material wholly or partially on wetlands.

Since the wetland involved was large (more than 12 contiguous acres in size), both state and federal wetland protection agencies became involved. The state, which acted first, took enforcement action against the unlawful road fill. The

Government control of wetland-impacting activities in New York

Case 1: A. Significant alteration of a 12-acre freshwater wetland involving fill

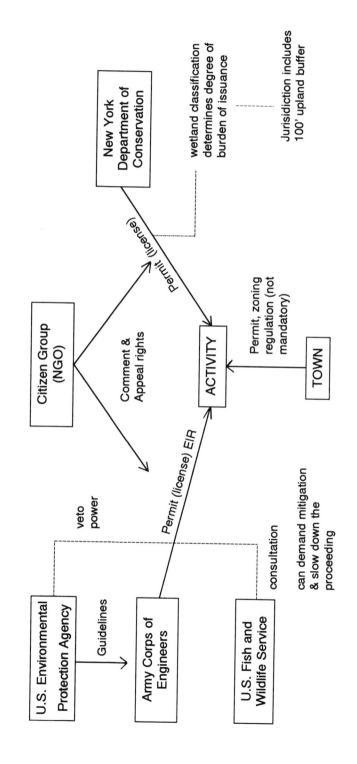

developer ultimately agreed (a) to pay a $10,000 civil penalty to the state, (b) to remove the fill, and (c) to revegetate the area of impact with indigenous wetland species of plants.

The scope of the development was, in addition, significantly reduced in size as a result of the state and federal permit proceedings. The developer agreed, in order to avoid lengthy administrative proceedings, to eliminate 25 of the 30 wetland-impacting lots. The administrative process the developer avoided by scaling down the project is illustrated in the schematic chart on the previous page.

The developer is required, for a major project involving a large wetland (in New York), to secure a permit from the U.S. Army Corps of Engineers (COE) and from the New York Department of Environmental Conservation (DEC).

Under Section 404 of the Clean Water Act, the process involves:

1. An Environmental Impact Review under the National Environmental Policy Act—a decision must be made by the COE whether to write an Environmental Impact Statement or make a formal determination (called a Finding of No Significant Impact) that none is required;

2. Public Notice;

3. A Public Interest Review and review under the stringent 404(b)(1) guidelines of the Environmental Protection Agency. There is also potential for delay imposed by the U.S. Fish and Wildlife Service;

4. Written Decision;

5. Potential veto by EPA, or lawsuit in federal court by opposing citizen groups, which could result in reversal of COE permit decision.

The state procedures are no less onerous, involving:

1. An Environmental Impact Review under the State Environmental Quality Review Act ("SEQRA"). Similar statutes exist in California and in a few other states;

2. Public Notice;

3. Public Hearing;

4. Decision based on factors contained in the state statute and DEC regulations;

5. Possible appeal by opponents in state court.

Had the wetland at issue been 12 acres in size and the area proposed to be filled less than 10 acres, in New York the regulatory situation would have been significantly different. As shown in the diagram opposite, because of jurisdictional limits imposed either by statute or agency regulation, alteration of a small wetland, even if it is a high quality wetland, is only marginally subject to government regulation, in New York essentially only at the local government level, if at all. There is often no local regulation specifically addressing wetlands. Local planning boards administer subdivision regulatory laws and assure consistency with local "zoning" and other land-use requirements.

Government control of wetland-impacting activities in New York

Case 1: B. Significant alteration of a 9-acre freshwater wetland involving fill

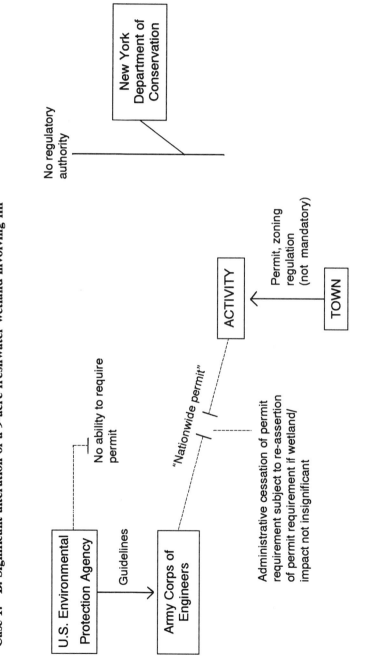

Case 2

Biddeford Pool, Maine is a small coastal community that is part of the larger City of Biddeford. It contains a large, productive salt marsh (primarily *Spartina alterniflora* and *S. patens*) that attracts large numbers of shore and sea birds, and a barrier beach and dune complex. The fringes of the salt marsh have been subject to increasing development pressure from small construction projects, each one too small to trigger mandatory federal permits, and since the COE has only two inspectors in the entire State of Maine, there is little chance of federal involvement. The state has an inactive, poorly funded wetland programme, and the local government encourages development. Local citizen groups have been unable to slow fringe development, and over 10 acres have been destroyed within the past two years.

One major problem is that there is not a unified regulatory overview of the coastal ecosystem. Dune and beaches are not regarded as wetlands. The State of Maine, moreover, takes a very narrow view of the upland extent of tidal wetlands, basically treating "high marsh" areas as though they were upland.

Case 3

Case 3 involves a massive Government-sponsored project in a tidal estuary that happens to include New York City, with the lower Hudson River. The State of New York, in partnership with the United States Department of Transportation and the City, proposed to construct a new eight-lane freeway (called "Westway") along the west side of New York City. The new road was to be built largely on earth fill placed in the river adjacent to the existing bank (which is mostly created of filled land dating from about 1880). A portion of the fill was to be placed in an area of old, now unused, shipping piers, called the "interpier area".

Because the project required the placement of fill in a "water of the United States", a 404 permit was required. Since this particular water body is also navigable, authorization under §10 of the Rivers and Harbors Act of 1899 was also required, though the procedures for decision-making are similar.

This case is an example of a situation in which one part of the Government is required to exercise regulatory authority over another part of the Government. Initially, the Army Corps of Engineers decided to grant the required permits, though another federal agency, the U.S. Fish and Wildlife Service, had objected, primarily because of evidence that the area proposed for filling appeared to be an important winter habitat for juvenile striped bass. This fish is an important sporting fish in the northeastern United States, and the Hudson River is one of its two major spawning and nursery habitats.

Although the permit was issued, the action was challenged by a collection of citizens groups, which argued that the Corps of Engineers had not adequately considered the striped bass issue in its Environmental Impact Assessment, or in its permit decision. The decision was overturned by a trial judge, and the Corps issued a second permit, which was again challenged and overturned. The trial court's decision was subsequently upheld by the United States Court of Appeals. Consequently, the project was effectively cancelled.

Proponents of the highway have complained that the concerns that stopped it are not significant, and complain about the negative economic impacts of the court decisions. Opponents have hailed the Westway decisions as an example of how citizens' participation can force environmentally responsible action in the face of unwillingness on the part of government regulatory personnel.

Problem areas

The three case studies have illustrated some of the problems that plague wetland protective regulation in the United States. There are others. In some states, few permits are ever denied, in part due to uncertainties about legal defensibility of outright permit denials under state law. There are inadequate field enforcement resources in either the federal or state programmes to provide sufficient regulatory oversight of private activities.

The federal wetland programme also suffers from a number of problems peculiar to it. There has been a lack of enthusiasm for administering 404 on the part of the Corps of Engineers supervisory personnel. This fact has created problems both from the standpoint of efficient administration of the programme and the regulated community. A related, and complex, issue is the uneasy interface between the Corps of Engineers' "public interest review" procedures and the 404(b)(1) guidelines, which are supposed to be controlling in 404 decision-making. There has been tension between the Corps and EPA over this issue and the degree to which permit applicants must demonstrate the absence of upland alternatives to the activity for which they are seeking a permit.

Enforcement of the 404 programme may be impeded by the Supreme Court's recent decision in United States v. Tull, in which the Court ruled that defendants in 404 enforcement actions are entitled to a jury trial. This limitation, which makes civil enforcement more expensive for the government, may be mitigated somewhat by a 1987 amendment to the Clean Water Act that confers administrative penalty-levying authority on the Corps. Another problem area is jurisdictional determinations. The Corps has never sufficiently formalized the process by which it makes jurisdictional determinations to avoid the potential for judicial review of its jurisdictional determinations. The end result may be a hodge-podge of different lower federal court opinions on the application of 404 to essentially identical biological systems.

Finally, the Corps' "mitigation" policy has driven permit applicants to distraction, and has also been criticized by environmental organizations. The acceptability of enhancement of a marginal wetland area to mitigate for loss of an area of better productivity, or creation of an artificial wetland to compensate for loss of a natural system, has long been controversial. The Corps' mitigation policy has sometimes been responsible for significant uncompensated losses of high quality wetland, and has also occasionally produced excellent trade-offs. It has also sometimes produced absurd results. In one recent case, for example, a developer in Connecticut whose contractor had placed rocks in a biologically unproductive area (which has been used for industrial purposes for many years) was required to build a *Spartina alterniflora* marsh immediately against a Corps of Engineers-owned hurricane barrier which was itself a massive mound of earth fill, and which will block much sunlight from reaching the new marsh.

Nevertheless, it must be said of the overall effort in the United States that it has slowed the destruction of wetlands, and has certainly created a heightened sense of wetland values. It has also created an industry, the wetlands consulting industry, which employs biologists and engineers in great numbers.

La loi égyptienne relative aux aires naturelles protégées

ABDEL AZIZ ABDEL HADY

Professeur à la Faculté de Droit, Université de Mansourah, Le Caire, Egypte

Introduction

La plupart des états du monde se sont intéressés—notamment au cours de la seconde partie de ce siècle—à la protection de l'environnement et à la conservation des ressources renouvelables et non renouvelable, dans l'intérêt des générations présentes et à venir.

C'est pourquoi un grand nombre de ces états ont promulgué des législations adéquates pour préserver les composantes naturelles de l'environnement: eau, air, sol, et les espèces végétales et animales.

Au niveau mondial, les états et les organisations internationales se sont aussi intéréssés à conclure des accords ou des traités et à adopter des résolutions pour promouvoir la coopération dans ce domaine.

Bien que l'étendue de la protection de l'environnement doit englober tous les éléments naturels de l'environnement en tant qu'ils constituent une unité écologique, il n'en reste pas moins qu'il existe certaines zones de cet environnnement qui nécessitent une protection spéciale en raison de leurs caractéristiques naturelles, géologiques ou géographiques, ou encore en tant qu'habitat ou lieux de migration[1] d'animaux marins ou terrestres, ou bien encore en raison de leur richesse en espèces menacées par les activités de l'homme, tels la pêche, la chasse, les opérations d'exploration ou d'exploitation de minerais et de pétrole, le développement économique et les progrès de la science et de la technique.

Le principe fondamental en la matière a été ainsi défini par la Déclaration de Stockholm de 1972: "L'homme a une responsabilité particulière dans la sauvegarde et la sage gestion du patrimoine constitué par la flore et la faune sauvages et leur habitat, qui sont aujourd'hui gravement menacés par un concours de facteurs défavorables. La conservation de la nature, et notamment de la flore et de la faune sauvages, doit donc tenir une place importante dans la planification pour le développement économique".

Pour toutes ces raisons, un nombre croissant d'états ont cherché à assurer une protection spéciale à ces zones d'intérêt écologique, par la désignation de superficies déterminées de terres, d'eaux intérieures ou littorales en tant qu'aires naturelles protégées destinées à préserver leurs éléments naturels contre la destruction et, partant, de conserver leur faune et leur flore[2].

En Egypte, les études menées dans ce domaine font apparaître qu'un nombre croissant d'espèces animales et végétales ont été exterminées ou ont disparu de son territoire, et que d'autres sont susceptibles de l'être. C'est la raison pour laquelle l'Organisme[3] des affaires de l'environnement, au sein du Conseil des Ministres, a préparé un projet de loi relatif à la protection des zones d'intérêt écologique; ce projet a été finalement adopté par l'Assemblée du peuple (le Parlement) en 1983.

Nous allons traiter des éléments principaux de cette loi (loi Nr. 102 de 1983 relative aux aires naturelles protégées).

La loi relative aux aires naturelles protégées est l'une des lois qui ont été adoptées en Egypte afin de protéger les milieux naturels et les espèces végétales et animales qui les composent. Cette loi vise de manière générale à conserver l'environnement dans certaines zones déterminées sur le territoire égytien.

Notre examen de cette loi sera concentré sur les points suivants: la définition de l'expression "aire protégée", les actions interdites dans ces zones, l'autorité compétente, le rôle des associations de l'environnement, le fonds des aires protégées et enfin les pénalités.

Définition de l'expression "aire protégée"[4]

Aux termes de l'article 1 de la loi mentionnée, on entend par l'expression "aire protégée" toute surface de terre, d'eau littorale ou intérieure, qui se caractérise par ce qu'elle contient en tant qu'êtres vivants (plantes, animaux ou poissons) ou en tant que phénomènes naturels d'une valeur culturelle, scientifique, touristique ou esthétique, bénéficiant d'un certain régime juridique de protection déterminé par décret du premier ministre, sur proposition de l'Organisme des affaires de l'environnement.

Depuis la promulgation de cette loi en 1983, quatre zones ont été désignées comme aires protégées: la région du Ras Mohamed et des deux îles de Tirane et de Sanafir dans le gouvernorat du Sinai Sud[5], la région du Nord d'El Arish et du Lac Bardawil dans le gouvernorat du Sinai Nord[6], la région d'El Umayed dans le gouvernorat de Marsa Matrouh, et la région de Gabal Elba dans le gouvernorat de la mer Rouge.

Il faut rappeler que l'exposé des motifs de la loi prévoit la création ultérieure d'autres aires protégées. On peut citer parmi celles-ci la région du Mont Sainte Catherine, dans le presqu'île du Sinai, la Région de Ras El Hekma dans la région du littoral Nord, etc.

Les actions interdites dans les aires protégées

Comme on l'a déjà mentionné, l'expression "aire protégée" s'applique à toute région bénéficiant d'un certain régime juridique de protection et relevant, pour la mise en oeuvre de ce régime, d'une autorité responsable désignée par la législation. Cette expression peut donc couvrir des institutions très différentes selon les pays[7].

En vertu de la loi égyptienne, il nous semble que l'expression d'aire protégée signifie l'aire où toute activité humaine doit être interdite afin de permettre le libre jeu des phénomènes naturels. Il s'agit d'un système fondé sur une série d'interdictions fixées par le législateur et applicables à toutes les aires protégées. Cependant, ces aires sont ouvertes au public.

L'article 2 de loi définit les actions et les travaux interdits dans les aires concernées. Il est notamment interdit:

- de chasser, de transférer, de tuer ou de déranger les êtres vivants terrestres ou marins, ou de procéder à des travaux susceptibles de les détruire;

- d'endommager ou de transporter des plantes sises dans l'aire protégée;

- de détruire des formations géologiques ou géographiques ou des zones considérées comme l'habitat d'espèces, ou lieu de leur reproduction;

- d'introduire des espèces exotiques, dans celle-ci;

- de polluer le sol, les eaux et l'atmosphère de l'aire protégée, sous n'importe quelle forme.

Il est aussi interdit d'élever des constructions, d'établir des entreprises, ou de tracer des routes, de faire circuler des voitures, ou de procéder à n'importe quelle activité agricole, industrielle ou commerciale dans l'aire protégée, sauf autorisation de l'autorité compétente.

On doit signaler que la protection imposée par la loi ne se limite pas à l'aire protégée mais qu'elle s'étend, conformément à l'article 3 de la loi, aux activités qui s'exercent dans les zones qui l'entourent[8], si ces activités sont susceptibles d'avoir des effets sur l'environnement de celle-ci. Parmi ces activités, nous citerons l'installation d'entreprises susceptibles de polluer ou de d'affecter les organismes vivants qui s'y trouvent.

L'autorité compétente

Conformément à l'article 4 de cette loi, le Premier ministre déterminera la ou les autorités administratives qui seront chargées de mettre en oeuvre ses dispositions[9].

C'est ainsi que le Premier ministre a désigné par le décret n. 1067 de 1983 l'Organisme des affaires de l'environnement près le Conseil des ministres comme l'autorité dont relèvent les aires protégées.

Dans chaque gouvernorat où la création d'une aire protégée est décidée, le décret ministériel effectuant la création de celle-ci établit un conseil d'administration, sous la présidence du gouverneur, composé des représentants des ministères concernés.

Ce conseil est investi des attributions prévues par la loi ainsi que par les décrets ministériels, toujours sous la direction générale de l'Organisme des affaires de l'environnement.

En effet, le travail de ce conseil ne se limite pas à faire respecter les interdictions mentionnées dans l'article 2 de la loi, mais s'étend à certaines autres fonctions. Il s'agit surtout d'établir les programmes et de faire les études nécessaires pour la gestion de ces aires, d'y faire des inventaires, d'administrer et coordonner les activités relatives à celles-ci, d'informer et de sensibliser le public sur les buts et objectifs de la création de ces aires, et d'échanger informations et expertise avec les autres états et les organisations internationales dans ce domaine.

Le rôle des associations de l'environnement

D'après le Professeur Despax[10], les droits liés à la protection de l'environnement sont diffus, c'est-à-dire qu'ils appartiennent en même temps à la collectivité et à chacun des membres qui la composent. C'est pour cette raison qu'il est nécessaire de concevoir des modalités nouvelles de protection de l'environnement. Dans cette perspective, il apparaît indispensable de mettre l'accent sur le droit d'intervention devant les instances administratives et juridictionnelles des groupements et associations s'étant assignées comme objectif la protection de la nature et la défense de l'environnement.

Pour encourager les associations égyptiennes de protection de l'environnement à assumer un rôle effectif dans le domaine de la protection de la nature et des ressources naturelles, l'article 5 de la loi a permis aux associations régulièrement constituées de se référer aux instances administratives et judiciaires dans le but de faire exécuter les dispositions de la loi et des décrets relatifs aux aires protégées.

Il y a lieu de noter qu'un grand nombre de législations étrangères concernant la protection de l'environnement prévoient le droit des associations pour la protection de l'environnement à exercer certaines attributions dans le but de protéger l'environnement naturel. Parmi ces législations, signalons celles de la France et des Pays-Bas.

Fonds des aires protégées

L'article 6 de la loi précitée prévoit la création d'un fonds spécial destiné à fournir les fonds nécessaires aux autorités qui s'occupent de l'exécution des dispositions de cette loi. Ce fonds sera alimenté par des fonds publics destinés à cet effet, ainsi que par des donations et autres subsides, et par les recettes produites par l'application des dispositions de cette loi.

Ces fonds seront utilisés dans les objectifs suivants: consolider le budget des autorités qui s'occupent de l'exécution de la présente loi, améliorer l'environnement des aires protégées, effectuer les études et recherches nécessaires dans ce domaine, verser des gratifications aux informateurs et aux agents qui décèlent les infractions tombant sous le coup de la loi.

Les pénalités

L'article 7 de la loi fixe les sanctions à infliger pour les infractions commises contre les dispositions de celle-ci.

En effet, le non respect de la loi ou des réglementations basées sur celle-ci peut entraîner une peine d'emprisonnement pour une période ne dépassant pas une année et/ou la condamnation à une amende de 500 à 5,000 livres égyptiennes. Dans certains cas, la condamnation peut être assortie d'une obligation pour le contrevenant de remettre en état les sites endommagés et la confiscation des machines, outils ou appareils utilisés lors de l'infraction.

De cette analyse, on peut dire que la loi égyptienne no. 102 de 1983 concernant les aires naturelles protégées constitue un pas important sur la voie de la protection de la faune et de la flore sauvages et de leurs habitats ainsi que des zones considérées comme des zones humides.

Notes

1. Cf. de Klemm, Cyrille 1980, La protection des zones d'intérêt écologique, In *Trends in Environmental Policy and Law*, IUCN Environmental Policy and Law Paper, No. 15, pp. 169-197; Lausche, Barbara J. 1980, *Guidelines for Protected Areas Legislation*, IUCN Environmental Policy and Law Paper No. 16; Lyster, Simon 1985, *International Wildlife Law*, IUCN Environmental Policy and Law Paper No. 22; Koester, Veit 1980, *Nordic countries: Legislation on the Environment with Special Emphasis on Conservation, a Survey*, IUCN Environmental Policy and Law Paper, No. 15; Franson, Robert T., *The Legal Aspects of Ecological Reserve Creation and Management in Canada*, IUCN Environmental Policy and Law Paper, No. 9; Kiss, A. Ch. 1977, Protection internationale de l'environnement, *Notes et études documentaires*, No. 4419-4420, la Documentation française, pp. 38-42.

2. Cf. Kiss, *op. cit.*, p. 41; cf. aussi Lausche, B.J., Justification for protected areas, in Lausche, *op. cit.*, p. 14; de Klemm, Cyrille, La protection des zones d'intérêt écologique, *op. cit.*, 171 *et seq.*

3 Cet organisme a été créé en 1982 par le décret du Président de la République no. 631 de 1982.

4 Sur ce point cf. de Klemm, *op. cit.*, p. 173; Lausche, B.J., Definitions for different kinds of protected areas, in Lausche, *op. cit.*, pp. 25-26.

5. Cf. Décret ministériel no. 1968 de 1983.

6. Décret ministériel no. 1429 de 1986.

7. Cf. Kiss, *op. cit.*, p. 40; Lausche, B.J., Prohibited and regulated activities for protected areas, in Lausche, *op. cit.*, 51 *et seq.*

8. "There is a growing number of examples where entire protected areas or certain zones are being adversely affected or destroyed by activities outside their boundaries ... The user of agricultural and industrial chemicals on adjacent lands may affect the aquatic and other habitat within a protected area ... protected areas near urban centres may be threatened by a variety of external activities" ... (Lausche, *op. cit.*, p. 57).

9. Sur l'établissement de l'autorité compétente chargée de la gestion des aires protégées, cf. de Klemm, *op. cit.*, p. 181.

10. Cf. Despax, M. 1979, Défense collective de l'environnement et recevabilité des actions en matière de pollution transfrontière, In *La protection de l'environnement dans les régions frontières*, OCDE, p. 199 *et seq.*

The Implementation of the Wetlands Convention in the Netherlands

Memorandum from the Minister for Agriculture and Fisheries, Mr G.J.M. Braks (dated 26 September 1985)

Summary

Section 1 of this memorandum on the implementation of the Wetlands Convention defines the concept "wetlands" within the meaning of the Wetlands Convention, and describes both the significance of wetlands with regard to their various functions and the threats to which these areas are exposed. Section 2 analyses the Wetlands Convention, showing that its provisions fall into three categories: those which apply to all wetlands, those governing inclusion in the List of Wetlands of International Importance, and those governing international cooperation.

Sections 3, 4 and 5 set out the relevant policy, referring to the categories of provisions outlined in section 2. Since I attach great importance to the general provisions of the Convention which apply to all wetlands—with particular reference to those concerning "wise use" and the establishment of nature reserves—policy on these subjects is dealt with first (section 3), demonstrating that much has been achieved with regard to both wise use and the establishment of nature reserves in wetlands. The Structure Plan for Nature Conservation and Protection of the Countryside contains various elements which are relevant to wetland policy. Many wetlands have already been allocated purposes and uses within the framework of physical planning which recognize and accord with the ecological significance of such areas. Using the customary consultative procedures I intend to foster this process. I shall also continue to encourage wise use by promoting appropriate acknowledgement of the ecological significance of wetlands in environment and water management policy and in multi-sectoral planning on large areas of open water. I shall carry on with the policy of establishing nature reserves through the use of instruments specifically geared to preservation, such as acquisition and designation under the provisions of the Nature Conservancy Act.

I shall promote appropriate formulation of policy with regard to relevant research. I believe that the provision concerning the increase of waterfowl populations can be realized through adherence to the provisions concerning wise use, the establishment of nature reserves and the conservation of wetlands. As to the training of competent personnel, I feel that the Netherlands is already doing this through the available courses for managers and wardens of public and private nature reserves.

With regard to designation for inclusion in the List of Wetlands of International

Importance (section 4), I feel that this step can only be taken if the conservation of such wetlands is promoted under national law, as provided for in the Wetlands Convention. This means that administrative agreement must be reached beforehand on the maintenance of the ecology of the areas concerned. It is against this background that the Netherlands will continue to designate suitable wetlands for inclusion in the List.

The Research Institute for Nature Management is to draw up a conspectus of areas which fulfil the relevant internationally-agreed criteria, as a scientific background for policy on both the general provisions of the Wetlands Convention and designation for inclusion in the List of Wetlands of International Importance.

Section 5 sets out policy on international cooperation. I feel that the establishment of a permanent secretariat is one of the measures which could be taken to increase the effect of the Wetlands Convention. The Netherlands will also continue to support international organizations involved in the study of wetland ecology and in research into the ecological relations between wetlands in the Netherlands and elsewhere.

I intend to ensure that more information is provided on wetlands when designating particular areas for inclusion in the List. The relevant educational establishments will also be requested to devote attention to wetlands, and where necessary give financial assistance with the production of educational materials (section 6).

1. The significance of wetlands

The collective term "wetlands" covers a wide variety of wet areas of which the ground of the substratum is, periodically at least, saturated with or covered by water. The Convention on Wetlands of International Importance especially as Waterfowl Habitat, hence referred to as the Wetlands Convention, defines wetlands as follows:

> "... areas of marsh, fen, peatland or water, whether natural or artificial, permanent or temporary, with water that is static or flowing, fresh, brackish or salt, including areas of marine water the depth of which at low tide does not exceed six metres."

Wetlands are often very rich ecosystems characterized by high levels of biological production. Good examples of this are artificial lakes, estuaries and deltas. Such production is closely linked to the fact that organic substances carried, for example, by tidal currents and rivers, sink down into shallow water. The resultant concentration of organic matter is broken down in and on the bottom. The productivity of wetlands makes them important to the fishing industry—serving as they do as breeding grounds and nurseries for various types of fish—and to waterfowl, which forage, rest, moult and breed on wetlands, sometimes in very large numbers.

Although the majority of wetlands consist of dynamic and extremely productive systems, some belong to another very valuable category which includes peatbogs and fens—areas low in nutrients. Besides their ecological significance, wetlands of both categories are of great public value from the point of view of water management, recreation and beauty.

Wetlands in one country often have features in common with those in others, thus possessing an international dimension. These common features can roughly be divided into three categories. The first is wetlands of the same type situated in two or more countries, of which the Waddenzee is a good example. Second, are physically-connected wetlands of different types located in two or more countries. These include wetlands situated upstream and others, such as tidal areas, lying downstream on the same river. The effect of pollution or interference with the flow of water is felt throughout the catchment area and the connecting wetlands. Finally there are wetlands which lie along the migration routes of birds. This type of common feature is, geographically speaking, the most wide-ranging. One such route is the Western Palaearctic migration route, which stretches from Greenland and Siberia over the Netherlands to southern Africa. The wetlands along such routes form a chain of stopping places and wintering areas. Each link in the chain is important, and its preservation crucial to the survival of the others.

In global terms wetlands are probably among the most threatened of ecosystems. Their importance is only gradually being realized, and wetlands are still being sacrificed on a large scale to industry, port development, housing construction, agriculture and other activities. Factors which affect the supply of water, such as the construction of dams for hydro-electric power or the canalization of rivers for shipping purposes, can have disastrous effects on the ecological character and thus the significance of wetlands. Effects of an equally serious but less visible nature can result from the accumulation of pollutants such as mercury and PCBs in sedimentation.

Thanks to its development and low-lying situation, the Netherlands boasts a relatively large number of large and small wetlands: estuaries, mud flats, marshes, fens and lakes. These vary both in type and size. Some are of international significance, particularly in connection with their location at the intersection of the migratory routes of waterfowl.

2. Origins and contents of the Wetlands Convention

As stated above, wetlands are extremely important in many respects. In recent decades awareness of their significance has become increasingly widespread and many countries have adopted policies specifically geared to these areas. At the same time it has been realized that international cooperation is crucial to the conservation of important wetlands. This was the reason behind the Wetlands Convention—the Convention on Wetlands of International Importance especially as Waterfowl Habitat, which was drawn up in Ramsar, Iran, in 1971. The Netherlands played an active role in the drafting of the Wetlands Convention, which it ratified in 1980 (Lower House 1976-1977, 14135/R 1946, no. 1-4).

The Parties which initiated the Convention took this step in the conviction that wetlands constitute a natural resource of great economic, cultural, scientific and recreational value, the loss of which would be irreparable. These considerations are linked to the ecological role of wetlands within, *inter alia*, water management as a whole, and as areas with distinctive flora and fauna. Special importance is attached to waterfowl; migrating as they do between their winter and summer habitat, these birds can be considered as part of the international heritage. The Parties wished to call a halt to the progressive encroachment on and loss of wetlands, through the combination of far-sighted national policies with coordinated international action. When the Wetlands Convention was drafted the main stress was—and is—on waterfowl, but provision was made in its application and implementation for emphasis to be placed on other animal and plant species. This has now been expressed in the criteria for the determination of the international importance of wetlands as proposed by the first Conference of the Contracting Parties at Cagliari in 1980.

The Wetlands Convention has such major implications for national policy that its main principles and provisions will be set out below before national policy is discussed. The provisions of the Convention fall into three categories:

I.   General provisions on all wetlands within the territory of a contracting Party (see section 3);

II. Provisions on designation for inclusion in the List of Wetlands of International Importance and provisions concerning all areas designated as such (see section 4);

III. Provisions relating to international cooperation (see section 5).

I.   The most important provision in the first category is that which promotes as far as possible the wise use of all wetlands within a contracting Party's territory (Article 3, paragraph 1). Wise use can be taken to mean taking account of or providing scope for the natural functions of wetlands.

     Among the Convention's other general provisions is that promoting the conservation of wetlands and waterfowl by establishing nature reserves (Article 4, paragraph 1). Other relevant provisions concern the encouragement of research and the exchange of data and publications (Article 4, paragraph 3); the increase of waterfowl populations through management (Article 4, paragraph 4), and the promotion of training of personnel competent in the fields of wetland research, management and wardening (Article 4, paragraph 5).

II. Under the Wetlands Convention, contracting Parties are obliged to designate suitable wetlands for inclusion in a List of Wetlands of International Importance (Article 2). A country must have designated at least one such wetland before it can become Party to the Convention. Criteria defining the term "suitable" were put forward at the Cagliari Conference. Under the Convention, the contracting Parties are obliged to formulate and implement their planning so as to promote the conservation of the wetlands included in the List (Article 3, paragraph 1). They must also inform the Secretariat of the Wetlands Convention at the earliest possible time of actual or potential changes in the ecological character of any wetland. The Convention allows a contracting

Party the right, because of urgent national interests, to delete or restrict the boundaries of wetlands included by it on the List. However, the country should as far as possible compensate for such a loss, and in particular should create additional nature reserves for waterfowl (Article 2, paragraph 5, and Article 4, paragraph 2).

III. The provisions concerning international cooperation are embodied in Articles 5 and 6 of the Wetlands Convention.

These provide, *inter alia*, for cooperation between two or more contracting Parties, within or outside the framework of conferences convened by the Parties on the conservation of wetlands. An example would be cooperation on wetlands extending over the territory of more than one contracting Party along a migratory route. Finally, the conferences convened by Parties can constitute a particularly effective instrument for the promotion of international cooperation and of effective national policy on the part of individual countries. The Wetlands Convention indicates the issues which should be covered by such conferences.

3. The general provisions of the Wetlands Convention

General provisions are the provisions which apply to all areas defined as wetlands. I set great store by these provisions since they are the chief guarantee of the conservation of wetlands. The following sections describe the extent to which the objectives of these provisions have been embodied in policy to date and the nature of my future policy in this field. Since I believe the wise use of wetlands and the establishment of nature reserves to be of particular importance, policy on these subjects will be dealt with first.

3.1 Wise use (Article 3, paragraph 1)

The importance of wetlands for many fields, for example for water management, has long been recognized in the Netherlands. In recent decades their ecological significance and their importance for research has also increasingly found expression in policy. There has moreover been a growing awareness that wetlands lining the migration routes of large numbers of birds (for example along the Western Palaearctic route) are of particular international importance. These considerations have been reflected in a trend in policy which is increasingly geared to the wise use of wetlands in the Netherlands.

The Structure Plan for Nature Conservation and Protection of the Countryside contains various elements which are relevant to policy on wetlands. Many wetlands fall into the category defined in the Structure Plan as "natural areas" and some into the category "major areas of outstanding natural interest". Government policy on these areas, as is apparent from the relevant government decision, is geared to providing them with adequate protection, which means that they cannot be encroached upon or used in such a way that their functions or values are impinged upon or lost, unless urgent public interests dictate otherwise. The Structure Plan also contains policy specifically directed towards large areas of open water. This will be discussed in more detail below.

Wise use may also entail active monitoring of ecological changes resulting from changes in the use of an area. Such monitoring would be designed to ensure optimal ecological development within the functions considered desirable for that area.

Policy decisions on development plans for an area are taken after consideration of all important factors, and an increasingly important role has been played here by the ecological significance of wetlands. Many wetlands—for example many lakes, fens and marshes and certain large areas of open water—have been assigned functions within the framework of physical planning which recognize and accord with their ecological importance. Such policy is reflected in policy documents, structure schemes, regional schemes, provincial policy documents and development plans.

It shall be my constant aim to ensure that the ecological significance of wetlands in the Netherlands is adequately recognized in physical planning. Where necessary I shall also foster this process at provincial and regional level in the consultative procedure provided for in legislation on physical planning.

Wise use of wetlands can moreover be achieved by applying the instruments contained in the Policy Document on Agriculture and Nature Conservation to agricultural land which forms part of wetlands. Such land is also included in the Priority List of areas referred to in the Policy Document. I shall continue to devote the requisite attention to wetlands within the framework of this Policy Document.

A further important factor with regard to wise use of wetlands is targeted application of legislation on the quality of the environment and water management. Of particular importance for the protection of wetland ecology are the Pollution of Surface Waters Act, the Noise Nuisance Act, the Waste Substances Act, the Air Pollution Act, the Soil Protection Act and the Water Companies (Ground Water) Act.

National policy planning in respect of the application of the above Acts takes the form of Indicative Multi-year Programmes (IMP). National and provincial water quality plans are also being drawn up. As announced in the policy document "More than the sum of the parts" (Lower House, 1983-1984 session, 18292 no. 1-2), the various national and provincial environmental plans are to be replaced by national and provincial environmental policy plans and an environmental policy implementation programme. This will create a better basis for a coherent policy on the protection of areas such as wetlands. The IMP on environmental protection for 1986-1990 published at the time of the 1986 Budget goes into this in more detail.

In the context of water management legislation, mention should be made of the Water Management Bill which is currently in preparation. This will introduce a new water management planning system which will facilitate a more coherent policy than is currently possible on such water management systems as include wetlands.

I shall promote optimal use of the scope for the protection of wetland ecology provided by environmental and water management legislation, including international regulations, particularly those of the EC and the International Commission for the Protection of the Rhine against Pollution. I shall moreover do all I can to ensure that the ecological significance of such areas is a significant criterion in central government's contribution to and evaluation of provincial plans.

Finally, special mention should be made of the policy on large areas of open water. A system of integral or multi-sectoral planning has been developed or is in preparation to deal with the problems unique to this field. It provides for wise use of large areas of open water through the management methods to be applied and the regulation and dove-tailing of activities with due regard to ecological factors. At present, plans for the various large areas of open water are as follows:

- **Waddenzee.** The policy is set out in the Policy Document on Development of the Waddenzee area, part (e) (Lower House, 1980–1981 session 13 933, no 53). Further details will be laid down in a general management plan and in sectoral management plans.

- **Eastern Scheldt.** The main lines of physical planning and management policy are set out in the Eastern Scheldt policy plan which has been adopted at three administrative levels, including the Water Control and Purification Boards. Further elaboration will take place during management planning.

- **Grevelingen.** Policy principles are laid down in the *New structure sketch of the Grevelingen basin.*

- **Krammer-Volkerak.** The Krammer-Volkerak Steering Committee is currently preparing a policy plan.

- **Western Scheldt.** The objective is an integral policy which would coordinate all the functions of the Western Scheldt basin. This will take place in consultation with the Belgian authorities. Conservation and where possible restoration of natural resources and features will play an influential role in planning.

- **Haringvliet/Hollands Diep.** Specific policy plans for this area are to be elaborated further within the framework of an integral management plan for the whole basin.

- **Peripheral lakes.** Plans are currently being prepared by the Steering Committee on the Development and Management of the IJsselmeerpolders' Peripheral Lakes (STIBRIJ). Planning has almost been completed with regard to the Gooimeer and the IJmeer.

- **Klein IJsselmeer.** A start will be made on planning once the Government has made a decision on the future of the Markermeer area.

Certain large areas of open water have now been designated as primarily nature areas within the framework of such integrated or multi-sectoral planning and/or physical planning and water management policy. These are the Waddenzee, the Eastern Scheldt and Grevelingen. The latter has also been designated as a prime recreation area.

I intend to continue the policy outlined above on large areas of open water.

3.2 Establishment of nature reserves (Article 4, paragraph 1)

The establishment of nature reserves is an important means of conserving wetlands. The Netherlands has two instruments at its disposal for establishing nature reserves as referred to in the Wetlands Convention. These are acquisition followed by state management or management by non-governmental nature conservation organizations (with the help of state subsidies) and designation as an area of outstanding natural importance or a national area of outstanding natural importance protected under the Nature Conservancy Act. Important wetlands, large areas of which have been acquired and turned into reserves, include: Engbertsdijksvenen, Wieden, Weerribben, Zwanenwater, Eilandspolder, Nieuwkoopseplassen, and the Zuidhollandse and Brabantse Biesbosch. Mention should also be made of areas which have been transferred to the State Forest Service or to non-governmental conservation organizations for management by the State Property Department of the Ministry of Finance. These include Texel salt marshes, areas outside the dykes along the Frisian IJsselmeer coast, the Zwarte Meer, Fochteloërveen and shallows in the Veerse Meer. Priority has already been accorded to wetlands with respect to designation under the Nature Conservancy Act. This is evident from the following examples: large areas of the Waddenzee, including Dollard, parts of the Eemmeer, salt marshes, mud flats and shallows in Haringvliet and Hollands Diep, Verdronken Land van Saeftinge, Deurnse Peel and Mariapeel.

I shall continue the policy of using both sector instruments for the establishment of nature reserves in wetlands.

3.3 Research (Article 4, paragraph 3)

For years now, targeted research has been in progress into the function and significance of Dutch wetlands. Research activities relevant to wetland policy are essentially extremely varied and wide-ranging. They vary from the purely scientific to the technical, and an important role is played by research on the various functions of the relevant areas. Research is moreover conducted on a great variety of types of wetlands.

Many research establishments are active in this field. Important work is carried out by such institutes as the Research Institute for Nature Management, particularly by its estuarine ecology department, the Institute of Limnology, the Delta Institute for Hydrological Research, the IJsselmeerpolders Development Authority, the Tidal Waters Division and the Inland Waterways section of the Government Institute for Sewage and Waste Water Treatment of the Public Works Department, Fisheries Research and the Netherlands Marine Research Institute. A research programme is currently being carried out in the North Sea and the Waddenzee under the auspices of the North Sea and Wadenzee Integrated Ecological Research Steering Committee (SEON). Research activities are not confined to the Netherlands; some extend beyond our frontiers. Most research of this kind concerns areas or aspects relating to wetlands in the Netherlands. It should be noted that university institutes are also active in the field of ecological research.

I shall promote an appropriate wetland research policy within the relevant frameworks.

3.4 Increase of waterfowl population (Article 4, paragraph 4)

It should be stated in advance that the provision in the Wetlands Convention whereby the contracting Parties are obliged to endeavour through management to increase waterfowl populations on appropriate wetlands is an exceedingly general one. In the first place, "waterfowl" is a very wide concept and it would be impossible to prescribe that efforts to increase populations be of an equal level in the case of each individual species. Secondly, in many cases it is extremely difficult if not impossible to influence bird populations, since the factors which determine population size very often extend beyond the borders of any one country.

I feel that the Netherlands complies with this provision by adhering to the provisions concerning wise use, the establishment of nature reserves and the conservation of wetlands included in the List of Wetlands of International Importance. This ensures to a great extent the presence of suitable breeding habitat for breeding birds and sufficient feeding and resting grounds for migrating and wintering birds.

As regards game, as referred to in the Hunting and Shooting Act, and hunting in wetlands, I believe that attempts should be made to protect and re-establish populations of species defined as game. Preventing damage caused by game can play a role here.

It could be ascertained to what extent hunting could be considered compatible with the management aims of wetlands falling under the Nature Conservancy Act, of wetlands owned by the State and of partly State-subsidized wetlands owned by non-governmental nature conservancy organizations.

3.5 Training of competent personnel (Article 4, paragraph 5)

Since it is extremely important that sufficient expertise exists concerning wetlands, the Wetlands Convention contains a provision to encourage the training of personnel and wardening. Such expertise is important not only in providing a sound basis for wetland policy but also for its proper implementation. Several hundred people are active in the management and wardening of Dutch reservations relevant to the Wetlands Convention, some employed by public bodies and others by non-governmental organizations. They may be considered competent by virtue of their training and experience. Training in research which could be relevant to wetlands is extremely varied and widely available. The existence of research institutes and cooperation between such bodies and universities constitutes a stimulus for expert research.

4. Designation for the List of Wetlands and the provisions concerning areas included in the List

Leaving aside the policy outlined above with regard to all wetlands within its territory, the Netherlands, by ratifying the Wetlands Convention, has placed itself under an obligation to designate wetlands of international ecological, botanical, zoological, limnological and hydrological significance for inclusion in the List of Wetlands of International Importance (Article 2).

To date, the Netherlands has designated seven areas for inclusion in the List. These are the Haardermeer (750 ha), the Groote Peel (900 ha), the Zuidwaard Biesbosch (1700 ha), Weerribben (340 ha), Boschplaat (4400 ha), Griend (100 ha) and the Waddenzee (250,000 ha).

I believe that areas should only be designated where it is possible to adhere to the Wetlands Convention provision that "the Contracting Parties shall formulate and implement their planning so as to promote the conservation of wetlands included in the List" (beginning of Article 3). This means that administrative agreement will first have to be reached on the maintenance of the ecology of the areas concerned. Parameters will have to be established within which nature conservancy planning can take place. Administrative agreement can be said to have been reached if:

(a) clear administrative agreements have been laid down concerning the main lines of development, land-use and/or management;

(b) the ecological significance of an area has been reflected in physical planning policy;

(c) an area has largely been secured through acquisition and subsequent management by a nature conservation organization or through application of the Nature Conservancy Act.

These conditions accord with the proposals put forward by the Government in Explanatory Momorandum No. 3-4 (Lower House, 1976-1977 session, 14135 (R 1046) p. 3416). The above provision has already been adhered to with respect to the areas designated to date.

A second provision concerning areas included in the List stipulates that the contracting Party shall arrange to be informed at the earliest possible time if the ecological character of a wetland is changing or is likely to change (Article 3, paragraph 2). In the Netherlands, the body with administrative responsibility guarantees that timely warning will be given of changes in the ecological character of an area.

The Netherlands cannot always comply with the third provision, which states that contracting Parties should as far as possible compensate for any loss of wetland resources where the boundaries of a wetland included in the List have been deleted or restricted in a Party's urgent national interest (Article 4, paragraph 2). In such cases compensation is not always a realistic option, either for reasons of a biological or technical nature or because of lack of suitable space in the Netherlands. In any case, given the provisions of Article 3, paragraph 1, deletion or restriction of the borders of a listed wetland will be an exceptional occurrence. Deletion or restriction is permissible for reasons of urgent national interest. Cases could also arise in which designated wetlands wholly or partially lose their ecological function and value.

Listed areas are also designated as quiet areas under Section 123 of the Noise Abatement Act, unless placed on a list of exceptions. In addition, certain activities not confined to one particular spot, such as fishing, are deemed to be normal maintenance activities within the meaning of the Noise Abatement Act.

I aim to continue designating suitable wetlands for inclusion in the List and, taking into account the Wetlands Convention, I shall give priority to waterfowl habitat. These will tend to be large areas and others which are of great importance under the Wetlands Convention. However, I shall only do so where the preservation of such areas can be guaranteed in national policy.

Before it is decided to designate an area, a procedure is followed involving inter-ministerial consultation, hearings at which local authorities put forward their views, and consideration by the national Land-Use Planning Agency. A designation is submitted together with a report detailing the reasons for the area's international importance under the Wetlands Convention and the probable consequences of its designation. The managers of the wetland in question are consulted on the report before the designation procedure. The procedure with regard to deletion or restriction of the boundaries of a listed wetland would resemble that of designation.

The Eastern Scheldt, including the Markiezaatsmeer and the Zwanenwater, is currently in the process of being designated. Parts (a) and (d) of the Structure Plan for Nature Conservation and Protection of the Countryside contain a proposal to designate the Grevelingen for inclusion in the List of Wetlands of International Importance; further consideration was felt necessary before designating the peripheral lakes and the Kleine IJsselmeer. The Explanatory Memorandum to the 1984 Budget moreover mentions other areas: the Oostvaardersplassen, other parts of the Biesbosch and the Verdronken Land van Saeftinge.

When choosing other areas for designation the following criteria will be used:

- fulfilment of the internationally-recommended criteria agreed at Cagliari;

- administrative agreement on the preservation of the ecology;

- geographic dispersal and varied types of terrain;

- areas which constitute units in spatial, functional, and ecological terms;

- promotion of optimal ecological conditions for migrants and other birds dependent on wetlands.

When determining priorities extra attention will be paid to wetlands which can be considered part or large areas of open water, especially those in the region of the former Zuiderzee and in the Delta area.

Working on the above principles, consideration is to be given to designation of the following areas in the next few years: Groote Wielen (Friesland), Oude Venen

(Friesland), de Deelen (Friesland), Lauwersmeer (Groningen/Friesland), a major area of outstanding national interest, Fochterloërveen (Friesland/Drenthe), Barger-veen (Drenthe), De Wieden (Overijssel), Engbertsdijksvenen (Overijssel), Lepe-laarsplassen (Almere), Kil van Hurwenen (Gelderland), Botshol (Utrecht), Nieuwkoopse Plassen (South Holland) and parts of the Haringvliet/Hollands Diep (South Holland). Some of these areas already fulfil the Cagliari criteria while at the same time forming part of a larger wetland.

The Research Institute for Nature Management has drawn up a conspectus of areas which can be considered of international importance according to the criteria recommended within the framework of the Wetlands Convention. I feel that a conspectus of this kind is important as a scientific background to policy-making concerning both designation of wetlands for inclusion in the List, and the general provisions of the Wetlands Convention as set out in section 3 above.

5. The provision on international cooperation

Ecological links between wetlands make international cooperation desirable if effective protection is to be given to these areas. The Wetlands Convention provides the pre-eminent framework for such cooperation.

Great importance is attached to the effective implementation of the Wetlands Convention. Improvements are needed, particularly the establishment of a permanent Secretariat, the promotion of regular consultation between contracting Parties, the ratification of the Convention by more States and the provision of mutual assistance in the implementation of the Convention. My Ministry currently makes Fl 25,000 a year available for the implementation of the Convention, and I intend to continue this financial support. It should be pointed out that a future goal is joint financing by all the States Parties to the Wetlands Convention. I shall also continue with active efforts to bring about measures to increase the effectiveness of the Wetlands Convention. The Netherlands has, for example, been given the role of pioneer in the working group set up by the Groningen Conference to examine the possibility of establishing a permanent Secretariat and to formulate proposals for amendments to the Convention. I shall do my best to ensure that decisions can be taken on these points at the next conference convened by the contracting Parties. As soon as the Paris Protocol, which provides for an amendment procedure, has been ratified by a sufficient number of States to enter into force—which is expected to happen shortly—the formal obstacles will in any case have been removed.

My Ministry also promotes research in wetlands outside the Netherlands which have a direct ecological link with areas such as the Waddenzee or the Delta area. Grants have been provided for ornithological expeditions by Dutch researchers to Mauritania, Tunisia, Guinea Bissau and Sierra Leone. Such expeditions are increasingly geared to the training of counterparts and the transfer of technical equipment and know-how necessary to the management of the relevant areas.

Knowledge of important wetlands and their ecological characteristics is used to evaluate projects financed by the Dutch government. Even where the government is only indirectly involved, however, steps will be taken to determine whether, and in what way, my Ministry can encourage business and organizations developing and implementing projects in wetlands outside the Netherlands to take sufficient account of the ecological aspects involved, since this will not only help to conserve wetlands but will improve the quality both of the projects eventually carried out and of the recommendations on which they are based.

Mutual assistance in the implementation of the Wetlands Convention can be provided, for example, in the form of expert technical assistance in the management of wetlands.

I believe that it continues to be vital to increase and disseminate knowledge of the world's must important wetlands and the threats facing them. Financial support to international organizations active in this field, namely the International Union for Conservation of Nature and Natural Resources (IUCN) and the International Waterfowl Research Bureau (IWBR) must be seen in this light.

6. Information and education on wetlands

The Wetlands Convention does not contain any provisions concerning information and education. Nevertheless, both are important to a sound policy on wetlands, since the bodies and individuals concerned must be properly informed of the function and value of wetlands if they are to act responsibly with regard to such areas. Knowledge is needed not only of the ecological issues, but also of the relevance of wetlands to, for example, water management, fishing and recreation. If the Wetlands Convention is to be properly implemented I feel that the contracting Parties have a responsibility in this field, as in others.

Designation of individual areas for inclusion in the List of Wetlands of International Importance could be the occasion, for example, for more attention to be devoted to publicity and information campaigns. My Ministry will also devote attention to wetlands in its general information activities.

In the field of education, the government's role is primarily to set parameters. Subsidies provided to a number of organizations such as the Nature Conservation Education Institute have enabled a network to be set up.

Les zones humides en droit marocain

MOHAMED ALI MEKOUAR
Président de la Société marocaine pour le droit de l'environnement
(SOMADE)

Introduction

Les zones humides sous leurs diverses formes—marais, marécages, tourbières, plaines d'inondation, plans d'eau artificiels[1]—constituent des écosystèmes utiles autant que fragiles. A plusieurs égards, elles sont d'une richesse insoupçonnable. Assurant la synthèse écologique entre la terre et l'eau, elles sont le "siège d'une vie intense de micro-organismes végétaux et animaux"[2]. Les poissons, pour leur reproduction, et les oiseaux, pour leur nidification, y trouvent refuge. Une grande variété d'espèces sauvages, rares ou menacées, y élisent leur habitat. La qualité de l'eau peut leur être due: en filtrant sédiments et produits chimiques, elles maintiennent une relative pureté de l'eau. Leurs fonctions protectrices sont reconnues: en régulant les niveaux d'eau, en ralentissant leur écoulement, elles épargnent aux humains bien des catastrophes naturelles. Paradis pour les botanistes et ornithologues, elles font également le bonheur des touristes, chasseurs et pêcheurs[3]. Précieuses, les zones humides le sont donc à tous points de vue: écologique, scientifique, économique, social, récréatif, etc.

Elles ne sont pas moins vulnérables pour autant. Soumises à de fortes pressions humaines au cours des décennies écoulées, elles ont nettement régressé dans les pays industrialisés et elles ont tendance, de plus en plus aujourd'hui, à subir le même sort dans la plupart des pays en développement[4]. Trop souvent asséchées pour les besoins du "développement", elles font en outre les frais des "remblaiements, endiguements, drainages, opérations coûteuses, à l'utilité discutable, (qui) ont eu des conséquences écologiques désastreuses"[5]. Leur surexploitation se traduit encore par l'eutrophisation et la pollution conduisant à la perte de biotopes. Au total, ce sont "d'immenses zones humides naturelles (qui) disparaissent, au prix d'un appauvrissement de la diversité génétique, des espèces animales et végétales, de la composition des populations"[6].

Malgré l'importance qu'elles revêtent, et en dépit des périls qu'elles encourent, les zones humides n'ont que faiblement, et bien tardivement, suscité l'intérêt des juristes. La doctrine, dans sa jeunesse, n'y a guère prêté attention[7]. Nul enthousiasme non plus, sauf exception , de la part des législateurs à leur endroit[8]. C'est au niveau international que l'essentiel a été fait jusqu'ici, notamment avec l'adoption de la Convention de Ramsar sur les zones humides d'importance internationale (1971)[9]. Des initiatives plus récentes prises depuis lors[10], bien que relativement isolées et d'un retentissement limité, dénotent cependant le souci grandissant qui se manifeste ici et là de préserver les zones humides contre la destruction systématique.

Mais, qu'en est-il au Maroc à cet égard? Ses zones humides, faute d'avoir été sérieusement recensées, demeurent assez méconnues. Quatre d'entre elles, parmi les plus importantes, figurent dans la Liste internationale de la Convention de Ramsar (le Maroc ayant adhéré à cette dernière en 1980). Il s'agit de la Baie de Knifiss (6500 ha), de la Merja Zerga (3500 ha), de la Merja Sidi-Boughaba (200 ha)—toutes trois situées sur le littoral atlantique—, ainsi que du Lac d'Affennourir (380 ha, au nord du pays)[11]. Pour le reste, une prospection récente a établi l'existence de quelque 82 zones humides d'importance inégale servant à l'hivernage des Anatidés[12]; et n'était la sécheresse qui a sévi ces dernières années, sans doute eussent-elles été plus nombreuses aujourd'hui.

Sur le plan du droit, rares sont les juristes marocains qui se sont, de façon toute incidente d'ailleurs, quelque peu intéressés aux zones humides[13]. S'ils suivent en cela la tendance dominante de la doctrine[14], c'est en partie à cause de la singularité de ces espaces que le droit, dans sa lenteur coutumière à réagir, n'a pas encore eu le temps d'apprivoiser. Mais un tel désintérêt est dû tout autant à l'absence de dispositions légales spécifiquement protectrices des zones humides: celles-ci, ignorées comme telles par le législateur, le sont de la même manière par les juristes aussi. Comment, dans ces conditions, le droit marocain les appréhende-t-il? Quel statut y ont-elles? De quelle protection peuvent-elles jouir?

Statut

Les zones humides n'ayant pas leur propre loi, c'est dans le droit des ressources naturelles, essentiellement, qu'il faudra rechercher les règles juridiques susceptibles de les gouverner, en raisonnant par analogie et en faisant des extrapolations.

Ainsi peut-on dire, quant à leur statut, que la grande majorité des zones humides font partie du domaine public de l'Etat. Ce principe est en effet clairement énoncé à l'article 1er du dahir du 1.7.1914 (modifié) relatif au domaine public dans les termes suivants:

> "Font partie du domaine public ...:—le rivage de la mer jursqu'à la limite des plus hautes marées, ainsi qu'une zone de 6 mètres mesurée à partir de cette limite; ...—toutes les nappes d'eau, qu'elles soient superficielles ou souterraines; les cours d'eau et les sources de toute nature;—les lacs, étangs, lagunes, marais salants et marais de toute espèce. Sont considérées comme rentrant dans cette catégorie, les parcelles qui, sans être recouvertes d'une façon permanente par les eaux, ne sont pas susceptibles en année ordinaire d'utilisation agricole (merjas, etc).); ...—les canaux de navigation, d'irrigation ou de dessèchement exécutés comme travaux publics;—les digues, barrages, aqueducs, canalisations et autres ouvrages exécutés comme travaux publics en vue de la défense des terres contre les eaux, de l'alimentation des centres urbains ou de l'utilisation des forces hydrauliques ...".

La lecture de ce texte ne laisse donc pas de doute que, en règle générale, toute pièce d'eau, quelle qu'en soit la nature, est incluse dans le domaine public hydraulique et qu'aucune zone humide ne saurait en être soustraite, en principe, fût-elle conçue de main d'homme. Confirmation en est donnée par le dahir du 1.8.1925 sur le régime des eaux, dont le premier article apporte ces précisions: il y est spécifié que le domaine public comprend aussi:

> "Le lit des cours d'eau permanents et non permanents, ainsi que leurs sources; celui des torrents et ravins dans lesquels l'écoulement des eaux laisse des traces très apparentes; les berges jusqu'au niveau atteint par les eaux avant le débordement et, en outre, les parties des cours d'eau soumises à l'influence des marées, toutes les surfaces couvertes par les marées de coefficient 120; les francs-bords au-delà des limites ci-dessous définies ... (largeur de 6 mètres ou de 2 mètres selon les cours d'eau)".

Aussi bien les zones humides sont-elles manifestement des portions du domaine public aquatique. Celui-ci étant naturel, sa délimitation ne soulève guère de difficultés particulières: elle dépend, comme on sait, "de l'application quasi-automatique des règles fixées par le législateur lui-même"[15]. Mais cette simplicité des choses n'est en réalité qu'apparente, le principe de la domanialité publique des eaux étant susceptible d'exceptions diverses que le législateur a dû très tôt consentir.

Effectivement, le régime institué par le dahir de 1914 était trop absolu pour survivre inchangé: l'appliquer à la lettre eût conduit, soudainement, à priver les individus et les groupes d'une eau qu'ils utilisaient, de tout temps, en vertu des règles et coutumes antérieures[16]. Aussi le législateur a-t-il dû faire marche arrière dès 1919 pour admettre que les titulaires de droits acquis puissent continuer à en bénéficier: "Sont maintenus les droits de propriété, d'usufruit ou d'usage légalement acquis sur le domaine public antérieurement à la publication du présent dahir" (article 2 modifié). Par le biais de cette disposition, il est donc parfaitement concevable que des zones humides soient privativement appropriées, de façon individuelle ou collective, dès lors que les bénéficiaires se sont vu officiellement reconnaître leurs droits sur elles[17]. Reste à savoir si les zones humides ainsi soustraites au domaine public représentent des espaces étendus ou minimes. En attendant qu'un inventaire soit établi, il est vraisemblable que les zones humides privées n'ont qu'une faible importance.

Les zones humides peuvent-elles, par ailleurs, être possédées par des associations? La question mérite d'autant plus d'être posée que les groupements de défense de l'environnement se chargent de plus en plus, dans certains pays, de la gestion des espaces naturels, tels que parcs ou réserves. Pareille évolution, toutefois, ne s'est pas encore produite au Maroc[18], de sorte qu'on imagine mal, dans l'immédiat, que des zones humides puissent être gérées par des associations, et encore moins devenir leur propriété. Cependant, une telle éventualité est théoriquement envisageable, à travers les dispositions du dahir du 15.6.1924 (en cours de révision) relatif aux associations syndicales agricoles. Ces dernières peuvent être créées à l'initiative tant de l'Administration que des personnes intéressées en vue, notamment, d'assurer la défense contre les inondations, de procéder à l'assèchement des marais et des terres marécageuses ou insalubres, ou de favoriser l'amélioration et l'entretien des ouvrages d'aménagement des eaux déjà existants (article 1er). A cet effet, elles ont le pouvoir d'acquérir, louer, transiger, emprunter, hypothéquer, vendre (article 7)[19]. Ainsi la loi leur donne-t-elle la possibilité de devenir propriétaires de zones humides aux fins "d'aménagement", mais il est douteux qu'il en soit ainsi en pratique[20].

Aussi les zones humides sont-elles, en définitive, essentiellement un bien public. Incluses en principe dans le domaine public aquatique, elles jouissent de la double garantie de l'inaliénabilité et de l'imprescriptibilité[21]. Leur utilisation privative, pour être exceptionnelle, demeure néanmoins possible, soit en vertu de droits acquis, soit par le biais d'un usage temporaire[22]. Un tel statut est-il pour faciliter leur protection?

Protection

Les zones humides, on l'a vu, n'ont pas de législation spécifique[23]. Les mesures protectrices, dans la sphère juridique, doivent dès lors être puisées aux diverses branches du droit de la nature, en particulier, mais aussi dans celui de la propriété foncière, dans la mesure où la maîtrise de la terre donne à ses titulaires le pouvoir d'en disposer. La structure du capital foncier n'est pas non plus indifférente à cet égard. La région du Gharb, par exemple, assez bien arrosée par rapport au reste du pays, comporte d'intéressantes plaines alluviales, mais dont la préservation est probablement desservie par le caractère relativement morcelé de la propriété rurale[24]. La loi s'efforce pourtant de limiter l'émiettement des exploitations agricoles dans les périmètres d'irrigation, en interdisant le morcellement des parcelles de moins de 5 ha[25, 26].

Quant à la législation relative à l'environnement naturel, elle peut être à plusieurs égards applicable aux zones humides, de manière partielle ou indirecte. Ainsi des textes sur les aires spécialement protégées. Le dahir du 11.9.1934 sur les parcs nationaux peut ainsi servir utilement à la sauvegarde des zones humides qui seraient comprises à l'intérieur d'un parc, car les terrains englobés dans pareils espaces sont en principe soustraits à toute forme d'exploitation et maintenus dans leur état initial[27]. Dans ce cadre légal, il existe un projet de création de parc national abritant une belle zone humide côtière dans la région de Massa, au sud d'Agadir[28]. De la même manière, la législation concernant les réserves n'est pas sans intérêt pour les zones humides. Dans les réserves de chasse[29], celle-ci est prohibée de façon temporaire ou permanente; cette forme de protection, à des fins cynégétiques et pour la reconstitution du gibier, profite également aux zones humides incluses dans les réserves[30]. Pareillement, les réserves de pêche peuvent jouer un tel rôle protecteur, en ce sens que leur création, dans "les eaux courantes ou stagnantes"[31], répond au même souci de conservation des espèces et de maintien des biotopes[32].

En dehors des textes régissant les aires protégées, on peut également faire état d'un certain nombre de dispositions visant plus largement à combattre la dégradation et la pollution du milieu aquatique. C'est ainsi qu'un arrêté du

6.12.1924 réglementant les extractions de sable et gravier dans le lit des cours d'eau soumet ces opérations à autorisation administrative préalable (article 1er). De manière plus précise, le dahir du 23.11.1973 formant règlement de la pêche maritime[33] interdit le rejet en mer de toute "substance ou appât toxique susceptible d'infecter, d'enivrer ou d'empoisonner les poissons, mollusques, oursins ou crustacés, ... ou de polluer les eaux" (article 18). Les usines installées sur le littoral sont également tenues de prendre les mesures de précaution qui s'imposent pour éviter de causer de tels dommages (article 19)[34]. Des dispositions similaires se retrouvent aussi dans le dahir du 11.4.1922 relatif à la pêche dans les eaux continentales[35], ainsi que dans le dahir du 1.8.1925 sur le régime des eaux[36]. A travers la sauvegarde des systèmes aquatiques découlant de ces différents textes, c'est aussi, dans une certaine mesure, celle des zones humides qui peut être assurée[37].

Il est par ailleurs des règles classiques dont la mise en oeuvre peut se révéler bénéfique pour les zones humides. On songe ainsi à certaines obligations foncières, comme la servitude d'écoulement des eaux qui pèse sur le propriétaire d'un fonds que traversent des eaux et dont il ne peut empêcher le libre écoulement[38], en élevant une digue ou en dressant des obstacles[39]; même s'il clôturait son terrain, il n'en serait pas moins tenu d'aménager des ouvertures dans le mur de séparation[40]. Les grands barrages, en revanche, édifiés par l'Etat pour les besoins de l'irrigation[41], ne sont pas astreints à de telles obligations, même si leur impact négatif sur les zones humides n'est plus à démontrer[42].

Du point de vue institutionnel, la sauvegarde des zones humides incombe essentiellement aux pouvoirs publics, cette compétence pouvant s'exercer au double niveau central et local. Concrètement, la gestion de l'environnement naturel relève de différents départements ministériels, en particulier celui de l'Agriculture (Direction des Eaux et Forêts), celui de l'Equipement (Direction de l'Hydraulique) et celui de l'Intérieur (Division de l'Environnement)[43]. La tutelle administrative et la gestion matérielle des zones humides peuvent donc se trouver partagées entre divers organes, ce qui n'est pas sans poser des problèmes de coordination inter-institutionnelle[44].

Conclusion

Au Maroc, comme partout ailleurs, les zones humides sont dépréciées: "leur image manque d'éclat et leur intérêt n'est pas évident"[45]. La conscience de leur importance est loin d'être prise, que ce soit par les décideurs ou par le public. La politique agricole leur est dans l'ensemble plutôt défavorable: soucieuse de stimuler la production, sans égard aux impacts écologiques[46], elle fait reculer les zones humides à mesure que, pour s'étendre, elle les conquiert[47].

L'inexistence de toute protection juridique spécifique n'est pas pour améliorer leur sort. Bien que bénéficiant des garanties que leur confère la domanialité publique, elles ne sont nullement à l'abri des empiètements. Et quoique certains textes leur soient indirectement applicables, ce n'est, au demeurant, que de manière ponctuelle et imparfaite[48].

L'adoption d'une loi sur les zones humides n'en apparaît alors que plus opportune, afin de les doter d'un statut juridique propre et de les soumettre à un régime protecteur particulier[49]. Parallèlement à la mise en place d'une telle législation, il conviendrait de faire la "toilette" de certains textes en vigueur, voire d'en abroger quelques-uns, en vue de les expurger de bon nombre de dispositons nettement préjudiciables au maintien des zones humides[50]. Ces mesures juridiques devraient s'accompagner d'une action de sensibilisation à l'utilité et à la fragilité de ces espaces naturels naguère déconsidérés mais depuis peu réhabilités.

Notes

1. Selon M. Prieur, 1984, *Droit de l'environnement*, Paris, Dalloz, p. 504, les zones humides recouvrent des espaces appelés, "marais, marécages, lagunes, estuaires, vasières, prairies inondables, tourbières, etc.". Pour la définition de ces espaces, voir le dossier spécial sur les zones humides dans le *Bulletin de l'UICN*, 16(10-12), 1985.

2. Morand-Deviller, J. 1987, *Le droit de l'environnment*, Paris, Que Sais-Je?, p. 69.

3. Pour plus de détails sur l'utilité des zones humides, voir le dossier précité dans le *Bulletin de l'UICN*, p. 116 s.

4. Klein, L. 1981, *Les zones humides*, mémoire de Strasbourg; Untermaier, J. 1979, La protection des zones humides au plan national, dans *La protection du littoral*, SFDE, Lyon, PPS, p. 183.

5. Morand-Deviller, J., précité, p. 69. La démoustication des zones humides, au moyen d'insecticides, est également source de nuisances pour ces espaces: Despax, M. 1980, *Droit de l'environnement*, Paris, Litec, p. 186 ss; voir aussi les développements que cet auteur consacre à l'assèchement des zones humides à des fins agricoles (p. 177 ss.)

6. Les zones humides sur la sellette, *Bulletin de l'UICN*, 16(10-12), 1985, p. 110.

7. Par exemple, Malafosse, J. de 1973, *Le droit de l'environnement: Le droit à la nature*, Paris, Monchrestien; et Lamarque, J. 1973, *Droit de la protection de la nature et de l'environnement*, Paris, LGDJ; écrivant tous deux leur ouvrage au début des années soixante-dix, n'y ont pas fait place aux zones humides.

8. Prieur, M., précité, p. 505. Il y a tout de même des exceptions: ainsi, aux Etats-Unis, il existe une réglementation spécifique sur les zones humides: Larson, J.S. 1985, Evaluer les avoirs liquides, *Bulletin de l'UICN*, 16(10-12): 119.

9. Cette Convention est le principal mécanisme de coopération internationale pour la sauvegarde des zones humides; elle a l'originalité d'être la seule dont l'objet est d'assurer la conservation d'un écosystème particulier et des espèces qui en dépendent. Aux termes de ses dispositions, les Parties contractantes désignent au moins une zone humide nationale à incorporer dans la Liste des zones humides d'importance internationale tenue à cet effet par l'UICN: Navid, D. 1985, Ramsar: la bouée de l'espoir, *Bulletin de l'UICN*, 16(10-12), p. 124; Groningue: vague ou vaguelette?, *Bulletin de l'UICN*, 15(4-6), 1984, p. 42; de Klemm, C. 1976, La protection internationale des zones humides, *Naturopa*, 24, p. 7. Pour une vue plus globale sur le droit international des zones humides: Baum, P., Principales activités des organisations inter-nationales en matière de zones humides, dans *La protection du littoral*, précité, p. 198 ss.; Lyster, S. 1985, *International Wildlife Law* (notamment p. 183 ss.).

10. Comme les recommandations du Comité des ministres du Conseil de l'Europe concernant: l'une les tourbières (R-81) et l'autre la fiche d'identification et d'évaluation des zones humides (Prieur, précité, p. 510). Notons aussi la Résolution 16/16 de l'Assemblée générale de l'UICN (Madrid, 1984) sur la conservation des zones humides (UICN, Résolution de la 16e session de l'Assemblée générale).

11. Convention on Wetlands of International Importance Especially as Waterfowl Habitat, List of Contracting Parties, IUCN Document, 151 p, Kew, CMC, July 1983.

12. Recensement hivernal d'oiseaux d'eau au Maroc. Janvier 1984, Direction des Eaux et Forêts/Institut Scientifique, Rabat, mars 1984.

13. Comme Bekrate, A. 1983, *La protection de la nature au Maroc*, Thèse de Bordeaux I (en étudiant les aires spécialement protégées) ou Mekouar, M.A. 1986, Système foncier et écosystèmes côtiers: entre terre et mer, le littoral balloté, *Revue marocaine de droit et d'économie du développement*, 12/1986, p. 137 (en étudiant le littoral).

14. Le même silence observé par la doctrine se remarque dans un ouvrage plus récent: Machado, P.A.L. 1982, *Direito ambiental brasileiro*, Sao Paulo, Ed. Revista dos Tribuais.

15. Rousset, M. (et autres) 1984, *Droit administratif marocain* (3è édition), Rabat, Imprimerie Royale, p. 462.

16. Avant l'instauration du Protectorat au Maroc, les eaux étaient régies par deux ordres de règles qui s'interpénétraient, celles du droit musulman (très élaborées) et du droit coutumier berbère (extrêmement diversifiées). La législation introduite au début du siècle est venue se juxtaposer aux règles antérieures, en évinçant nombre d'entre elles, mais sans pouvoir les supprimer en bloc, de sorte qu'aujourd'hui encore cohabitent les trois systèmes juridiques. Sur cette question: Sonnier, A. 1983, *Le régime juridique des eaux au Maroc*, Paris, Sirey; Decroux, P. 1960, Le régime des eaux, *Gazette des Tribunaux du Maroc*, 10/Juin 1960; Roche, P. 1965, Le régime juridique des eaux et irrigation au Maroc, *Revue juridique et politique Indépendance et Coopération*, janvier–mars 1965.

17. La reconnaissance des droits privatifs d'eau ne peut intervenir qu'au terme d'une enquête administrative effectuée par une commission spéciale dans les conditions fixées par un arrêté viziriel du 1.8.1925: Maarouf, R, 1983, *La protection de la ressource en eau au Maroc*, Thèse de Bordeaux I, p. 101. Cet auteur précise en outre que la preuve d'un droit acquis est à la charge de celui qui s'en prévaut et qu'elle doit être rapportée devant la commission d'enquête. Il doit s'agir d'un véritable droit, et non pas seulement d'un intérêt, fût-il sérieux (ainsi le tribunal de Casablanca, par jugement du 13.2.1922, a refusé de reconnaître à des maraîchers des droits privatifs sur une rivière qu'ils utilisaient, alors même qu'ils présentaient pour eux un grand intérêt). Il faut en outre que le droit invoqué ait été légalement acquis, en vertu d'une concession ou d'une possession paisible (ayant duré 10 ou 30 ans selon les cas, mais cette condition n'est pas toujours rigoureusement exigée par la jurisprudence: une possesssion durable, mais pas forcément décennale, suffit parfois, comme en a décidé le tribunal de Rabat par un jugement du 14.2.1924, dans une affaire où le demandeur avait coutume, depuis de longues années, de couper des graminées dans un marécage) (Maarouf, précité, p. 100 s.).

18. Mekouar, M.A. 1987, Associations et environnement, *Journée d'étude sur le droit et l'environnement*, SOMADE, Casablanca, février 1987.

19. L'article 6 ajoute que les propriétaires et usagers peuvent être tenus de faire partie d'une association syndicale, et que si leurs terrains sont compris dans un périmètre de dessèchement, ils peuvent être admis à se libérer de leurs charges moyennant délaissement d'une partie de leurs terres au profit de l'association.

20. Pascon, P. (et autres) 1984, *La question hydraulique*, Rabat, p. 31.

21. Article 4 du dahir de 1914 sur le domaine public.

22. Le dahir du 30.11.1918 règlemente les occupations temporaires du domaine public: l'utilisation privative est subordonnée à la délivrance unilatérale d'une autorisation administrative; plus rarement, elle peut être accordée par une convention de concession. Le dahir de 1925 sur le régime des eaux prévoit précisément ce type de concessions conventionnnelles, par exemple pour l'exploitation des sources d'eau minérale (Rousset, précité, p. 470). Bien que les zones humides ne soient pas expressément visées par ce texte, rien n'empêche, en théorie, qu'elles puissent faire l'objet d'une utilisation privative dans les conditions du droit commun.

23. Il existe cependant un texte sur les merjas du Gharb (parcelles inondées à certaines périodes de l'année, surtout lors de grandes pluies): le dahir du 27.8.1956 aux termes duquel ces merjas

doivent être incorporées au domaine privé de l'Etat au fur et à mesure de leur assèchement (article 1er). En contre-partie "de l'abandon, par elles, de leurs droits d'usage sur les territoires correspondants, les collectivités riveraines recevront la pleine propriété du 1/3 des parties asséchées" (article 2). C'est donc manifestement un outil juridique conçu pour supprimer ces zones humides.

24. Meziane, R. 1984, *Le droit de l'environnement au Maroc*, Thèse de Bordeaux I, p. 19, parle de parcellisation des exploitations, dont la superficie ne dépasse guère 4 ha en général; La question hydraulique, précité, p. 22.

25. Dahir du 25.7.1969 formant code des investissements agricoles; ce même texte interdit le morcellement des grandes propriétés lorsqu'il conduit à la création d'unités de moins de 5 ha.

26. Précisons que, depuis 1966, dans le cadre de la "réforme agraire", les attributaires de parcelles de 5 ha sont tenus de se regrouper en coopératives; la même obligation pèse, depuis 1969, sur les bénéficiaires de parcelles de 5 ha provenant des terres collectives traditionnelles, reçues au titre de la distribution des terres (décret du 25.7.1969). Sur ce point: Bekrate, précité, p. 233; *La question hydraulique*, précité, p. 49 ss.; Decroux, P. 1972, *Droit foncier marocain*, Rabat, La Porte; Meziane, précité, p. 243; Popp, H. 1984, *Effets socio-géographiques de la politique des barrages au Maroc*, Rabat, p. 49..

27. Bekrate, précité, p. 122 ss.; Meziane, précité, p. 145 ss.

28. Naturopa (Faits nouveaux-nature), no 86-6 (1986), p. 3: "Le parc comprendra un large éventail d'habitats, dont certains revêtent une grande importance pour les oiseaux migrateurs, tels que les ibis chauves". Selon l'UICN, l'ibis chauve est quasi endémique à la région de Massa, où vivent la majorité des individus recensés (364 sur une population mondiale estimée à 400): Portas, P. 1983, *De la protection de l'ibis chauve* (Geronticus eremica) *à la création du parc national de Massa*, Gland, UICN, 1983.

29. Dahir du 21.7.1923 sur la police de la chasse (article 4), complété par l'arrêté du 3.11.1962 portant réglementation permanente de la chasse (article 11), ainsi que par les arrêtés annuels portant ouverture de la chasse.

30. En particulier, lorsque ces réserves sont permanentes et bénéficient ainsi d'une protection durable, comme dans l'île de Skhirat (dite "île des oiseaux"), l'îlot du "Pharaon" (au large d'Essaouira), ou la baie du Khnifiss. Au sujet de ces réserves, S. Benjelloun ("La protection de la faune sauvage au Maroc", communication au Symposium international sur la gestion et la conservation de la faune sauvage méditerranéenne, Fès, Avril 1983) écrit: "Situées le long de la voie de migration sur la côte atlantique, ces réserves sont des lieux d'escale et d'hivernage de milliers d'oiseaux d'eau venant d'Europe en période hivernale ... Les données quantitatives de la distribution des espèces de la sauvagine montrent que ces zones humides représentent un échantillon important du patrimoine international constitué par l'aire de répartition des oiseaux d'eau".

31. Article 5 du dahir du 11.4.1922 sur la pêche dans les eaux continentales.

32. Bekrate, précité, p. 116.

33. Celle qui est "faite à la mer et sur les côtes ainsi que dans les lagunes classées par décret hors des eaux courantes et stagnantes du domaine public terrestre"—article 1er du dahir.

34. Lahlou, A. 1983, *Le Maroc et le droit des pêches maritimes*, Paris, LGDJ, p. 70.

35. Article 6 et, surtout, article 7 qui dispose: "Il ne pourra être accordé d'autorisation d'établissement d'usine à proximité des eaux du domaine public terrestre ... qu'à la condition que les eaux résiduaires de ces usines ... ne seront en aucun cas déversées dans les eaux. Toutefois, l'arrêté d'autorisation fixera les conditions moyennant lesquelles ces eaux, après avoir été rendues inoffensives ou propres à la vie animale, pourront exceptionnellement être déversées dans les eaux du domaine public terrestre".

36. Article 21: "Il est interdit ... de faire des dépôts dans le lit des cours d'eau ...; de jeter ... des matières nuisibles à l'hygiène publique et à l'alimentation des animaux".

37. Observons que la préservation des zones humides peut aussi résulter de la protection des espèces qui y vivent. Au Maroc, nombre d'oiseaux dépendant de ces zones (balbuzard pêcheur, busard des roseaux, busard cendré, poule sultane, flamant rose, spatule blanche, ibis chauve, ibis falcinelle, cigogne blanche, demoiselle de Numidie, avocette, échasse, erismature, tadorne, etc.), sont protégés par la législation cynégétique.

38. Dahir du 2.6.1915 sur les immeubles immatriculés (article 110-112) et dahir du 1.8.1925 sur le régime des eaux (article 7).

39. Decroux, précité, p. 347; Maarouf, précité, p. 114.

40. Article 112 du dahir de 1915.

41. Benhadi, A. 1977, La politique marocaine des barrages, dans *Les problèmes agraires au Maghreb*, Paris, CRESM/CNRS.

42. Popp, précité; Laalou, A. 1985, *Impact des barrages sur l'environnement au Maroc*, mémoire de l'INAU, Rabat, p. 90: "L'implantation des barrages ... ne fait naturellement qu'entraîner l'assèchement des marais abritant des effectifs importants d'oiseaux et par conséquent la disparition de leurs zones de nourriture, d'escale et de nidification". Toutefois, les retenues de barrages peuvent également servir de zones de repos pour les migrants (p. 94). Le code des investissements agricoles (dahir de 1969), instrument de la politique d'irrigation, comporte divers encouragements à "l'assainissement", dont les zones humides font parfois les frais: aménagements, défrichements, défoncements, nivellements, drainage, dragage, dérivation, entre autres travaux destinés à la mise en valeur des terres agricoles (rendue obligatoire dans les périmètres d'irrigation), contribuent à des degrés divers à la régression des zones humides, non seulement dans les régions irriguées, mais aussi dans les régions cultivables en sec (où l'Etat peut délimiter des secteurs "d'assainissement" dans lesquels on procède à l'élimination des "eaux de surface en excédent", afin de protéger les propriétés agricoles menacées par les crues—article 35 du dahir du 25.7.1969).

43. Mekouar, M.A. 1987, L'Administration de l'environnement face au changement, dans *Les services publics marocains face au changement*, Toulouse, P.I.E.P., p. 167.

44. Meziane, précité, p, 198 ss.; Bekrate, précité, p. 178: "la coordination des actions ministérielles demeure, en l'état actuel des choses, notoirement défaillante sur le plan politique. Chaque ministère se trouve prisonnier de ses propres compétences et n'éprouve le besoin de coordonner avec les autres départements qu'à condition que cette coordination ne vienne pas limiter ses pouvoirs".

45. Campagne pour les zones humides, *Bulletin de l'UICN*, 16(10-12) 1985, p. 122.

46. Mekouar, M.A. 1987, *Droit, agriculture, environnement: stimuler la production dans le respect de la nature*, Communication au Séminaire sur la protection de l'environnement et la gestion des ressources naturelles, Meknès, juin 1987.

47. En plus des avantages accordés par le Code des investissements agricoles, l'impôt agricole n'est plus levé depuis quelques années. De surcroît, les attributaires de terres distribuées qui ne les exploitent pas peuvent en être dépossédés. Enfin, la mise en valeur des terres agricoles est obligatoire en général, ce qui empêche de les laisser à l'état d'abandon (article 5 et 50 du dahir du 25.7.1969). Pareilles dispositions ne sont guère, a priori, avantageuses pour les zones humides.

48. La législation protectrice des espaces naturels est d'ailleurs, dans l'ensemble, fort peu appliquée; Bekrate, précité, p. 149 ss.

49. On observera que le projet de loi sur la protection et la mise en valeur de l'environnement (1985), s'il comporte bien un chapitre sur "les zones spécialement protégées, les paysages et les sites", ne fait aucune mention expresse des zones humides.

50. Comme le dahir de 1956 sur les merjas du Gharb, ainsi que la plupart des textes qui organisent l'assèchement et "l'assainissement".

The Conservation of Wetlands in Great Britain

DAVID WITHRINGTON

Nature Conservancy Council, Peterborough, U.K.

Types of wetlands in Great Britain

Some 35 estuaries around the coast of Great Britain support internationally important numbers of waterfowl in winter and on migration to and from their Arctic breeding grounds. Peat bogs, especially the blanket bogs of north and west Britain, are important examples of globally scarce habitat and support significant breeding populations of wading birds. Water supply reservoirs and flooded gravel pits also provide a winter refuge for many hundreds of thousands of water birds.

Rivers and their catchments are at the heart of freshwater ecosystems. In Britain most of the lowland rivers and their floodplains have been extensively modified by man. Only a few remnant areas of fen, water meadow, marshland and grazing marsh retain typical wetland flora and fauna. Many of these areas are reserves owned by voluntary or statutory nature conservation bodies. Lakes, ponds and disused canals all contribute to the habitat for wetland wildlife.

The Ramsar Convention defines wetlands to include shallow seas up to a depth of six metres. There are a number of areas of marine conservation interest around the coast of Britain, particularly on the western seaboard, which are little modified by human activities. Current survey programmes will show which of these are of national importance for their wildlife.

Pressures on wetlands

Wetlands were once a more extensive feature of Britain's landscape. In 1637 the area of fenland in East Anglia was 3,380 sq. km but today it is less than 10 sq. km, because of drainage and reclamation for agriculture. More than half of lowland peat bogs have been lost due to peat cutting and reclamation for forestry or agriculture. Recent pressures are illustrated by the loss of conservation interest of 10% of lakes identified as nationally important in 1967 due to nutrient enrichment. These losses of habitat are having consequences for species: for instance since 1950, four of our 43 native dragonflies have become extinct and 11 have declined significantly.

Because of surpluses of food in the European Community, the pressures from drainage and agriculture are now declining, but other developments are gaining momentum. These include:

- Afforestation of peat bogs in northern Britain;

- Acidification of upland lakes and rivers from air pollution;

- Enrichment of lowland lakes and rivers from sewage effluents and agricultural fertilizers;

- Pollution of rivers from farm wastes (silage liquor and intensive livestock units);

- Pollution from fish farms in lakes, rivers and sea lochs;

- Intensification of inshore fisheries, e.g. suction dredging of shellfish;

- Reclamation of estuaries for industrial and port developments;

- Proposals for tidal barrages for energy generation;

- More intensive use of wetlands for water sports.

The legal and administrative framework for wetland management

In England and Wales, the management of reservoirs and water supplies, inland fisheries, river management and flood protection, sewage treatment and water pollution control is undertaken by ten public Water Authorities. Some 210 low-lying agricultural areas are managed by statutory Internal Drainage Boards. Coastal fisheries are regulated by 12 Sea Fisheries Committees. Governmental responsibility is divided between the Secretary of State for the Environment, the Secretary of State for Wales and the Minister of Agriculture. The Government have published proposals (July 1987) for the privatization of the 10 Water Authorities to provide water supplies and sewage treatment. They intend to create a National Rivers Authority to regulate water abstraction, water quality, fisheries and flood protection.

In Scotland water quality is regulated on the mainland by seven River Purification Boards. Water supply, sewage treatment and flood protection is undertaken by Regional and Islands Council (local authorities). Government responsibility rests with the Secretary of State for Scotland, who also has direct control over coastal fisheries.

Canals and some balancing reservoirs are administered by the British Waterways Board. Navigation is in the hands of a variety of public bodies.

Various Acts of Parliament contain provisions for the control of abstractions and impoundments, land drainage, water quality and fisheries. These are administered by the bodies listed above.

Developments other than those involving drainage, agricultural and forestry activities, require planning permission from the local authority. The conservation status of the site is taken into account and on internationally important wetlands there would normally be a public inquiry under the aegis of the Secretary of State.

Protection of wetlands

The Nature Conservancy Council* is the official body in Great Britain responsible for promoting the conservation of wildlife habitats (including wetlands). This is done in a number of ways:

- Notifying Sites of Special Scientific Interest to their owners and occupiers under the Wildlife and Countryside Act 1981. At present there are 4,500 sites covering 7% of the countryside.

- Ensuring the management of the most important of these sites in the public interest by the creation of National Nature Reserves and the provision of wardens. At present there are some 230 NNRs covering over 160,000 hectares.

- Giving financial support to other bodies to establish nature reserves.

- Offering management agreements to landowners and occupiers with appropriate payments to maintain the special conservation interest of designated sites. Last year the NCC spent over £5 million on these agreements.

- Giving advice to local authorities on proposed developments affecting Sites of Special Scientific Interest and giving evidence to public inquiries on the nature conservation case.

- Giving practical guidance to Water Authorities and Internal Drainage Boards on the exercise of their statutory duty to "further" the conservation of flora and fauna.

The Government have designated eight Environmentally Sensitive Areas (ESAs) under the Agriculture Act 1986. These are areas where the maintenance or adoption of certain agricultural methods will help to conserve the flora and fauna. Agriculture Departments offer agreements to farmers, with management prescriptions worked out by the NCC. Two large wetland areas—The Broads in East Anglia, and the Somerset Levels and Moors—have been designated as ESAs.

The Secretary of State has the power to make orders under Section 29 of the Wildlife and Countryside Act 1981 to prohibit specified operations on sites of nature conservation interest, especially those of national or international importance. These orders provide for up to a maximum of 15 months for the NCC to resolve disagreements with owners and occupiers and conclude a management agreement. On SSSIs without an order, operations have to be notified to the NCC but can go ahead after four months without the NCC's consent. In all cases, if planning permission has been obtained from the local authority, the order or the designation can be ignored.

---

* On 1 April 1991, the Nature Conservancy Council was replaced by separate agencies for England, Scotland and Wales, with a joint Nature Conservation Committee to deal with matters affecting Great Britain as a whole, e.g. international work.

Thirty-one wetlands in the U.K. have been designated under the Ramsar Convention. The NCC has drawn up a candidate list of 129 sites. This may be added to when non-bird criteria are developed. Before designation, the NCC has to carry out local consultations and prepare a detailed case for each site for the Secretary of State. A programme exists for Special Protection Areas under the EC Directive 79/409 on the Conservation of Wild Birds; most Ramsar sites will also qualify under this Directive. Both designations rely on the legislative protection afforded to SSSIs. However, their international status is likely to carry more weight at planning inquiries.

Certain species of wildlife which depend on wetlands are among those protected from taking or killing under the Wildlife and Countryside Act 1981, though their habitats can be destroyed. These wetland species include 42 birds (with a further 14 protected in the summer months only), three newts (*Triturus* spp.), the natterjack toad (*Bufo calamita*), the fen raft spider (*Dolomedes plantarius*), one butterfly, one dragonfly, one moth, one fish, the otter (*Lutra lutra*), the common porpoise (*Phocaena phocaena*) and two dolphins. No species of wild plant may be uprooted or destroyed except with the permission of the landowner. In addition, there are 62 species of plant which may not be picked or offered for sale; a number of these depend on wetlands. Certain alien species of plant and animal may not be released into the wild. A review of protected species is carried out every five years by the Nature Conservancy Council and recommendations for deletions from or additions to the listed species are made to the Secretary of State.

Enforcement of the laws on habitat protection is undertaken in England and Wales by the Nature Conservancy Council and in Scotland by the Procurator Fiscal on the advice of the NCC. Enforcement of the laws on species protection is principally in the hands of the police: most county Constabularies have appointed Wildlife Liaison Officers.

Conservation initiatives

In addition to the work carried out by the Nature Conservancy Council as the official body, a wide range of voluntary conservation organizations make a substantial contribution to the conservation of wetlands, principally by establishing nature reserves and involving the public in educational activities and practical management and protection projects.

Special publications have been issued to assist in the conservation of wetlands, notably guidelines on river engineering and the management of canals. In England and Wales from 1987 all the regional Water Authorities are making surveys of wildlife in river corridors before undertaking any major river works, using a methodology developed by the NCC. The NCC is cooperating with local authorities and water authorities on schemes for removal of phosphates and other pollutants entering selected lakes of nature conservation importance. In parts of the Broads phosphate stripping is supplemented by mud pumping of the polluted sediment and re-establishment of zooplankton.

Action required to improve the conservation of wetlands

The problems of wetlands are broadly the same as those facing conservation as a whole. Various forms of "economic" development are pursued which directly or indirectly damage the environment. In Britain, support for conservation will probably ensure that no major wetland site will be destroyed without a public debate.

Reduction in Government grants for agricultural drainage and reclamation have reduced pressures on wetlands and further measures within the European Community to restrict cereal production are likely to be beneficial. Reduction in subsidies and tax relief for afforestation and a system of licensing would reduce pressures on peat bogs in northern Britain. Developments which require planning permission, such as barrages and industrial developments, will probably go ahead, even on internationally important wetlands, in so far as they are equated with economic progress.

The laws governing water quality are fairly comprehensive, but have not been fully implemented. The Control of Pollution Act 1974 gives the Secretary of State powers to issue regulations on the storage of polluting substances on farms and industrial premises and to designate water source protection zones. The same Act gives Water Authorities and River Purification Boards duties and powers to remedy and forestall pollution injurious to fauna and flora. The main problem is in finance and manpower to improve sewage treatment and inspect and police farm pollution. The last five years have seen a significant deterioration of water quality, particularly in rural rivers. The Government's proposals for the establishment of a National Rivers Authority may provide the opportunity for tackling the problems of water quality in our rivers and coastal waters and making sure that the requirements of wildlife are taken into account along with drinking and bathing waer. Directives of the European Community in these areas have been effective; it would be helpful if the EC addressed itself to the problems of eutrophication, particularly phosphates.

France: Axes d'action du Ministère de l'environnement

M. GALLEMANT

Direction de la protection de la nature, Ministère de l'environnement, Paris, France

La panoplie des moyens juridiques applicables à la protection des zones humides en France a été déjà largement évoquée au cours de ce Colloque, aussi me contenterai-je de les énumérer, sans avoir la prétention d'être exhaustif.

- L'Etat, tout d'abord, dispose de la loi sur les parcs nationaux, de la loi du 10 juillet 1976 sur la protection de la nature et en particulier des réserves naturelles et des arrêtés de biotope, d'un opérateur foncier sur le littoral et les rivages des grands lacs: le conservatoire de l'espace littoral et des rivages lacustres. Il peut par exemple, dans le cadre des plans d'exposition aux risques naturels, préserver de l'urbanisation des zones inondables dans les lits majeurs des cours d'eau.

- Les collectivités locales ont également la possibilité d'agir sur la conservation des zones humides: les communes, grâce à leur plan d'occupation des sols, les départements avec la taxe départementale des espaces naturels sensibles, enfin les régions qui peuvent instaurer des politiques autonomes d'acquisiton et de gestion d'espaces naturels comme c'est le cas dans le Nord du Pas de Calais ou en Alsace. Je citerai ici les parcs naturels régionaux, qui bien que ne pouvant servir directement à la protection des zones humides, permettent par leur rôle de coordination et de concertation entre leurs membres d'aboutir à la mise en place de politiques cohérentes de protection et de gestion des espaces naturels.

- Pour terminer ce rapide inventaire, je me dois de citer le rôle, de plus en plus important, que peuvent jouer les associations de protection de la nature ou même de chasseurs grâce notamment aux réserves naturelles volontaires, aux réserves libres et aux conservatoires des sites régionaux qu'elles mettent en place. Pour le Ministère de l'environnement, l'enjeu actuel de la protection des zones humides, n'est donc pas de créer des instruments réglementaires nouveaux mais plutôt de coordonner les moyens actuels et les acteurs qui les maîtrisent.

D'autres axes d'action sont également poursuivis par le Ministère de l'environnement:

- Tout d'abord et ainsi que l'ont signalé plusieurs intervenants, il s'agit de lever les obstacles à la protection des zones humides: aides publiques et avantages fiscaux accordés au drainage de ces zones, impôts fonciers élevés dans les régions des marais, héritage d'une époque où ces secteurs étaient considérés comme les plus riches pour l'agriculture. Bien entendu dans ce but des négociations sont entreprises avec le Ministère de l'agriculture, le Ministère des finances ou le Ministère de l'intérieur.

- En outre, une utilisation économique et sociale viable, conservant les caractéristiques fondamentales des zones humides est un atout majeur de protection de ces zones fragiles: dans ce but et afin de proposer des solutions alternatives à l'assèchement ou à l'abandon des zones humides, tous deux synonymes de banalisation et de dégradation de la richesse écologique, le ministère apporte également une aide à la recherche de systèmes de gestion de ces zones qui préservent leur intérêt biologique.

Il s'appuie pour cela largement sur le réseau des espaces protégés, comme autant de territoires d'expérience, et veut promouvoir une large diffusion des résultats acquis, ce que traduit en particulier la création, à la direction de la protection de la nature, d'un atelier technique des espaces naturels.

A terme, il s'agit de construire une véritable ingénierie du milieu naturel—enfin, une réflexion préalable a été engagée sur les possibilités de développement de contrats de gestion avec des agriculteurs en vue de la protection des zones naturelles sensibles et en particulier des zones humides. Sur ce sujet, il convient, en effet, d'avancer avec beaucoup de prudence car, comme l'ont souligné d'autres intervenants, ce type de pratique présente d'importants risques de "dérapages" défavorables.

Pour illustrer mon propos, je pense que la présentation d'un exemple concret d'application de ces divers instruments vous permettra de mieux comprendre la politique menée par le Ministère de l'environnement en matière de protection des zones humides.

Je vous parlerai donc du programme de protection et de gestion des marais de Carentan.

Cette zone humide complexe de plus de 20 000 ha est située en Normandie et coupe pratiquement en deux la presqu'île du Cotentin. Elle est constituée essentiellement de prairies inondables, de tourbières et de vasières, pour la partie en aval de la baie des Veys.

Elle présente un grand intérêt floristique, bien que le site botanique majeur, la tourbière de Baupte, ait été pratiquement détruit par une immense carrière. Mais elle est surtout connue pour sa grande richesse ornithologique, à la fois comme zone de nidification—râle des genets, grand courlis, anatidés—et comme zone de passage et d'hivernage sur l'axe de migration de la mer du Nord à l'Atlantique.

Cet intérêt a justifié son inscription au préinventaire des zones de protection spéciale de l'avifaune migratrice au titre de la Directive 79/409 de la C.E.E.

Conscient des menaces qui pesaient alors sur les marais et de la nécessité, pour protéger cet ensemble, de faire appel à de multiples moyens et à de multiples acteurs, le Ministère de l'environnement a mis en oeuvre en 1983 un programme pluriannuel, impliquant la participation de nombreux partenaires nationaux et locaux—conseil général, communes, associations de protection de la nature, associations de chasseurs, de pêcheurs, scientifiques, ONC, WWF, CEMAGREF.

Ce programme de plus de 4 M.F., qui a obtenu un financement de la C.E.E. au titre des actions communautaires pour l'environnement, a pour but de comprendre le fonctionnement de cet écosystème complexe, afin de le gérer et de le protéger.

Il regroupe donc des actions très variées:

- En matière d'hydraulique—puisque c'est un point fondamental pour les zones humides: étude de fonctionnement du système, recherche d'une gestion hydraulique compatible avec les intérêts des différents partenaires, acquisition de droit d'eau sur des ouvrages.

- En matière de biologie—inventaire très complet des sites majeurs pour la faune et la flore, à protéger en priorité, et étude de l'influence des diverses activités humaines sur la richesse du milieu.

- En matière d'agriculture—études de systèmes viables d'exploitation de la prairie naturelle.

- En matière de modes de gestion complémentaires des espaces naturels—élevage de troupeaux rustiques, récolte des roseaux.

Les résultats de ce programme, qui s'achève, ont permis la rédaction d'un "livre-blanc" qui décrit le fonctionnement et l'état des marais et propose aux différents acteurs des hypothèses d'évolution et des solutions de gestion et de protection.

L'aboutissement de ce programme sera une "charte" des zones humides par laquelle chacun des partenaires s'engagera à mettre en oeuvre les moyens dont il dispose pour gérer les marais de Carentan.

Ainsi la plupart des instruments que j'évoquais au début de mon intervention seront-ils utilisés, de façon coordonnée, pour réaliser un ensemble cohérent et fonctionnel de conservation et de gestion.

L'adoption de la charte permettra alors à la France de notifier à la Commission des Communautés européennes les marais de Carentan en tant que zone de protection spéciale de l'avifaune au titre de l'article 4 de la Directive 79/409 de la C.E.E.

Je pourrais vous donner d'autres exemples de cette politique concertée et contractuelle en faveur des zones humides: c'est ainsi que sont ou devraient être gérés la Camargue, la Brière, le Marais Poitevin, la Brenne, ou la Sologne.

Mais pour conclure ce rapide exposé en ouvrant le débat, je veux vous faire part des principales questions que se pose le Ministère de l'environnement en matière de droit de la protection des espaces naturels en général et des zones humides en particulier:

- Tout d'abord quelle peut être la portée juridique d'un engagement contractuel du type des "chartes", en particulier de celles des parcs naturels régionaux?

- Dans le même ordre d'idée, quelle serait la valeur, en droit international, de la notification d'une zone humide, soit au titre de la Convention de Ramsar, soit au titre de la Directive 79/409 sans que cette zone soit protégée par des mesures réglementaires en droit interne?

- Quelle serait la meilleure forme de contrat à passer avec des propriétaires ou des agriculteurs pour la gestion conservatrice des milieux naturels?

- Enfin, ne faudrait-il pas en France, à l'instar de ce qui existe dans d'autres pays, un instrument réglementaire spécifique permettant la protection des zones humides contre les atteintes dont elles sont l'objet, en particulier pour les zones humides de petites tailles ou à caractère diffus?

La campagne zones humides du WWF France

J.F. TERRASSE

Directeur scientifique du WWF France, La Garenne, France

En 1985, l'Union internationale pour la conservation de la nature (UICN) et le WWF international lançaient la campagne pour la protection des zones humides.

C'est dans ce cadre que la section française du WWF adressait un appel d'offres à près d'une centaine d'organismes, essentiellement des associations de protection de la nature regroupées au sein de la Fédération française des Sociétés de protection de la nature (FFSPN), des associations ornithologiques, la Fédération des parcs naturels régionaux, des parc nationaux, etc. ... couvrant l'ensemble de la France.

Le WWF France leur demandait de lui proposer des projets sur la protection des milieux naturels entrant dans la catégorie des zones humides mais aussi des espèces menacées liées à ces habitats ou non. Trois consultants étaient engagés pendant plusieurs mois pour rencontrer les auteurs de ces projets, étudier leurs propositions et rédiger les dossiers à l'intention d'un Comité consultatif de 30 personnes constitué à cet effet et comprenant des scientifiques, des juristes, des représentants des associations, de l'administration et des universités.

Ce Comité présidé par le Dr Luc Hoffmann, Vice-président du WWF international, avait la tâche difficile de sélectionner les meilleurs projets et les plus importants pour lesquels le WWF France, récemment réorganisé, devait rechercher les financements nécessaires à leur réalisation tout en assurant leur promotion dans les médias à l'intention du grand public afin d'obtenir son adhésion à cette entreprise.

Grâce au remarquable et efficace réseau d'associations couvrant l'ensemble de la France, un nombre important de projets de qualité était proposé au WWF France: 89 projets concernaient la protection des zones humides (milieux), et 50 celle des espèces menacées, dont 21 étaient liées aux zones humides (8 mammifères, 9 oiseaux, 2 reptiles, 2 amphibiens).

Cette réponse positive acquise en quelques semaines traduisait également la forte demande des associations et l'absence de financements publics pour des projets d'importance nationale, voire internationale.

Sur les 89 projets de protection des milieux, 40 étaient sélectionnés. Sur les 21 dossiers d'espèces liées aux zones humides, 5 (loutre, cigogne blanche, râle des genêts, sternes) étaient retenus, et 7 (ours, bouquetin des Pyrénées, chauves-souris, busard cendré, vautor fauve, gypaète barbu, tortue d'Hermann) sur les 29 projets concernant des espèces terrestres.

Les financements sollicités pour la réalisation de ces projets s'échelonnaient de 5.000 à 1.000.000 de francs.

On peut répartir les 89 projets concernant les zones humides en 5 grands groupes (tableau 1).

(a) Recherche (inventaires, études préliminaires)

Sur 15 projets, seulement 2 ont été sélectionnés, le Comité ayant jugé que le financement de la recherche n'était pas une vocation prioritaire du WWF. Mis à part un petit projet d'étude en vue de l'aménagement d'un étang littoral de la Côte d'Azur, le principal projet, présenté par l'Institut de Droit de l'Environnement, concerne le sujet essentiel de l'impact des politiques agricoles sur les zones humides.

(b) Maîtrise foncière (achat, location)

L'importance du nombre des projets présentés (16 achats, 7 locations) traduit une grosse demande des associations réalisant que seule la maîtrise foncière permet une gestion planifiée. 13 projets étaient sélectionnés représentant une proportion importante du budget total (9 achats, 4 locations).

Ces opérations, où le WWF ne devient ni propriétaire ni locataire, mais permet à l'association gestionnaire de le devenir, impliquent la participation quasi obligatoire d'autres partenaires: collectivités locales, Conservatoire du littoral, Fédération départementale des chasseurs, Office national de la chasse, Office national des forêts, Ministère de l'environnement, Délégation régionale à l'architecture et à l'environnement (DRAE) ...

Une certaine naïveté et un manque évident d'expérience en matière d'acquisition d'espace en milieu rural, l'apparition de conflits d'intérêts avec d'autres usagers (chasseurs, élus) faisaient rapidement échouer 4 projets importants. D'autres étaient réalisés (l'un malgré l'opposition des chasseurs en Meuse, l'autre grâce à leur appui dans la Manche) et cinq autres sont en attente avec une chance raisonnable d'aboutir.

(c) Gestion (aménagement)

C'est un lieu commun de dire qu'un pays comme la France est fait de paysages façonnés par l'homme. Les marais, les prairies humides, les étangs, les tourbières, sont exploitées d'une manière traditionnelle (pâturage, fauche, pisciculture) depuis des siècles. Que ces activités disparaissent ou se modifient et l'évolution de la végétation modifie rapidement non seulement le paysage, mais aussi la composition de la flore et de la faune souvent dans le sens d'un appauvrissement de la diversité. Il est donc normal que les associations se préoccupent de la gestion dans le sens d'une diversité génétique maximum.

L'utilisation de races rustiques pour maîtriser la végétation à un stade choisi (vache nantaise en Brière, boeuf écossais et chevaux de Camargue au Marais Vernier et en Brenne, moutons à l'Ile de Ré, etc. ...) est une méthode en plein développement permettant d'allier économie et conservation du milieu. D'autres

Tableau 1

La campagne zones humides du WWF France

Septembre 1985 – Septembre 1987

Projets proposés	Nombre	Pourcentage	Sélection	Budget	En cours	Terminé	Echec
Recherche (Inventaire, études préliminaires)	15	17	2	183.000	1	1	0
Maîtrise foncière (achat, location)	23	26	13	2.105.000	5	4	4
Gestion (aménagement)	12	13	7	744.000	4	3	0
Equipement (Observatoire, bateau, optique, etc. ...)	15	17	5	668.000	2	3	0
Information (dépliant, brochure, audiovisuel)	24	27	13	542.000	6	7	0
Total	89	100	40	3.498.000	18	18	4

aménagements de type hydraulique permettent de rétablir le fonctionnement des zones humides abusivement drainées ou de recréer des sites de nidifications pour des espèces sensibles (sternes, flamants roses).

(d) Equipement

Un autre souci des associations gestionnaires d'un espace protégé: comment permettre son accès au public, favoriser la découverte de la nature, utiliser cet espace comme un outil pédagogique. Les 5 projets sélectionnés concernent la construction d'observatoires et de bâtiments d'accueil sur des sites déjà en réserves en Camargue, en Brenne, en Vendée, dans les Landes et en Alsace.

(e) Information

Complémentaire du précédent, ce type de projets répond à la forte demande d'un public de plus en plus nombreux qui souhaite recevoir sur les lieux de la découverte toutes les informations nécessaires à la compréhension de ce qu'il observe: audio-visuels, films, brochures, dépliants, réalisés par les associations et qui s'ajoutent aux nombreux documents élaborés et diffusés par le WWF.

Conclusion

Deux ans est une durée bien trop courte pour une campagne de ce type et il est évident qu'elle se poursuivra longtemps encore.

Néanmoins, cette durée a été suffisante pour réaliser, avec une structure très légère, près de 50% des objectifs de la campagne. Le WWF France n'a pas la prétention d'avoir "sauvé" les zones humides mais la campagne a créé une dynamique nouvelle et apporte un complément pratique et concret à d'autres actions comme celles lancées avec le concours de certaines DRAE. Elle a permis de créer de nouveaux liens avec les associations, l'administration, les élus, qui débouchent sur de nouvelles actions sans doute mieux ciblées et mieux préparées.

La campagne du WWF a été à l'origine de centaines d'articles dans la presse sur le rôle et l'intérêt des zones humides. Cette campagne est tombée au bon moment, avec les problèmes de la déprise agricole et du devenir des terres marginales, et a servi de révélateur des besoins immenses en ce domaine.

De vastes zones humides sont à vendre en France depuis un an et il y a là une opportunité à saisir.

Bien entendu le WWF poursuivra cette campagne même si de nouveaux thèmes d'une actualité plus brûlante apparaissent.

Conclusions de la première partie

La recherche juridique

JEAN UNTERMAIER

Professeur à l'Université Jean Moulin Lyon III, Lyon, France

La Conférence internationale de Lyon (23-26 septembre 1987) sur les problèmes juridiques de protection des zones humides a confirmé, s'il en était besoin, l'importance du droit, dans tous les pays, pour la conservation de ces zones. Il a été souligné également que le droit des zones humides pouvait apporter une utile contribution à la science juridique en général ainsi qu'au développement de notre connaissance de l'environnement, de la société et de leurs relations mutuelles.

Cependant, les travaux de la Conférence ont révélé des lacunes, certes normales dans un domaine qui ne suscite que depuis peu de temps l'intérêt des juristes, mais néanmoins préoccupantes.

En ce qui concerne le droit positif de la protection et de la gestion des zones humides, les données dont nous diposons sont très incomplètes. En de nombreux Etats sinon des régions entières, l'information fait entièrement défaut ou presque. Certains mécanismes d'un intérêt considérable pour les zones humides, en particulier le droit coutumier, sont fort mal connus. De surcroît, dans une écrasante majorité de pays, nous manquons de renseignements sur les modalités d'application de la législation. Enfin, le traitement même de l'information juridique disponible laisser à désirer: d'une part les études, voire les simples commentaires de la législation sont rares; leur diffusion, d'autre part, n'est pas correctement assurée.

Ces constatations ont conduit les participants à reconnaître la nécessité d'une intensification de la recherche en droit des zones humides, ce qui implique la mise en oeuvre de certains moyens.

Le développement de la recherche en droit des zones humides

Si la Conférence de Lyon ne pouvait avoir pour mission d'établir un programme de recherche, elle se devait en revanche de présenter des suggestions.

A. Plusieurs disciplines ou sous-disciplines juridiques qui concernent plus directement que d'autres les milieux naturels ou peu humanisés, devraient en tant que telles faire l'objet de travaux approfondis.

On a mentionné, entre autres:

- le droit rural, public et privé: réglementation du drainage et de l'aménagement foncier en général, législation des baux ruraux;

- le droit privé, souvent négligé par les spécialistes de l'environnement en dépit de l'intérêt qu'il peut présenter dans le contexte du développement de protections non réglementaires;

- le droit financier et fiscal: les débats ont mis en évidence qu'il contenait souvent des entraves à la conservation; de plus, des recherches devraient être conduites en ce secteur, en collaboration avec d'autes disciplines (économie, sociologie politique), afin d'étudier les mécanismes de péréquation et de mettre au point de nouveaux procédés de financement de la protection;

- la science administrative: étude des processus de décision dans le domaine de l'aménagement du territoire et de la gestion des ressources et des milieux naturels;

- le droit international, y compris le droit communautaire.

B. Divers mécanismes, institutions ou problèmes méritent une attention particulière; par exemple:

(a) Les obstacles juridiques à la protection des zones humides, lesquels ne sont évidemment pas seulement d'ordre financier ou fiscal. De plus, il serait opportun de s'attacher aussi aux dispositions favorables, afin d'en permettre le maintien ou, à défaut, le remplacement sans dommage pour l'environnement.

(b) Parmi les mécanismes particulièrement importants pour les zones humides, ont été cités:

- le principe de compensation (mitigation) et ses modalités d'application;

- les servitudes de droit privé et les servitudes administratives. Ces dernières posent, en plusieurs pays, la difficile question de leur indemnisation éventuelle;

- les techniques et les institutions de planification, d'aménagement et d'utilisation du sol en général;

- les mécanismes conventionnels.

(c) Les inventaires scientifiques; étape préliminaire de toutes les politiques modernes de protection, ils suscitent maintes interrogations; ainsi:

- comment intégrer les résultats dans la planification et les décisions d'aménagement du territoire?

- comment passer, si cela s'avère souhaitable, de l'inventaire à la protection de la zone considérée?

(d) Il a encore été relevé que le problème de la définition juridique des zones humides demeurait en suspens tant dans une majorité de droits nationaux qu'au plan international; en conséquence, la réflexion sur des critères d'identification doit être poursuivie.

Des participants ont d'ailleurs émis des propositions en ce sens et évoqué la possibilité de constituer un atlas international ou une cartographie (écologique et juridique) des zones humides.

(e) Enfin, l'unanimité s'est faite sur la nécessité d'étudier concrètement l'application du droit de la conservation; il est en effet paradoxal de constater que souvent l'on ne dispose d'aucune indication sur l'efficacité des règles ou des institutions de protection.

Au total, il est clair que les axes de réflexion ne manquent pas. Se pose dès lors le problème des moyens de la recherche en science juridique.

Conclusions de la deuxième partie

La pratique

FRANÇOISE BURHENNE-GUILMIN

Chef du Centre du droit de l'environnement de l'UICN, Bonn, Allemagne

Le Professeur Untermaier vous a parlé des thèmes à approfondir; je suis persuadée que vous enrichirez la liste des thèmes qu'il vous a soumis. Je voudrais maintenant vous livrer quelques réflexions sur les moyens nécessaires à une mise en chantier d'une telle tâche.

Il me semble évident qu'après l'intérêt qu'a suscité l'échange de vues que nous avons eu, le dialogue devrait continuer.

Ma première conclusion est donc la nécessité de continuer et d'élargir la communication entre les juristes intéressés par les problèmes des zones humides ou ceux qui s'en occupent activement. C'est l'idée, entendue au départ, d'une conférence permanente, ou plus simplement, d'un réseau de spécialistes.

Ce réseau pourrait avoir plusieurs fonctions:

● D'une part, il aurait une fonction d'échange d'informations entre ses membres, pour leurs propres bénéfices.

● D'autre part, il pourrait, lorsque cela se révèle nécessaire, et sur demande, fournir un apport technique à la Convention de Ramsar, dans le cadre des recommandations de la Conférence des Parties sur l'utilisation rationnelle des zones humides.

● En outre, ce réseau pourrait servir de moteur à un processus d'approfondissement des thèmes juridiques dont nous avons parlé plus haut.

● Enfin, il pourrait servir à l'établissement d'un dialogue juridique qui ne serait pas seulement Nord/Nord mais également Nord/Sud.

Nous sommes en face d'un problème qui, par beaucoup d'aspects, est réellement mondial. Or, il est évident à celui qui a travaillé dans le domaine sur une base comparative qu'il y a une énorme lacune dans notre information sur le droit des pays en voie de développement.

Cependant, une analyse législative, aussi nécessaire et utile qu'elle soit, ne permet pas de connaître et de comprendre le fonctionnement pratique et l'efficacité des institutions. Il faut pour cela de vraies études de terrain pour lesquelles un réseau de correspondants est également indispensable.

Ma seconde conclusion anticipe déjà sur la création du réseau.

Aucune des tâches que j'ai suggérées plus haut ne peut se réaliser sans l'accomplissement d'un travail de base sur la question. Il ne s'agit pas seulement de l'établissement d'une documentation ou d'une banque de données, mais bien de l'établissement de ce qui j'appelle l'état juridique de l'environnement. Nous faisons bien à l'heure actuelle des rapports ou des bilans sur l'état de l'environnement. Ils brillent par l'absence—et pour cause—d'analyses de la situation juridique.

Je sais que c'est une tâche qui se rapproche peut-être de celle de Sisyphe, mais je ne pense pas qu'elle soit impossible, car elle peut être faite brique par brique et degré par degré.

Dan Navid nous a par exemple dit qu'une information succincte sur les aspects nationaux de la protection serait déjà une contribution appréciable aux travaux de la Convention de Ramsar.

C'est un début. Au-delà de cet immédiat se situe un inventaire des mécanismes nationaux utilisés pour la protection des zones humides. A l'horizon lointain se dessinent des analyses comparatives—la recherche, en somme, de deux buts: d'une part, celle de l'avancement de la science juridique de la protection de la nature, que je ne considère pas du tout comme un but théorique en soi, mais bien pratique; d'autre part, l'avancement du droit de la protection de la nature sur le terrain.

Les deux buts se rejoignent: il s'agit principalement de développer des législations adéquates là où il y a, soit des obstacles, soit des vides juridiques.

L'idée n'est pas utopique. Il est une foule de mesures pratiques qui pourrait y contribuer. Je pense ici, par exemple, à un réseau de coordination des programmes universitaires ou de recherche: un autre réseau de communication à créer.

Je suis persuadée que le noyau moteur d'une telle initiative pourrait être constitué par le programme du droit de l'environnement de l'UICN, la SFDE et le Centre de droit de l'environnement de l'Université Jean Moulin. Mais bien d'autres, j'en suis sûre, se joindraient à ceux-ci.

Annexe 1

Questionnaire relatif aux problèmes juridiques de protection des zones humides

1 Votre pays compte-t-il une ou plusieurs zones humides que l'on peut considérer, au point de vue écologique, comme:

        exceptionnelles   Oui / Non

        très intéressantes   Oui / Non

        moyennement intéressantes   Oui / Non

2 Le statut foncier des zones humides

    2-1 La propriété des zones humides

        2-1-1 Les zones humides de la liste (p. 188) ou certaines d'entre elles sont-elles la propriété de l'Etat ou d'une autre personne publique?

        2-1-2 ... la propriété de personnes privées?

        2-1-3 ... la propriété d'organismes d'intérêt général?

        (Organismes privés ou de nature indéterminée. Par exemple: association de protection de la nature, fondation reconnue d'utilité publique.)

        2-1-4 ... ou sont-elles insusceptibles d'appropriation au sens habituel du mot?

        (Considérées, par exemple, comme des "choses communes".)

    2-2 Régime de protection des zones humides et système de propriété

        2-2-1 Existe-t-il des dispositions juridiques propres aux zones humides appartenant à l'Etat ou à d'autres personnes publiques?

        2-2-2 ... ou la réglementation s'applique-t-elle, au contraire, indifféremment aux zones publiques ou privées?

    2-3 Les politiques d'acquisition foncière

        2-3-1 L'Etat ou d'autres personnes publiques ou des organismes d'intérêt général ont-ils procédé à l'acquisition de zones humides à des fins de protection?

2-3-2 Ces actions foncières sont-elles importantes?

2-3-3 Le cas échéant, à quels obstacles se heurtent-elles?

2-4 Zones humides et structures foncières

2-4-1 Certaines régions humides ou zones humides sont-elles caractérisées par l'existence ou la prédominance de grandes, voire de très grandes propriétés?

2-4-2 Existe-t-il des dispositions réglementant la division des propriétés foncières rurales ou visant à empêcher leur morcellement?

2-4-3 Existe-t-il des institutions permettant des actions collectives ou une gestion coordonnée des propriétés rurales privées?

2-5 Zones humides et fiscalité foncière

2-5-1 Existe-t-il un impôt foncier?

2-5-2 Existe-t-il des impositions frappant les terres incultes, à l'abandon, ou insuffisamment exploitées?

(Au sens du présent questionnaire, le mot "imposition" désigne indistinctement les impôts, taxes, redevances, taxes parafiscales, etc. Veuillez préciser, le cas échéant, la personne ou l'organisme *bénéficiaire* de ces prélèvements.)

2-5-3 D'une manière générale, pensez-vous que la fiscalité soit, dans votre pays, favorable (ou plutôt favorable) au maintien en l'état des zones humides ou estimez-vous, au contraire, que la fiscalité constitue une incitation à l'assèchement ou à la transformation de ces zones?

3 La protection des zones humides

3-1 Les zones humides ou certaines d'entre elles, font-elles l'objet d'une législation ou d'une réglementation spécifique?

(Par exemple: loi sur la protection des zones humides; loi sur les tourbières).

3-2 A défaut d'une législation spécifique, le droit général de la protection de l'environnement contient-il des dispositions particulières applicables aux zones humides ou à certaines d'entre elles?

(Par exemple: dans une loi sur les produits chimiques, un article sur l'utilisation des pesticides dans les zones humides; dans la législation relative aux réserves naturelles, un régime spécial pour les réserves naturelles concernant les zones humides.)

3-3 Aires naturelles protégées et zones humides (voir table ci-contre)

3-3-1 Certaines institutions de protection des milieux naturels concernent-elles des zones humides?

Tableau 1

Aires naturelles protégées et zones humides (question 3-3)

La question 3-3 demandait d'indiquer quels types d'aires protégées sont utilisées pour chaque type de zones humides. La version originale du questionnaire comprenait un tableau, divisé en cases, où les types de zones humides apparaissaient horizontalement, et les types d'aires protégées verticalement. Il suffisait donc de marquer les cases appropriées, et d'expliquer la réponse. Le tableau ci-dessous indique les types d'aires protégées et les types de zones humides en question.

Types d'aires naturelles protégées	*Types de zones humides*
Parc national	Lac
Parc régional	Etang
Réserve naturelle	Cours d'eau
Réserve cynégétique	Plan d'eau artificiel
Réserve halieutique	Marais de l'intérieur
Autre réserve à but particulier	Marais du littoral
	Mangrove
Site ou monument naturel	Autre zone humide littorale[1]
Zone protégée par des documents d'urbanisme ou d'aménagement du territoire	Tourbière
	Prairie inondable
Autre aire naturelle protégée	Autre milieu inondé ou inondable[2]
	Autre type de zone humide

1. Par exemple, vasière, pré salé, saline.
2. Par exemple, forêt riveraine, plan d'eau temporaire ou épisodique.

3-3-2 Lesquelles et quels types de zones?

(Veuillez utiliser le tableau ci-dessous en cochant la case correspondante et commenter votre réponse.)

3-4 Les autorités de protection

3-4-1 La protection des zones humides relève-t-elle de l'Etat ou d'une autre autorité publique[1]?

Etat

Région ou Etat membre

Collectivité locale

Autorité autre que l'Etat ou les collectivités locales[2]

3-4-2 Dans le cas où l'Etat est compétent en matière de protection des zones humides, ces compétences sont-elles exercées par un ministre spécialisé en matière de protection de la nature ou par un autre ministre?

3-4-3 Les compétences de l'Etat sont-elles exercées par un ministre spécialisé en matière de protection de la nature ou par un autre ministre?

(Par exemple: ministre de l'agriculture, ministre de l'aménagement du territoire, etc.)

3-5 Votre pays compte-t-il des zones humides que vous jugez intéressantes par leur superficie et/ou leurs qualités écologiques et qui ne disposent *d'aucune* protection spécifique?

3-6 Existe-t-il des servitudes protégeant ou pouvant concourir à la protection des zones humides?

(Par exemple: interdiction d'édifier le long d'un fleuve des clôtures ou ouvrages susceptibles de gêner l'écoulement des eaux; interdiction de construire des ouvrages susceptibles de modifier le régime hydraulique.)

3-7 Zones humides et protection des espèces

3-7-1 Certaines espèces animales ou végétales inféodées aux zones humides sont-elles protégées?

3-7-2 Lesquelles?

(Ne citer, le cas échéant, que les espèces strictement dépendantes d'un milieu humide.)

---

1. Veuillez cocher la case correspondante.
2. Par exemple: Agence nationale, organisme agréé, conservatoire, etc.

3-8 La protection de telle ou telle zone humide peut-elle être réalisée par voie de *convention* entre, d'une part, l'Etat ou une autre collectivité ou institution publique ou privée (par exemple, association de propriétaires) et des personnes privées, d'autre part?

3-9 Existe-t-il des dispositions fiscales ou réglementaires concourant à la protection ou fournissant une gestion écologiquement satisfaisante des zones humides?

(Par exemple: taxes ou autres impositions affectées à l'acquisition de zones humides; obligation d'effectuer les travaux d'entretien des berges d'un cours d'eau en se conformant à diverses obligations.)

3-10 Existe-t-il des usages ou des dispositions coutumières concourant à la protection ou favorisant une gestion écologiquement satisfaisante des zones humides?

(Par exemple: droit de pâturage collectif dans les prairies inondables.)

3-11 Existe-t-il des procédures permettant la création ou l'aménagement de zones dans le but de favoriser des espèces animales ou végétales liées aux milieux humides?

(Par exemple: création d'îlots artificiels pour la nidification des sternes, de vasières pour les limicoles; aménagement de milieux ouverts pour l'hivernage des grues.)

3-12 Lorsque sont réalisés de grands travaux d'équipement (par exemple: construction d'une autoroute, d'un barrage hydro-électrique), est-il possible de réaliser également des aménagements susceptibles de limiter ou de compenser l'impact de l'ouvrage sur le milieu naturel?

3-13 En cas de destruction ou de dégradation illégale d'une zone humide, existe-t-il des procédures de remise en l'état ou de restauration du milieu?

3-14 Dans les zones alluviales subissant des crues périodiques, existe-t-il une protection du champ d'inondation?

3-15 Les zones humides et la jurisprudence

3-15-1 Les juridictions de votre pays ont-elles eu l'occasion d'intervenir en matière de protection des zones humides?

3-15-2 Quels commentaires cette jurisprudence vous inspire-t-elle?

3-16 Protection des zones humides par l'éducation des personnes concernées

3-16-1 Existe-t-il des lignes directrices préparées par l'administration, des organisations agricoles ou de protection de la nature relative à la gestion écologique des zones humides?

(Par exemple, éviter de cruper la végétation aquatique en période de nidification)

3-16-2 Si c'est le cas, indiquer la mesure dans laquelles ces lignes directrices sont observées:

par les autorités administratives

par les particuliers

4 Les activités susceptibles de détruire ou de dégrader les zones humides

4-1 La réglementation des activités susceptibles d'affecter les zones humides

4-1-1 Ces activités sont-elles réglementées?

4-1-2 Selon quelles modalités? (voir tableau ci-contre)

4-1-3 *L'élevage* dans les zones humides fait-il l'objet d'une réglementation particulière?

4-2 *La chasse* dans les zones humides fait-elle l'objet d'une réglementation particulière?

4-3 *La pêche* dans les zones humides fait-elle l'objet d'une réglementation particulière?

4-4 Lorsqu'elle existe, la réglementation des introductions ou réintroductions d'espèces animales ou végétales comporte-t-elle des dispositions spéciales pour les zones humides?

4-5 Les opérations d'assainissement, de drainage, d'assèchement

4-5-1 Peuvent-elles être réalisées par:

l'Etat

une autre autorité publique

un organisme particulier bénéficiant d'une aide ou d'une reconnaissance officielle[1]

(Veuillez répondre par oui ou par non et commenter votre réponse.)

4-5-2 Peuvent-elles bénéficier de l'expropriation?

4-5-3 Peuvent-elles bénéficier d'autres prérogatives de puissance publique?

4-5-4 Peuvent-elles être imposées par une autorité publique ou privée, pour des motifs:

agricoles

sanitaires

---

1. Par exemple: association syndicale de propriétaires.

Tableau 2

La réglementation des activités susceptibles d'affecter les zones humides (question 4-1)

La question 4-1 demandait d'indiquer les méthodes utilisées pour contrôler certains types d'activités. La version originale du questionnaire comprenait un tableau, divisé en cases, où les méthodes de contrôle étaient indiquées horizontalement, et les activités verticalement. Il s'agissait donc de marquer les cases appropriées, et d'expliquer la réponse. Plusieurs cases pouvaient être marquées pour la même activité. Pour les activités qui sont soumises à des controles généraux, il était demandé de mentionner les dispositions spécifiquement applicables aux zones humides, ou l'absence de telles dispositions.

Opération ou activité	*Modalités de la réglementation*
Agriculture (principalement)	Autorisation de l'Etat
1. Assèchement/suppression d'une zone humide	
2. Assainissement/drainage	Autorisation de la région ou de l'Etat fédéré
3. Changement de culture ou du mode d'exploitation agricole. Intensification de l'exploitation.	Autorisation émanant d'une autre autorité
4. Remembrement rural	
5. Autres travaux d'aménagement rural	Autorisation d'une autorité de protection de l'environnement
Exploitation	
6. de la tourbe	
7. de la végétation aquatique (roseaux par exemple)	Consultation d'une autorité de protection
8. d'autres produits naturels	
9. de matériaux	Etude d'impact
Depot de	
10. déchets ménagers	Autre forme de réglementation
11. déchets industriels	
Circulation	Pas de réglementation
12. du public	
13. des bateaux	
14. des aéronefs (survol)	
Ouvrages et installations	
15. pisciculture	
16. base de loisirs	
17. construction à usage d'habitation ou autre	
18. barrage	
19. autres ouvrages hydrauliques	
20. autres ouvrages (par ex. lignes électriques)	
21. prise d'eau	
22. rejet d'eau	

de protection contre les eaux

de production d'énergie

autres

pour n'importe quel motif d'intérêt général

(Veuillez répondre par oui ou par non et commenter votre réponse.)

4-5-5   Peuvent-elles bénéficier d'un régime fiscal favorable?

(Par exemple: exonération totale ou partielle des taxes foncières; déductions diverses; crédits d'impôt, etc.)

4-5-6   Quelle est l'autorité compétente pour définir l'assiette et pour fixer le taux des impositions susceptibles d'affecter les zones humides?

(Le mot "imposition" est utilisé dans le sens indiqué à la question 2-5-2.)

4-5-7   Peuvent-elles bénéficier d'aides:

de l'Etat

d'un Etat fédéré ou d'une région

d'une autre autorité publique

d'un organisme d'intérêt général[1]

d'une organisation internationale ou d'une institution supranationale

(Veuillez répondre par oui ou par non.)

Quelles formes ces aides peuvent-elles revêtir?

Subventions

Prêts à des conditions spéciales

Autres

(Veuillez répondre par oui ou par non.)

4-5-8   Peuvent-elles être financées par une imposition spéciale?

(voir questions 2-5-2 et 4-5-6.)

4-5-9   Sont-elles soumises à étude d'impact?

---

1. voir question 2-1-3.

5   Questions générales

5-1   (Le cas échéant) L'absence de protection spéciale des zones humides dans votre pays s'explique-t-elle par l'absence de problèmes de conservation ou par d'autres considérations?

5-2   Quelles observations la législation de votre pays concernant les zones humides, considérée dans son ensemble, vous inspire-t-elle?

5-3   Comment pensez-vous qu'il soit possible de l'améliorer?

Définitions

Aire naturelle protégée: Territoire soumis à un régime juridique spécifique dans un but de protection de la nature. Au sens du présent questionnaire, l'expression "aire naturelle protégée" désigne aussi bien des espaces bénéficiant d'une protection générale (par exemple: parcs nationaux, parcs naturels régionaux, state parks, réserves naturelles) que des réserves à but particulier (par exemple: réserves cynégétiques, réserves botaniques ...).

Assainissement agricole: Ensemble des opérations ayant pour objectif l'évacuation de l'eau considérée comme excédentaire dans le sol, y compris l'établissement de rigoles, de fossés et de conduits collectifs permettant l'écoulement des eaux, en particulier des eaux de ruissellement et de celles venant du drainage.

Assèchement: Opération aboutissant à la disparition d'une zone humide.

Champ d'inondation: L'expression désigne les zones plus ou moins régulièrement submergées par les crues d'un cours d'eau. Synonymes: lit majeur (en français), flood plain (en anglais).

Décentralisation: Système d'administration consistant à permettre à une collectivité humaine (commune, département, région, etc. ...) de s'administrer elle-même sous le contrôle de l'Etat. Une collectivité décentralisée dispose de la personnalité juridique, d'autorités et de ressources propres.

Déconcentration: Système consistant à confier certaines compétences de l'Etat central à des autorités qui sont en fonction dans différentes circonscriptions administratives.

Drainage: Opération ayant pour but l'évacuation de l'eau considérée comme excédentaire dans le sol, en général par un système de drains enterrés. En anglais, le terme "drainage" désigne les trois types d'opérations respectivement qualifiées en français de: drainage, assainissement agricole, aménagement de rivière.

Etat: Dans le présent questionnaire le terme désigne indifféremment un Etat unitaire ou un Etat fédéral. Dans le cas d'un Etat fédéral, les collectivités politiques qui le composent (Etat américain, canton suisse, Land, etc.) sont désignées par l'expression: Etat fédéré.

Région humide: Territoire présentant une certaine unité bio-géographique et possédant une importante concentration de zones humides. Exemple: la Dombes (France), qui compte un millier d'étangs répartis sur un territoire de 110.000 hectares environ.

Remembrement rural: Opération consistant à imposer aux propriétaires ruraux, dans le cadre d'un plan d'ensemble des échanges de parcelles de terrains dispersés, en vue d'aboutir à une structure foncière moins morcelée.

Zones humides: Zones de marais, marécages, tourbières ou eau libre, qu'elles soient naturelles ou artificielles, permanentes ou temporaires, que l'eau soit stagnante ou courante, douce, saumâtre ou salée, incluant les eaux côtières jusqu'à une profondeur de six mètres à marée basse.

Liste des catégories de zones humides visées dans le questionnaire[1]

Lacs

Etangs

Cours d'eau[2]

Marais et marécages

Plans d'eau artificiels

Tourbières

Zones humides littorales (par exemple: prés-salés, vasières, milieux lagunaires, mangroves). Milieux inondés ou inondables (par exemple: prairies inondables, creux d'eau temporaires, forêts riveraines).

---

1. Cette liste, établie essentiellement à partir des zones humides européennes, *n'est pas limitative*.
2. S'agissant de rivières, fleuves, torrents, etc., le questionnaire se préoccupe surtout des parties peu profondes de ces cours d'eau: berges, gravières, bras morts ...

Annex 2

Questionnaire on legal issues relating to the conservation of wetlands

1 Does your country contain one or more wetlands which can be considered, from the ecological point of view, to be:

Exceptional	Yes/No
Very interesting	Yes/No
Moderately interesting	Yes/No

2 Wetlands in the law of real property

    2-1 Property in wetlands

        2-1-1 Are the types of wetlands listed on p. 198 (or any of them) the property of the State or other public bodies?

        2-1-2 ... the property of private persons?

        2-1-3 ... the property of public interest asociations?

        (Associations of a private or indeterminate character, such as nature conservation organizations, recognized public interest groups.)

        2-1-4 ... or are they not susceptible to acquisition in the accepted sense of the term?

        (For example, are they subject to communal rights?)

    2-2 The system of protection of wetlands and the property regime

        2-2-1 Are there any legal provisions specifically applying to wetlands owned by the State or other public bodies?

        2-2-2 ... or do such provisions apply to such areas whether in public or private ownership?

    2-3 Land acquisition policies

        2-3-1 Has the State, or have other public bodies or public interest associations, undertaken the acquisition of wetlands with a view to protecting them?

        2-3-2 Are these acquisitions of significance?

2-3-3   When they occur, what obstacles must be overcome?

2-4   Wetlands and the system of land ownership

2-4-1   Are any wetland regions or wetlands characterized by the existence of large or even very large land-holdings?

2-4-2   Are there any legal rules which regulate the division of rural land-holdings or which aim to prevent their fragmentation?

2-4-3   Are there any institutions which allow collaborative action or coordinated management in respect of privately-owned rural land?

2-5   Wetlands and land taxation

2-5-1   Does a land tax exist?

2-5-2   Is there any tax burden imposed on uncultivated, abandoned or insufficiently worked land?

(For the purposes of this questionnaire, the word "tax" includes all taxes, duties, dues, production or other levies, etc. Please specify, where appropriate, the person or body benefitting from these deductions.)

2-5-3   In general terms, is it your opinion that the tax system in your country is favourable (or on the whole favourable) to the maintenance of wetlands in their present state or that the tax system amounts to an incentive to the reclamation or alteration of such areas?

3   Protection of wetlands

3-1   Are wetlands (or any of them) the subject of specific legislation or regulation?

(For example, wetland protection law, laws concerning peat-bogs or turf-moors.)

3-2   In the absence of specific legislation, does the general law of environmental protection contain any provisions particularly applicable to wetlands or to certain wetlands?

(For example, a section in an Act dealing with chemicals which regulates the use of pesticides on wetlands; or special provision in protected areas legislation for such areas in respect of wetlands.)

3-3   Protected areas and wetlands (see Table 1, opposite)

3-3-1   Do any of the existing mechanisms for the protection of natural sites apply to wetlands?

3-3-2   If so, which mechanisms and to which types of area do they apply?

Table 1

Protected areas and wetlands (Question 3-3)

To answer Question 3-3, respondents are asked to outline which types of protected area are used for each type of wetland. The original version of the Questionnaire included a chart marked into boxes, with the types of wetland along the top, and the types of protected area along the side. Respondents were asked to tick the appropriate boxes, and to explain their answers. This table lists the types of protected area and the types of wetland involved.

Types of protected area	*Types of wetland*
National Park	Lake
Regional Park	Pond/Mere
Nature Reserve	Water-course
Hunting Reserve	Man-made body of water
Fishing Reserve	Inland marsh
Other Reserves established for specific purposes	Coastal marsh
	Mangrove
Natural Site or Monument	Other coastal wetland[1]
Site protected by applicable land-use planning schemes	Peat-bog
	Grassland susceptible to flooding
Other Protected Area	Other site flooded or susceptible to flooding[2]
	Other types of wetland

1. For example, mudflats, saltings, salt-marsh
2. For example, riverine forest, temporary or periodic body of water

3-4   Authorities with responsibility for protection

3-4-1   Is protection of wetlands the responsibility of the State or of another public authority[1]?

State

Region or component State (in federal systems)

Local Authority

Authority other than State or local authority[2]

3-4-2   Where the State has responsibility for the protection of wetlands, is this responsibility exercised at the central level or devolved upon other authorities?

3-4-3   Are the responsibilities of the State discharged by a Minister with specific responsibility for the protection of nature or by another Minister?

(For example, Minister for Land-Use Planning, etc.)

3-5   Does your country have any wetlands which (in your opinion) are of interest by virtue of their extent and/or of their ecological qualities but which enjoy *no* specific protection?

3-6   Are there any land obligations which contribute to or are compatible with the protection of wetlands?

(For example, prohibitions on the construction on a riverside of enclosures or other works which may impede the flow of water; prohibition on construction of works which may affect the hydrology of a water-course.)

3-7   Species protection and wetlands

3-7-1   Are any animal or plant species associated with wetlands protected?

3-7-2   If so, which?

(Only list those species *strictly* dependent on wetlands.)

3-8   Are any wetlands protected by means of an agreement between the State, or other authority or public or private institution (such as an association of land-owners), and private persons?

3-9   Are there any tax or regulatory provisions which coincide with the protection or which contribute to the ecologically acceptable management of wetlands?

---

1. Please tick as appropriate.
2. For example, national agency, designated organization.

(For example, taxes or other charges used for acquisition of wetlands; duty to maintain the banks of a water-course.)

3-10 Are there any usages or customary rules which coincide with the protection or which contribute to the ecologically acceptable management of wetlands?

(For example, communal grazing rights in water-meadows.)

3-11 Are there any procedures providing for the establishment or management of areas with the purpose of encouraging plant or animal species associated with wetlands?

(For example, creation of artificial islands as nest sites for terns; mudflats for waders; management of open spaces as watering grounds for cranes.)

3-12 In the carrying out of major engineering works (such as the building of a highway, or dam for the generation of hydro-electric power), is it also possible to make arrangements which may limit or compensate for the impact of the project on the natural environment?

3-13 Are there procedures for reinstatement or restoration of wetlands which have been illegally destroyed or degraded?

3-14 In alluvial areas subject to periodic flooding, is there any legal protection for the flood-plain?

3-15 Wetlands and case-law

   3-15-1 Have the courts in your country played any role in the protection of wetlands?

   3-15-2 What remarks have you to offer on their intervention?

3-16 Protection of wetlands through the education of the persons involved

   3-16-1 Are there any guidelines issued by the public authorities, agricultural organizations or nature conservation bodies setting out instructions for the ecologically sound management of wetlands?

   (For example, avoiding the cutting of aquatic vegetation during the nesting season.)

   3-16-2 If so, please indicate the extent to which these guidelines are observed:

      by public authorities;

      by private persons.

4 Activities which may lead to the destruction or degradation of wetlands

  4-1 Control over activities which may affect wetlands

    4-1-1 Are these activities controlled?

4-1-2 By what means? (See Table 2, opposite)

4-1-3 Is *stock-farming* on wetlands the subject of specific control?

4-2 Is *hunting* on wetlands the subject of specific control?

4-3 Is *fishing* on wetlands the subject of specific control?

4-4 If there is any control over the introduction or re-introduction of plant and animal species, does that control contain any special provision for wetlands?

4-5 Drainage and reclamation operations

4-5-1 May these be carried out by:

> The State
>
> Another public authority
>
> A private organization enjoying official support or recognition[1]

(Please reply Yes or No, and explain your answer.)

4-5-2 May these operations be furthered by the use of compulsory purchase powers?

4-5-3 May these operations be furthered by means of other privileges accorded to public authorities?

4-5-4 May such operations be insisted upon by any public authority or private person for any of the following subjects?

> Agriculture
>
> Public Health
>
> Flood Protection
>
> Energy Production
>
> Other
>
> For any public purpose

(Please reply Yes or No, and explain your answer.)

4-5-5 May such operations take advantage of a favourable tax regime?

(For example, total or partial exemption from land taxation, deductions, tax-credits, etc.)

4-5-6 Which authority is responsible for establishing the tax base and assessing the rates of taxes which may fall on wetlands?

---

1. For example, a land-owner's association.

Table 2

Control of activities which may affect wetlands (Question 4-1)

To answer Question 4-1, respondents are asked to outline which types of operations or activities are controlled by each of a series of methods. The original version of the Questionnaire included a chart marked into boxes, with the methods of control along the top, and the activities or operations along the side. Respondents were asked to tick the appropriate boxes, and to explain their answers. Several ticks are permitted for each type of activity or operation, as appropriate. For activities which are the subject of general control (such as hunting, fishing, waste disposal, etc.), it is important to refer to provisions relating particularly to wetlands or to the absence of such provisions.

Types of operations or activities	*Methods of control*
Agriculture 1. Reclamation/destruction of wetland 2. Drainage 3. Change of cultivation or type of agricultural activity; intensification of use 4. Land consolidation 5. Other forms of rural management	Authorization by the State Authorization by region or component state (in a federal system) Authorization from other authority
Exploitation 6. of peat 7. of aquatic vegetation (e.g. reeds) 8. of other natural products 9. of materials	Authorization by environmental protection authority Consultation with a protection agency
Deposit of: 10. household waste 11. industrial waste	Impact assessment
Access 12. by the general public 13. by boats 14. overflight by aircraft	Other type of control No control
Works and installations 15. fish-farming 16. leisure facilities 17. residential or other building 18. dams 19. other hydraulic installations 20. other installations (e.g. electric power lines) 21. extraction of water 22. discharge of water	

(The word "taxes" is used here in the sense explained in connection with question 2-5-2.)

4-5-7 May such operations benefit from the assistance of:

> The State
> The region (or the component State in a Federal system)
> Other public authority
> Public interest association[1]
> International organization or supra-national institution
>
> (Please reply Yes or No.)

What form may such assistance take?

> Subsidies
> Loan of special terms
> Other
>
> (Please reply Yes or No, and explain your answer.)

4-5-8 May such operations be financed by the raising of a special tax?

(See questions 2-5-2 and 4-5-6.)

4-5-9 Are such operations the subject of an environmental impact assessment?

5 General Matters

5-1 (Where applicable) Is the lack of special protection for wetlands in your country explained by the absence of conservation problems or by other factors?

5-2 What remarks have you to offer as to the wetlands legislation in general in your country?

5-3 How, in your opinion, can it be improved?

---

1. See Question 2-1-3.

Definitions

Decentralization: An administrative system which allows communities (districts, regions, departments) the right to administer their own affairs under the supervision of the State, so as to invest these communities with legal personality and with responsibilities and resources of their own.

Devolution: A system of entrusting certain responsibilities of the State to the authorities operating in the appropriate districts.

Drainage: (a) Operations intended to remove from the soil water which is deemed to be excessive whether by means of a system of land drains, a system of open drains, ditches, or pipes permitting water to run off, particularly running water; and (b) River management operations. (Drainage thus covers the content of the following French terms, *"drainage"*, *"assainissement agricole"* and *"aménagement de rivière"*.)

Flood-Plain: The area which is flooded regularly by the overflowing of a water course.

Land Consolidation: The process by which rural land-owners are obliged to exchange scattered parcels of land in order to produce a more concentrated land-holding in accordance with an overall plan.

Protected Area: An area which is the subject of a special legal regime established with a view to conservation of nature. For the purposes of this questionnaire, the term "protected area" includes both areas enjoying protection of a broad character (for example, national parks, regional parks, state parks, nature reserves) and reserves established for a particular purpose (game reserves, botanical reserves).

Reclamation: Operations designed to achieve the removal of a wetland.

State: For the purpose of this questionnaire, the term "State" includes both unitary and federal States. Note that the component parts of a federal State (states of the United States, Swiss cantons, German *Länder*, etc.) are referred to as "component states in the federal system".

Wetland Region: Area possessing a degree of biogeographical unity and including a significant concentration of wetlands. For example, the Dombes (France), which comprises about 1000 ponds scattered over an area of 110,000 ha or thereabouts.

Wetlands: Marshes, fens, peat-bogs or open water, whether natural or man-made, permanent or temporary, with stagnant or running water, whether salt, brackish or fresh, including those coastal waters which at high tide achieve a depth of six metres.

List of categories of wetlands dealt with in this Questionnaire[1]

Lakes

Ponds

Water-courses[2]

Marshes and fens

Man-made bodies of water

Peat-bogs

Coastal wetlands (e.g. saltings, mud-flats, lagoons, mangroves)

Flooded areas or areas liable to be flooded (e.g. flood-plains, hollows which fill with water from time to time, riverine forests)

---

1. This list, which is based primarily upon European wetlands, is *not to be regarded as exhaustive.*
2. Such as rivers, streams, mountain streams, etc. The question is particularly concerned with the shallower parts of water-courses, such as banks, gravel-beds and ox-bow lakes.

Annexe 3

Liste des participants / List of participants

ABDEL AZIZ, Abdel Hady
  Professeur, Faculté de Droit, Université de Mansourah, 13 rue 251, Maadi - Le Caire, Egypte

ALVAREZ, Arenas Ramon
  Seccion de Recursos y Asuntos, Pieltain Legales, Gran Via de San Francisco 35-41, Madrid 28005, Espagne

BERNE, André
  Ingénieur du Génie Rural des Eaux et Forêts, 6 rue du Clos Jennetil, 45100 Orléans, France

BIBER, J. Pierre
  Comité Suisse pour la protection des oiseaux, Blauensteinerstr. 33, 4053 Basel, Suisse

BLAISE, Louis
  Délégué Régional à l'architecture et à l'environnement, DRAE Rhône-Alpes, 19 rue de la Villette, 69425 Lyon Cedex 03, France

BOUGRINE, Mohamed
  Délégué du Ministère de l'Agriculture, Service des Eaux et Forêts, Agadir, Maroc

BOUTEFEU, Emanuel
  Chargé de mission à la DRAE Rhône-Alpes, 19 rue de la Villette, 69425 Lyon Cedex 03, France

BRIFFAUD
  Laboratoire CINA, UA 366 - CNRS, 31000 Toulouse, France

BROYER, Joël
  Chargé d'études à la Direction départementale de l'Equipement de l'Ain, rue du Moyen Age, 01330 Villars-les-Dombes, France

BURHENNE, Françoise
  Head of IUCN Environmental Law Centre, Adenauerallee 214, 5300 Bonn 1, Allemagne

BURHENNE, Wolfgang E.
  Chairman of IUCN-CEPLA (Commission on Environmental Policy, Law and Administration), Adenauerallee 214, 5300 Bonn 1, Allemagne

DE CARA, Jean-Yves
Maître Assistant à l'Université Jean Moulin Lyon III, 15 Quai Claude Bernard, 69239 Lyon Cedex 02, France

CAUDAL, Sylvie
Assistant à l'Université Jean Moulin Lyon III, 15 Quai Claude Bernard, 69239 Lyon Cedex 02, France

COQUILLARD, Hervé
Centre d'étude des sciences de l'environnement - Lyon I, 43 Boulevard du 11 Novembre 1918, 69622 Villeurbanne, France

CORREIA da SILVA, Joao
Servicio Nacional de Parques Reserves et Conservacao da Natureza, Rua da Lapa no 73, 12000 Lisbonnes, Portugal

DALL, Stéphanie
Norbert H Dall & Associates, 1225 Eight Street Suite 485, Sacramento, California 95814, U.S.A.

DALL, Norbert
Norbert H Dall & Associates, 1225 Eight Street Suite 485, Sacramento, California 95814, U.S.A.

DAVIGNON, Jean-François
Maître-Assistant à l'Université L. Lumière Lyon II, Avenue de l'Université, 69500 Bron, France

DEBRUGE, Jean
Service de la Conservation de la Nature, Ministère de la Région Wallonne, Avenue Albert 1er 187-B, 5000 Namur, Belgium

DEJEANT-PONS, Maguelone
Administrateur au Conseil de l'Europe, 9 rue de Nazareth H2, 34080 Montpellier, France

DE KLEMM, Cyrille
Expert Consultant auprès de l'UICN, 21 rue de Dantzig, 75015 Paris, France

DHRUBA BAR SINGH, Thapa
Secretary, Ministry of Law and Justice, His Majesty's Government of Nepal, P.B. 828, Kathmandu, Nepal

DIENG, Papa Meissa
8 rue J. Mermoz, 67100 Strasbourg, France

DUGAN, Patrick J.
Wetlands Programme Coordinator, IUCN, Avenue du Mont Blanc, 1196 Gland, Suisse

FORSTER, Malcolm J.
International Division, Environment Group, Freshfields, Whitefriars, 65 Fleet Street, London EC4Y 1HS, Grande-Bretagne

FRANCK, Claude
Attaché de Gouvernement, Ministère de l'Environnement, 24 Ceinture des Rosers, 2446 Howald, Luxembourg

FROMAGEAU, Jérôme
Assistant à l'Université Paris XI, 24 rue Saint Charles, 75015 Paris, France

GALLEMANT, M.
Ministère de l'Environnement, 14 Boulevard du Général Leclerc, 92524 Neuilly-sur-Seine Cedex, France

JIMENEZ, Garcia Herreira
Consejeria de Agriculture, Direccion General de Montes Casa y Pesca, c/Alargos 31, Civoao Real, Espagne

KHAMBANONDA, Chalermsath
Department of General Management, Faculty of Business Administration, Ramkhamhaeng University, Bangkok, Thailand

KISS, Alexandre
Directeur de Recherche au Centre National de la Recherche Scientifique (CNRS), 29 rue du Conseil des Quinze, 67000 Strasbourg, France

KOESTER, Veit
Ministry of Environment, National Forest and Nature Agency, Slotsmerken 13, 2970 Horsholm, Denmark

LAMBRECHTS, Claude
Secrétaire général de la Société française pour le droit de l'environnement, 5 rue Goethe, 67000 Strasbourg, France

LARSSON, Torsten
Senior Administrative Officer, Natural Environment Protection Board, Box 1302, 171 25 Solna, Suède

LEBRETON, Philippe
Professeur, Laboratoire de Biologie végétale, Université Lyon I, 43 Boulevard du 11 novembre 1918, 69622 Villeurbanne, France

LE DUC, J. Patrick
Fédération française des Sociétés de protection de la nature, 58 rue Vaugerard, 75006 Paris, France

LETHIER, Hervé
Ministère de l'environnement, 31 rue de Buci, 75006 Paris, France

LEVY-BRUHL, Viviane
    Chargée d'études à l'Institut de droit de l'environnement, 14 Avenue Berthelot, 69007 Lyon, France

MAFFEI, Maria Clara
    Viale Dedei 1000 - 120 Viale, 43100 Parme, Italie

MAJEROWICZ, Simone
    Université Jean Moulin Lyon III, 15 Quai Claude Bernard, 69239 Lyon Cédex 02, France

MARTIN, Jean-Paul
    Assistant à l'Université Jean Moulin Lyon III, 15 Quai Claude Bernard, 69239 Lyon Cédex 02, France

MEGRET, Alain
    Chargé des relations extérieures au Ministère de l'Environnement, 14 Boulevard Général Leclerc, Neuilly-sur-Seine, France

MEKOUAR, Mohamed Ali
    Président de la Société marocaine pour le droit de l'environnement, 7 rue Général Roques, Casablanca 01, Maroc

MICHANECK, Gabriel
    Riksorganisation för Naturvand, B.P. 6400, 11 382 Stockholm, Suède

MOLINA VICENTE, Pedro
    Consejeria de Agriculture, Direccion General de Montes Caza y Pesca, c/ Duque de Lerma 3, 45004 Toledo, Espagne

NAVID, Daniel
    Secretary-General, Ramsar Convention Bureau, IUCN, Avenue du Mont Blanc, 1196 Gland, Suisse

PALLE UHD, Jepsen
    Wildlife Administration, Ministry of Agriculture, Standvejen 4, 841 c Ronde, Denmark

DIGIOVINE, Guiseppe
    Professeur, Université de Brescia, Faculté Economique et Commerciale, Corso G. Mameli 27, 25122 Brescia, Italie

PELERINS, Jacqueline
    Institut du droit de l'environnement, 14 Avenue Berthelot, 69007 Lyon, France

PENNING, H. Job
    Ministry of Agriculture and Fisheries, P.B. 20401, 25000 EK-The Hague, Pays-Bas

PETITPIERRE, Anne
Avocat, 15 rue Toepfer, 1206 Genève, Suisse

PLANCON, Annick
Juriste à la Délégation Régionale à l'architecture et à l'environnement, 10 rue des Chaux, 69430 Francheville, France

RAMSDEN, H.T.
Law Adviser to the Rand Water Board, 3 Fraser Street Johannesburg 2001, B.P. 1127, Johannesburg 2000, Afrique du Sud

RATSIMANDISA, Gabriel
Institut de droit de l'environnement, 14 Avenue Berthelot, 69007 Lyon, France

SARAGATAL, Jordi
Directeur, Parc National del Aiguamalls de l'Emperdà, El Cortalet, 17486 Castello d'Empuries, Espagne

SARCRIVA da COSTA, Carlos
Liga Para a Proteccao da Natureza, Estrado Do Calhariz de Benfica 187, 1500 Lisbonne, Portugal

SARIN, L. Manohar
Professor, Faculty of Law, Giessen, Hein-Heckroth Str. 5, 6300 Giessen, Allemagne

SCHWARTZ, Suzanne
Office of Wetlands Protection, 401 M. Street SW, Washington, D.C. 20460, U.S.A.

SESTIER, Jean-François
Assistant à l'Université Lumière Lyon II, Avenue de l'Université, 69500 Bron, France

SMART, Michael
Assistant Secretary-General, Ramsar Convention Bureau, IUCN, Avenue du Mont Blanc, 1196 Gland, Suisse

SOMMER, Jerzy
Professor, Research Group on Environmental Law, Institute of State and Law, Polish Academy of Sciences, SO 138 Wordaw - ul, Kuznicza 46147, Pologne

SOULIER, Martine
Institut de droit de l'environnement, 14 Avenue Berthelot, 69007 Lyon, France

STEVER, Donald W.
Professor of Law, Pace University School of Law, 78 North Broadway, White Plaine, New York 10603, U.S.A.

STRAVOPOULOS, Nicki
Department of Environmental Protection, Ministry of Agriculture, 2 Acharnon Street, 10176 Athenes, Gréce

TASNEEYANOND, Edy
Legal and Foreign Affairs Division, Office of Mercantile Marine Promotion Commission, Bangkok, Thailand

TASNEEYANOND, Panat
Professor, Law Faculty, Thammasat University, Rachan R.D., Bangkok, Thailand

TERRASSE, Jean-François
Directeur scientifique du WWF France, 60 rue Sartoris, 92250 La Garenne, France

TIMOSHENKO, Alexandre S.
Officer-in-Charge, Environmental Law and Institutions Unit, UNEP, P.O. Box 30552, Nairobi, Kenya

TOLENTINO, Amado S.
Environmental Law Consultant, National Environmental Protection Council, 6th floor, Philippine Heart Center, East Avenue, Quezon City, Philippines

TOMASI
Assistant à l'Université Jean Moulin Lyon III, 15 Quai Claude Bernard, 69239 Lyon Cédex 02, France

TRYZNA, Thaddeus
California Institute of Public Affairs, PO Box 10, Claremont, California 91711, U.S.A.

UNTERMAIER, Jean
Professeur à l'Université Jean Moulin Lyon III, Directeur de l'Institut de droit de l'environnement, 14 Avenue Berthelot, 69007 Lyon, France

VOISIN, Catherine
Assistante à l'Université Jean Moulin Lyon III, 15 Quai Claude Bernard, 69007 Lyon, France

VON DER ASSEN, Ferdinand
Responsable des Relations Extérieures, Ministry of Agriculture and Fisheries, PB 20401, 25000 EK The Hague, Pays-Bas

WENGER, Edith
Chercheur, Auen Institut, Josefstrasse 1, 7750 Rastatt, Allemagne

WITHRINGTON, David
English Nature, Northminster House, Peterborough PE1 1UA, Grande Bretagne

ZAHRI, Saïd
Ministère de l'Agriculture, Direction des Eaux et Forêts, Rabat, Maroc